How to Defend Humane Ideals

HOW TO DEFEND HUMANE IDEALS

Substitutes for Objectivity

James R. Flynn

UNIVERSITY OF NEBRASKA PRESS

LINCOLN AND LONDON

*Acknowledgments for the use of previously
published material appear on page ix.*

*© 2000 by the University of Nebraska Press
All rights reserved
Manufactured in the United States of America*

*Library of Congress
Cataloging-in-Publication Data
How to defend humane ideals:
substitutes for objectivity /
James R. Flynn.
p. cm.
Includes bibliographical references and index.
ISBN 0-8032-1994-6
(cl.: alk. paper)
ISBN 978-0-8032-1795-9
(pa.: alk. paper)
1. Humanistic ethics.
2. Social sciences and ethics.
I. Flynn, James Robert, 1934–
II. Title.
BJ1360.F58   2000
171'.2 – dc21
99-045984*

To Emily

CONTENTS

Acknowledgments

Thanks are due to many. To those at the Hoover Institution for hosting a scholar with views so opposed to their own; Lewis B. Stuart for funding the visit; Thomas and Mary Sowell for their company; Milton Friedman and Gary Becker for discussions over tea. To the Psychology and Philosophy Departments at Liverpool for office space and seminars. To Nicholas Mascie-Taylor and Nicholas Mackintosh of Cambridge for the opportunity to address the 1995 Galton Institute Symposium. To Charles Pigden, Kai Nielsen, Bill Dickens, Steve Ceci, and Jeremy Waldron for comments on the manuscript, above all, Jeremy Waldron. To Denis Dutton for bringing me to the attention of the University of Nebraska Press. To the University of Otago students who took Political Studies 401, on which this book is based, particularly Debbie Clapshaw, Stephen Dougherty, and Angela Warburton, who wrote honors essays that helped clarify my thinking and their thinking about Plato, Sumner, and Nietzsche, respectively.

Earlier versions of chapters 1, 4, 5, and 9, now much revised, appeared in *Philosophical Quarterly*, *Kant-Studien*, the *American Philosophical Quarterly*, and *Political Theory Newsletter*. Chapter 8 is largely from "Group Differences: Is the Good Society Impossible?" by James R. Flynn (1996), *Journal of Biosocial Science*, 28, 573–585. Reprinted with the permission of Cambridge University Press.

How to Defend Humane Ideals

INTRODUCTION

THE PROBLEM

I

Truth-Tests and What We Have Lost

This book was written by someone committed to humane-egalitarian ideals who thought he wanted a truth-test to defend them; now, after fifty years of reflection, he believes that there is something better. The struggle to fabricate ethical truth was abandoned not without pain: the notion of a higher court of appeal that would force antihumane people to choose between humane ideals and reason exercised a powerful attraction, and evidence of withdrawal symptoms will not be hard to find. Several perceptions about ethical truth-tests dictated their demise: that they must satisfy conditions that appear contradictory; that they have a darker side; that alternative uses of reason in moral debate are possible. The journey this book records is very much a personal odyssey, but despite that, it may have some larger significance. Ever since the sixteenth century, thinkers have been walking away from ethical truth, and the prevailing mood was captured by Max Weber when he pleaded with youth not to lose all their ideals along the way. Whether I am a good guide to an alternative defense of humane-egalitarian ideals, one that justifies them without corrupting them, is for the reader to judge.

An alternative defense depends on transcending the limitations of philosophy. I intend to argue that ethical truth-tests and proofs and so-called moral facts carry no rational conviction and, therefore, cannot justify any particular set of ideals, much less provide a defense of humane-egalitarian ideals. If that were the last word, Weber could lead us all in a chorus of despair without dissonance. But it is not the last word. Philosophy can come to its own rescue by way of an analysis that demonstrates the relevance of logic and social science to moral and political debate. Their potential liberated, logic and social science can then provide the arguments we need, arguments against opponents ranging from racists to contemporary thinkers who have persuaded many that egalitarian ideals self-destruct in practice (witness Herrnstein and Murray's *The Bell Curve* and its more than three hundred thousand readers). As this implies, the argument will reach substantive conclusions: that the great post-Enlightenment project—justice for all races and classes, the reduction of inequality, the abolition of privilege—has both moral dignity and social relevance. I will also address current issues like the redistribution of wealth, the welfare state, and affirmative action.

The above strategic plan dictates all that follows. The remainder of this chapter serves as an introduction that clarifies the status of moral ideals (including our own) in the absence of ethical truth. Thereafter, the book is divided into two parts linked by a transitional chapter. Part 1 reveals the limitations of philosophy and includes chapter 2, which argues that Plato's case for ethical truth has a contradiction at its core; chapter 3, which argues against all attempts to make a case for objective status in ethics; and chapter 4, which claims that there is a darker side to ethical truth and uses Kant as a case in point. Chapter 5 is the transitional chapter. It uses philosophical analysis to derive an agenda that reveals the potential of logic and social science for moral and political debate. Part 2 actually puts logic and social science to work, that is, it uses them to argue against various antihumane and antiegalitarian opponents. It includes chapter 6, which rebuts racist ideals and the Social Darwinism of William Graham Sumner; chapter 7, which criticizes the evolutionary ethics of Raymond B. Cattell and the elitist ethics of Nietzsche, our most elusive and disturbing opponent; chapter 8, which defends egalitarian ideals against the counterattack of *The Bell Curve*; and chapter 9, which urges postmodernists to acknowledge their humane ideals and conquer their repugnance for science so that they can defend them. Finally, chapter 10 provides a summary and acknowledges problems that are probably beyond reason and, therefore, allow only personal or conventional solutions.

An explanation of why certain thinkers are included and others omitted may make these pages seem less eccentric. Every thinker included was chosen because analysis of his or her work contributed to the development of my own approach to defending humane ideals. That is why Plato, Moore, Brink,

Sturgeon, Gewirth, Rawls, Kant, Nielsen, Hare, Jensen, Sumner, Nietzsche, Herrnstein, Murray, and Iris Marion Young get space and why Dworkin, Nozick, Anscombe, Blackburn, Cohen, Foot, Geech, Parfit, Sen, Michael Smith, Wiggins, and Bernard Williams, plus others, do not. It is not that I have no disagreements with the thinkers omitted; for example, I believe that concepts like natural rights simply confuse moral debate. But discussion of such issues would have blurred the focus on finding valid arguments against the antihumane. All the thinkers omitted (even Nozick) include all human-kind within their circle of moral concern. So none of them are antihumane, as I use the term, and none of them, as far as I can determine, address opponents like Nietzsche.

WHAT WE CAN NO LONGER SAY

Preliminaries over, the work of this chapter begins. The quest for ethical truth arises when we confront opponents whose basic ideals clash with our own. Moral debate presents us with two kinds of disputes, one that arises out of conflicting basic ideals, the other out of disagreements about facts or means to ends. The latter may arouse strong emotions, but at least they are resolvable in principle. Imagine two people, both of whom hold humane-egalitarian ideals and accept that society should help lower-income groups toward a life of minimal decency. One may favor the welfare state, the other attacks its flaws and favors topping up low incomes by cash transfers. They may castigate each other as liberal and conservative, but they share the same basic ideal and may well agree on the data that will settle whose means best realize the common end. Now imagine either of these people confronted by a Nietzschean who cares nothing for the lot of ordinary people, who be-lieves that human beings must earn the right to have their needs taken into account by becoming creative geniuses. This engenders a dispute of a more fundamental sort, a conflict between egalitarian ideals on the one hand and elitist ideals on the other that no simple appeal to data can resolve. And yet, precisely because we so much loathe ideals antihumane and cruel, it is here that we desire a resolution above all.

Some prefer to call a person's basic ideals "first principles" or "funda-mental moral intuitions." Moreover, they would be quick to point out that moral reasoning is often not as tidy as I have implied. A moral philosopher may explicitly state his or her first principles, say, the greatest happiness of the greatest number, and then derive moral judgments on lesser matters from such principles, but few people are moral philosophers. And even moral philosophers, when confronted with a new situation, sometimes find they possess moral reactions or intuitions of which they were unaware, something like suppressed first principles that lurk below the level of consciousness. Nonetheless, everyone reveres certain great goods that are not mere means to ends, and, therefore, while partially artificial, the concept of basic ideals or first principles is a useful one. It reveals that someone like Nietzsche, who banishes everyone but an elite from his circle of moral concern, is a very different opponent from someone who disagrees with us about whether the minimum wage is an optimum policy for benefiting unskilled workers.

Ethical truth-tests offer us the prospect of total victory over our most loathed ideological opponents. This is because they confer objective status on the ideals they endorse, and our hope, of course, is that they will favor our ideals and not those of some opponent. They have a poor relation that does the same job, namely, proofs that humane ideals have objective status. The former are analogous to the scientific method, which tests the truth-status of competing theories, while the latter are more like demonstrations in geometry, arguments that the rejection of humane ideals is somehow contradictory. In this chapter, when I speak about the status of our ideals in the absence of ethical truth, that wording really means in the absence of both truth-tests and proofs. The longer formula would be tedious. However, both will eventually get their due, and both will be subjected to critical examination over the next two chapters.

I have said that ethical truth-tests confer objective status on our ideals. Objective status is the same in ethics as it is in the realm of fact. Assume that the scientific method has handed down a verdict about conflicting hypotheses. The earth looks flat, but the Greeks noticed that when a ship approached port, the top of its mast was the first thing visible, as if it were climbing a curved surface. The evidence in favor of the earth's roundness versus its flatness is now overwhelming, and, therefore, all rational people ought to accept it whether they find it attractive or not. Romantics may find it pedestrian, preferring to believe that missing persons cannot be located because they have fallen off the earth's edge. The residents of Zion, Illinois, believe it is contradicted by the Bible, so in their town flatness makes a last stand. Nonetheless, as these examples show, every person must accept the scientific method's verdict or abandon rationality. Note the implications of the last phrase: a truth-test can confer objective status in the light of reason, but it cannot coerce people into being rational; it can resolve disputes in theory but not necessarily in fact. We may confront a racist with overwhelming evidence that all blacks are not mentally or emotionally immature, but the racist may be too stubborn to look at the evidence. It may take a Martin Luther King Jr., leading blacks in a bus boycott, blacks who visibly demonstrate intelligence, courage, and maturity, to melt the racist's stereotypes. Philosophy can settle disputes only between rational opponents. Other tactics must be used to condition people to be more rational and settle disputes in practice.

Plato exemplifies how ethical truth-tests function, that is, how they can be used to test conflicting basic ideals and show that only one set of ideals has objective status. Plato thought that the Form of Human Society contains the perfect or just state of human society and that dialectic could help us read the contents of the World of Forms. He thought that his own concept of justice matched the content of the Form and that Thrasymachus's concept was its antithesis. If we accept that the Forms are a test of what is truly or objectively just and that they endorse Plato's concept of justice, they give him a victory on behalf of his ideals of the most satisfying sort. They impose on all humanity a rational ought that activates a moral ought. However much Thrasymachus, that worshiper of tyrants, loathed Plato's roughly humane concept of justice, he would have to agree that he ought to accept it, just as he must accept that the earth is round rather than flat or abandon reason. And once his reason committed him to accept Plato's concept of justice, he would have to accept the moral imperative encapsulated in that ideal: rulers ought to promote the welfare of all, not rule simply in the interests of the stronger party.

We now understand the attraction of an ethical truth-test. It acts as a higher court of appeal, and if it vindicates our basic ideals, it gives us one big victory that routs all our loathed ideological opponents without further ado. The truth-test embodies a rational ought that coerces our opponents not only to abandon their ideals but also to accept ours. Accepting our ideals entails accepting a moral ought that commands them to behave humanely.

This prepares us to discuss one of the most contentious issues in moral philosophy. What is the status of our ideals in the absence of an ethical truth-test? The debate is complex because it takes place on two levels. What are the logical consequences of having no rational advantage whatsoever over our opponents? What are the logical consequences of having a rational advantage that falls short of a case for ethical truth? I believe that a case for ethical truth conveys a unique rational advantage on behalf of our ideals, one so different in kind from any other that once the first debate is settled, the second is clarified. Therefore, I will begin by analyzing the situation in which we lack any rational or epistemological advantage over our opponents, a position often called "ethical skepticism." And I will focus my analysis by asking a question. When we make assertions about our basic ideals, for example, say that people ought to accept them, to whom are those assertions directed? What exactly is the targeted audience?

The fundamental issues about the logical consequences of ethical skepticism are these: whether or not it entails nihilism, and whether or not it allows universal assertions that tell all people they ought to accept certain basic ideals. These issues divide thinkers into three schools: those who believe ethical skepticism does entail nihilism; those who reject nihilism and believe ethical skepticism allows universal assertions; those who reject nihilism and believe ethical skepticism does not allow universal assertions or, at least, believe it turns those assertions into empty words.

Dostoyevsky in *The Brothers Karamazov* says that if God is dead, anything is allowable. My old professor Leo Strauss used to say that if there is no ethical truth, the most cherished moral ideals collapse into the category of mere whim or desire, that risking one's life to pull a child out of the path of an oncoming car becomes indistinguishable from van Gogh's mad whim to cut off his ear. This school of opinion holds that ethical skepticism entails nihilism in the sense that it becomes irrational to take duties seriously, both duties in general and humane ideals in particular. If there is a truth-test, there are objective moral duties; if there is none, there are no duties at all. We may be passionately committed to principles that tell us we should act humanely, but the message of those principles is deceptive. They are like illusions whose content deceives.

This argument is logically incoherent and should be labeled the *nihilist fallacy*. Even in the absence of a truth-test, people may internalize humane ideals and be deeply committed to them; if so, why should they not take on humane behavior as a self-imposed duty? Commitment to a moral principle is a commitment to a duty, and it is far more serious than one's taste in soft drinks, which no one confuses with a self-imposed duty. Perhaps a humane skeptic cannot tell Nietzsche he ought to accept humane ideals. However, that hardly entails the proposition that a humane skeptic must tell himself he ought to abandon them. To say the latter would be to assume that lack of objective status entails that humane ideals have subjective status. However, what shows something to be either objective or subjective is that it has either passed or failed a truth-test. Therefore, if ethical skepticism is correct, there is no such thing as objectivity *or* subjectivity.

Dostoyevsky and Strauss assume that ethical skepticism entails treating humane ideals as if they had flunked a nonexistent truth-test. Clearly that is a mistake. If there is no such thing as ethical truth, it may be foolish to say humane ideals ought to be accepted by those who loathe them, but it would be equally absurd to say they ought to be dismissed by those who cherish them. Once again for emphasis: in the absence of a truth-test, no moral ideal, humane or otherwise, can either pass or fail. A self-imposed duty to be humane may seem worthless to the antihumane, but for us it is worth precisely what it is worth to us. That may be a great deal. It may demand that we lay down our lives to avoid antihumane consequences. It is not like some kind of hallucination that has flunked a truth-test, a sort of failed perception revealed as illusory and worthy of being dismissed.

The fact that ethical skepticism does not logically entail nihilism does not forbid nihilism as a psychological reaction. Someone reared in an atmosphere of faith and whose life has been entirely God-centered may find that loss of faith robs the world of all that engaged his or her passions. Similarly, someone who has always presumed that humane ideals were in accord with ethical truth may find lack of objective status unbearable, and his or her commitment to humane ideals may wither away. Self-imposed duties may seem too pale a shadow of truth-imposed duties. People must, I fear, come to terms with such a loss, just as they must come to terms with the death of a loved one, and philosophical analysis cannot dictate the outcome. What it can do is make certain that a logical mistake does not influence our psychology, that ethical skepticism does not plunge us into despair because we mistakenly believe it logically entails nihilism.

I owe D. Z. Phillips and H. O. Mounce (1970) a debt for calling my

attention to a second school of thought based on Wittgenstein or, more accurately, on an interpretation of Wittgenstein's fragmentary and scattered
writings on ethics. In his "Lecture on Ethics," Wittgenstein (1965) analyzes
the grammar of moral language. He asserts that calling something "good"
or "right" in an ethical sense is identical with saying it is good in an absolute
sense. His concept of absolutely good equates with my definition of objectively good. That is, Wittgenstein asserts that calling your basic ideals good
implies that everyone ought to accept them whether they actually do so or
not, that they ought to be accepted independently of people's tastes and incli-
nations. Wittgenstein makes it clear that he sees no prospect of making a case
for ethical truth; indeed, he calls such a notion a chimera. Therefore, he must
choose between two alternatives: accepting moral ideals and making universal assertions that tell all people they ought to accept them, or giving up
moral ideals and embracing nihilism. Rush Rhees (1965) has no doubt that
Wittgenstein rejected the nihilistic alternative. This seems plausible in the
light of Wittgenstein's remarks, both in his "Lecture" and in conversation
with Friedrich Waismann (1965), that he has the highest regard for those
who use ethical terms in an absolute sense.

What views Wittgenstein held is of course secondary to the question of
whether moral grammar really traps us into making universal assertions. If
he is correct, the very fact that I am committed to humane ideals forces me
to assert that all people ought to accept them whether they loathe them or
not—which means that I cannot say what I wish to say: that I am committed to humane ideals as self-imposed duties and yet, in the absence of ethical
truth, reject universal assertions on their behalf. There are two possible lines
of attack: disputing Wittgenstein's interpretation of conventional moral usage, or accepting his interpretation but arguing that such usage does not decide the question. The former looks unpromising. Conventional moral assertions take the form of "Thou shalt not kill" or, to add qualifications, "You
ought not kill human beings except under certain extenuating circumstances
such as self-defense." These assertions are apparently directed to all people,
not just those who happen to accept that killing is wrong. This feature of
moral usage may be called its absolute grammar, or its categorical grammar,
or its objective grammar, or what have you, but the point is clear. It seems
peculiar to say, "Those who accept the principle that killing is wrong ought
not to kill."

Therefore, I will argue that conventional moral usage is not decisive of what it makes sense to say in the absence of ethical truth-tests. My argument can be adumbrated as follows: when we say people ought to do something, we should specify whom we are addressing; that done, our use of "ought" should have some coherent meaning; there are only three coherent uses of the word "ought" in this context, namely, the rational, the methodological, and the moral; when addressing people who loath our ideals, the absence of a truth-test eliminates all three of these uses; therefore, conventional moral usage is incoherent and should be revised. The revision I have in mind is that we stop making universal assertions that all people, including the antihumane, ought to accept humane ideals, which puts me into the third school of thought concerning the logical consequences of ethical skepticism.

I have no illusions about the contention that humane people cannot, in the absence of a case for objectivity, tell all humanity that they ought to be humane. It is distasteful. It is controversial in the sense that I know of no other philosopher who has argued for it in detail. There are passages in Gilbert Harman (1977) that appear supportive. Among novelists who are also moralists, John Barth in *The Sot-Weed Factor* and *End of the Road* may take a similar view. I no more despise his support, if such it be, than Strauss despised Dostoyevsky. But Barth is atypical, just as I am atypical of philosophers. Those who believe nothing new is likely to be true have been forewarned.

Once the notion that ethical skepticism entails nihilism has been rejected, there is no problem about telling that fragment of humanity who are committed to humane ideals that they ought to behave humanely. However, those who on the strength of their own commitment to humane ideals say that "all people ought to behave humanely" are targeting a wider audience, namely, one inclusive of people like Nietzsche who loathe humane ideals. Wittgenstein himself recognizes that it makes no sense to advise people to act on moral principles until they actually hold those principles. Therefore, he alters his message to read, "all people (including Nietzsche) ought to accept humane ideals." Now if we say that, precisely what meaning adheres to the word "ought"? Three possibilities exist, that the word is used in a rational sense, or a methodological sense, or a moral sense.

The rational ought pertains only when there is a rational or evidential case that all people should accept something. Once again, one can say to a flat-earther, "You ought to accept that the world is round" because the scientific method plus evidence is on our side. In other words, we have an epistemological case, a case in terms of a truth-test. The absence of ethical truth removes the rational ought from contention and brings us to the methodological ought.

The methodological ought pertains when an appropriate method, one all parties to a dispute must accept as appropriate, dictates a resolution to the dispute, so that we can say, "Having agreed to this method, and having agreed that this method properly applied has this outcome, we ought to accept this outcome." An epistemological method is a special case of generating a methodological ought, and when it disappears in ethics, what remains? I will argue that lacking an *epistemological* method of resolving conflicts about basic ideals, the only remaining alternative is a *psychological* method. The best way to appreciate this is to shift from a conflict of ideals between two people to a conflict within a person, someone who is torn from within by opposing sets of basic ideals.

Plato believed that the youth of his day were torn between his humane concept of justice (rulers should attempt to perfect the ruled) and the Social Darwinist concept of Thrasymachus (the stronger have a right to exploit the weaker). He offered them an epistemological method of choosing, namely, dialectic as a road to ethical truth. But if he had been unable to offer them an epistemological method, what could they have fallen back on but a psychological method, the method of "look into yourself and clarify your commitments?" A more prosaic example may drive the point home. Imagine that you read of a particularly horrible and senseless murder, perpetrated by someone without obvious psychological problems and whose background reveals no extenuating circumstances. Assume you are not a hard determinist and feel free to allocate praise and blame. Despite the fact that you have always thought of yourself as thoroughly humane, you are overwhelmed with the sense that such a criminal deserves punishment for punishment's sake. So you find yourself torn by a clash between the ideal of a humane criminal code, one based purely on deterrence of crime and reformation of the wrong-doer, and the conviction that such a person ought to be punished no matter what deterrence and reformation dictate. For many people, the crimes of Hitler meant an agonizing reappraisal of their views on punitive justice. If we could have safely isolated him and saw no hope of his reformation, would we really have vetoed punishment in favor of maximizing his happiness?

When torn by conflicting ideals, and with no rational considerations to tip the scales in favor of one ideal, what choice does a person have but to look inward and ask himself or herself certain questions? Questions like, Does either of these ideals awaken a sense of moral revulsion? Given two people, one of whom lives by the first ideal and the other by its opposite, whom do I admire most? Which of these two ideals would I want to inculcate in my children? All of these questions are ways of clarifying my commitments, isolating the moral principles to which I am truly committed.

A psychological method will give different results when applied by different people. If you are the one torn between a nonpunitive and a punitive concept of justice and ask yourself, "What ideals do I want to inculcate in my children?" you may recoil from the notion of punishment for punishment's sake even in the case of Hitler. You may equate it with a revenge ethic you want to have no part in your children's psyche. Someone closer to Hitler's deeds, a Jewish American who lost all of her European relatives in concentration camps, may react differently. She may find that while she normally accepts a nonpunitive concept of justice, she deeply believes that it is overridden in the extreme case of crimes against humanity. The students I taught many years ago in eastern Kentucky had moral "intuitions" that told them that if someone from another clan committed murder, the relatives of the murdered person had a right to revenge. Nietzsche looked into himself and found that crimes by the great against ordinary people were no crimes at all.

Which is to say that even after everyone's commitments have been clarified, people find themselves committed to a variety of conflicting moral principles. Therefore, in the absence of ethical truth or an epistemological method, we cannot say all people ought to accept humane ideals and be using the methodological ought. After all, if you agree that a psychological method is the appropriate method in the absence of a truth-test, and you agree that each person has applied the method properly, you should accept the outcome: different people really are committed to different basic ideals, and you can give no methodological reason for telling them all to accept humane ideals. You may object that the psychological method was not properly applied and that if it were, unity would have been achieved. For example, you may say, "All those who want to punish someone for punishment's sake should imagine themselves in the shoes of the criminal" and argue that if they do, no one would be willing to punish. This line of argument will be examined in detail in chapter 7. For now, let me express skepticism: I doubt that Simon Wiesenthal would be shaken by imagining himself in the dock as Hitler or that Nietzsche would be moved by empathizing with the sufferings of herd men. If it is conceded that the psychological method, properly applied, will not bring unity, we must move on from the methodological ought to the moral ought.

The moral ought pertains when certain prerequisites are met, most notably when the person to whom it is addressed *can* perform the act advised. It makes no sense to tell a poor person that she should endow a university or someone who cannot swim that he should save a drowning child. Assume no ethical truth-test, assume no unifying method, and assume we are addressing people committed to antihumane ideals. Under what conditions could they act on moral advice to accept humane ideals? If after Nietzsche looked within himself and found ordinary people no more significant than insects, what would we think if we said to him, "You ought to accept humane ideals," and he replied, "Well I will then." The only plausible hypothesis would be that he was not himself to the point that his mind was unhinged. Does it make sense to give moral advice that only the insane can take? Imagine that a friend and comrade whom we greatly admire told us one day that he had abandoned humane ideals and accepted Nietzsche's antihumane elitist morality. And when we said, "For God's sake why," he replied, "Well, yesterday someone told me that all people ought to accept such antihumane ideals." We would, I think, suspect either that he had been deceptive all along about where his commitments lay or that he had taken leave of his senses.

If, without a truth-test, moral advice to accept humane ideals joins a class of utterances in which people cannot do what they are advised, is that moral advice not tainted? It is true that the impediment is not financial or physical incapacity but rather psychological, so let us add a case characterized by psychological incapacity. Assume that a woman was torn between two people and, after looking deep within herself, found an affection so profound that she chose one of them as a partner for life. Would you advise her that she ought to accept the other, purely because your love for him or her was the greater? Would not your advice constitute an absurdity as profound as advice that she should flip a coin or be swayed by whose name came first in the alphabet? I believe that none of us would want to populate this class of utterances with a new member, were our emotions not in control of our intellects. We want so very much to say that all people should accept humane ideals, and, therefore, we refuse to face the question of to whom the advice is directed.

If the advice is not to be directed to the antihumane, an alternative is to direct it to ourselves. But since we already accept humane ideals, it does not ask us to do anything, so rather than genuine moral advice, it is really a kind of cheerleading. Chanting "all people ought to accept humane ideals" may well arouse the passions of a partisan crowd and prepare them to confront their foes on the playing field, but like all mass oratory, it is best done when ✓ critical intelligence is on holiday. Perhaps the advice is directed to no one at all, in which case it does not matter much.

There are a few more steps before the string of using the moral ought is played out. Wittgenstein granted that it made no sense to say that people ought to behave humanely unless they accepted humane ideals, and, therefore, he said they ought to accept them. If it makes no sense to say people ought to accept humane ideals unless they find within themselves a commitment, the next step would be to say that they ought to find such a commitment. But since it is absurd to advise someone to find something that is not there, we immediately move to the final step: that the commitments of the ✓ antihumane ought to be altered by a conversion experience. But however fast we run, the same question pursues: Who is being advised that they ought to provide a conversion experience, so as to convert the antihumane?

If people find humane ideals repugnant, they can hardly be expected to commit themselves to the task of altering their commitments. They approve of the way they are. If one believes in God, the advice to alter the commitments of the antihumane can be addressed to Him or Her, in the hope that many Pauls will be struck from horses on the road to Tarsus. Failing that, must not the advice be directed to us, the humane? Now, for the first time, the moral ought makes sense. Given our self-imposed duty to act humanely, we ought to try to convert everyone to humane ideals, because that will make a more humane world. We must try to influence the psychology of the antihumane from without, which brings us back to Martin Luther King Jr. His tactics are worth trying when truth is on our side. We should force whites to confront the evidence that all blacks are not immature by presenting whites with the public spectacle of blacks behaving maturely. His tactics are also worth trying when we appeal to the heart rather than the mind. They are less likely to work, of course. Introducing Nietzsche to ordinary people of great dignity and courage, perhaps a couple struggling to give their children a better life than they enjoy, will not convert him if his love affair with creative genius makes him despise all that he sees. But we must try.

Now we see how conventional moral usage must be altered to bring it into line with what reason dictates in the absence of ethical truth. Universal assertions targeting humane advice to all people must give way to saying, "Those who can ought to behave humanely and ought to attempt to convert those who cannot," which reads, "Those who accept humane ideals ought to behave humanely and ought to attempt to convert the antihumane." This may seem feeble compared to the categorical thunder of conventional usage, the rousing "All people ought to accept humane ideals." However, when we realize that conventional usage translates into "All people, both those who can and those who cannot, ought to accept humane ideals," the novelty of the new should be less of a deterrent than the absurdity of the old.

No doubt some will say that the new usage has sacrificed the essence of morality. But how much has been lost? There are still self-imposed duties that bind us to sacrifice self-interest and even our lives for our ideals. There is still the mission to remake the world and all humankind in the light of our ideals. When raising children, parents will still say, "You ought not to pull your little sister's hair" on the assumption that they are preaching ideals their children will internalize and thereby render relevant for themselves. The only sense in which morality has been lost is that reflective people will give up universal assertions. I am happy to concede that morality has been lost in that sense, so long as it remains in all the other senses described. They can withdraw the label "morality" from us, but the substance will remain and be quite enough for the human race to get on with the business of living. We can also turn the tables by asking why they cherish the right to give moral advice to people who cannot take it. Has not the essence of moral advice departed, rather like the Cheshire Cat when the body had gone and only the smile remained?

Thus far we have assumed that the absence of ethical truth equals no rational advantage over our opponents. But this book will argue that such is not the case; that is, I myself will try to provide a rational advantage that falls short of a case for ethical truth. To anticipate, racist ideals are either logically incoherent, ignore evidence, or must count human traits as irrelevant that no one really believes to be irrelevant. William Graham Sumner's enthusiasm for the misery of the undeserving poor either violates his own concept of justice or necessitates an indefensible theory of human motivation. Raymond B. Cattell espouses an evolutionary ideal that, contrary to his intention, obligates us to endorse artificial intelligence as the highest form of "life." Nietzsche holds two ideals that, in the light of modern social science, can be shown to be mutually exclusive in practice, and the more fundamental of the two cannot be used to organize a human society. The meritocracy scenario of Herrnstein and Murray is operationally incoherent.

This preview takes us to the second level of the debate about the status of our ideals in the absence of an ethical truth-test. Assuming that the ideals of our opponents can be shown to be defective and that our humane ideals can be shown to be defensible, should not our defeated opponents accept humane ideals? If so, a rational advantage other than an ethical truth-test can do the work of a truth-test, that is, lend our ideals a status epistemologically equivalent to objective status.

To assess this possibility, we must take stock of what alters, and what remains the same, in the transition from no rational advantage to a rational advantage of the above sort. Our opponents may become demoralized because, insofar as they respect reason, they can no longer use their ideals to delineate the future of humankind. We can take a deep satisfaction in this. However, our opponents can still maintain that we have given them no reason to join us in attempting to mold humankind in accord with our ideals. Simply because humane ideals can be operationalized without counterproductive consequences, without logical inconsistency, without turning one's back on the truths of social science, gives no one a reason to espouse and promote them who finds them repugnant. Our method of assessing ideals is essentially negative rather than positive. We score critical points off our opponents. But however many we score, we do nothing to promote humane ideals from nonobjective to objective status, do nothing to show that someone ought to create a more humane world even though they lament every step in that direction. Which is to say, we have done nothing to bring the crucial rational ought into play, the rational ought that imposes a commitment to humane ideals; we have done nothing *epistemological* to fixate belief in humane ideals.

What about the *psychological* method? Have we affected our opponents' psychology in some way that would give them a proclivity toward humane ideals when they look within? The best way to determine that is to imagine them answering the questions that constitute the psychological method. Nietzsche would still feel revulsion for those who cater to the happiness of herd animals, admire only the great, be filled with horror at a child of his who suffered from the soul-superstition of believing that all people are worthy of concern. Sumner would still find absence of middle-class virtues insipid. The racist would still be revolted at the notion of contact with those who wear the color black. The psychology of our opponents would remain essentially unaltered.

It is one thing to overcome revulsion and accept an ideal because reason, either through a truth-test or proof, imposes it on you. That is the essence of following reason, whether it entails a theism you despise as childish, or a scientific theory you find ugly, or a morality you dislike. It is another thing to commit yourself to a loathed ideal simply because it possesses certain limited rational attributes. The fact that humane ideals, subjected to the full glare of science, possess internal coherence, both logical and operational, gives no one a reason to accept them. Such attributes have nothing to do with the human content of a morality, whether it incorporates moral concern for all, or only the great, or only a certain class, or only whites. Ethics is not geometry.

Our opponents would face a dilemma if they were left with no viable alternative to a humane way of life. But assuming that they can adapt to the loss of a crusading mission, they can seek whatever human, intellectual, physical, and sensual gratification their social surroundings allow. In terms of personal ties, they can indulge their preference for their favored group, seeking out creative artists, people who are self-reliant and thrifty, whites only, and eschew the company of those they dislike. This may seem to be essentially a life of enlightened self-interest, and that is a life-style some find unsatisfactory. However, whatever its limitations, people of this sort would hardly find it more satisfying to supplement it with attempting to promote humane ideals. They would probably do best to embrace a limited form of eroscentrism. Eroscentrism is an ethic in which moral concern is concentrated within the circle of personal love relationships, with no concern or diminished concern outside that circle. It may seem a poor alternative to an all-embracing morality like humanism. But those committed to it think the reverse: they find moral concern outside the circle of love artificial and alien. Let us wait to see whether we can use reason against them (chapter 10).

As conceded, this chapter does not reach traditional conclusions about the status of ethical ideals, and, therefore, it is important that I at least locate my position on the traditional philosophical map. To do this, I will borrow something from J. L. Mackie (1977, 20–30), namely, his distinction between conditional and unconditional truth. Ethical propositions can be said to be true in a conditional sense if they contain judgments or advise actions that are in accord with a standard or principles a certain group of people happen to share. They cannot be true in an unconditional sense unless some one set of principles, say humane ideals, is a product of knowledge. Because there is no such thing as an ethical truth-test (my term), our ideals cannot be either true or false in an unconditional sense. Since they are not unconditionally true, we cannot say that all people should accept humane ideals. Since ethical principles are not unconditionally false, we are not logically driven to nihilism. As for using true in a conditional sense, I believe this is so different that, if we are to use it at all, it should be used only as an adjective, for example, an act or judgment is truly humane, or truly Nietzschean, and so forth. However, I do not really care about conditional uses of true, just so long as it is granted that they have no relevance to what I consider to be the central issue: whether it makes sense to say that all people should accept humane ideals.

The reader now knows where I stand and has been forewarned what to expect. I will offer those who espouse humane-egalitarian ideals a rational advantage over their loathed opponents. But psychology remains crucial: you either sympathize with the sufferings of ordinary people or you do not. I have nothing up my sleeve that will give people a good heart. And since a lot of people do not have good hearts, we must abandon the categorical grammar of conventional moral language, the "Thou shalt nots" that tell everyone that they ought to be humane. There is no mystery why conventional usage has so powerful a hold. Prephilosophical peoples often believe that only the members of their own tribe are fully human and, therefore, believe that all real people accept their mores. Until recently, Western philosophy did little to erode such beliefs because it argued that our own mores possessed objective status. To go beyond what prephilosophy and philosophical mistakes have embedded in our moral grammar is a necessary, if painful, step along the road of understanding, unless, of course, I am mistaken. At least my analysis is easy to evaluate because it is based on a single contention: only objective status or commitment can activate the moral ought in the sense of imposing a duty on a concrete person. When both of these are absent, the moral ought simply cannot activate itself.

WHY WE MUST CHANGE

The controversy about usage is important. No good can come of a moral usage that made sense when ethical truth was thought possible lingering on when truth-tests have been abandoned. For example, recall those who believe ethical skepticism entails nihilism. Archaic conventional usage offers them a chance to do mischief. They can argue that holding moral ideals at all entails categorical grammar; that categorical grammar is logically incoherent without ethical truth (or some other prop for objective status); and that, therefore, the absence of ethical truth logically entails holding no moral ideals at all. In other words, revising conventional usage is necessary so that the nihilist fallacy can be perceived for the fallacy it is. On the other hand, the importance of moral usage should not be exaggerated. What we have lost with the death of ethical truth in terms of language is insignificant compared to what has been lost in moral debate. What we have lost above all is that wonderful longed-for verdict that, assuming it endorsed humane ideals, would force all humanity to choose between accepting our ideals and abandoning rationality. We have lost that one big victory over all of our ideological opponents that would either convert them or convict them of unreason or immorality or both. Philosophical analysis plus social science may offer substitutes for the objectivity conferred by ethical truth, but no substitute can ever fully compensate for its loss.

PART ONE

THE LIMITATIONS OF PHILOSOPHY

2

Plato and Thrasymachus

Plato commands our attention for several reasons. The presence or absence of ethical truth is important, and his is the greatest case for ethical truth ever made. Sadly, his case ends in a contradiction, one shared by all attempts to derive a truth-test, or at least all those attempts made thus far. Then there is the sheer delight Plato offers: once every part of *The Republic* is understood in the context of the whole, it has an austere beauty akin to the highest kind of sculpture. It seems incredible in this day of mass education that some people go to their graves without ever having learned to love Plato.

Plato summarizes his case for ethical truth in *The Republic*. In that dialogue, the theme is justice, and preliminary definitions are offered by Cephalus and Polemarchus and Thrasymachus. The debate about justice uses arguments from a tradition that was old when truth-tests were born and that has survived their demise. It has a special significance for us, as will be evident in chapter 5. The young men present find this kind of argumentation unsatisfactory and challenge Plato to tell them what justice really is and why it is good in itself. Moreover, in order to refute Thrasymachus, Plato must show that the ruling class of his ideal state is united by knowledge of the good. The demand for a case for ethical truth comes from all quarters. When the method of attaining ethical truth is made explicit, we find that Plato has been gently leading us down that path all along. Plato criticizes his theory of ethical truth in a later dialogue, namely, *The Parmenides*. As Bertrand Russell says, it is the greatest example of self-criticism in the history of Western philosophy. Clearly, Plato thought he had answers to the problems he posed. However, we do not have them, and, in fear and trembling, I will suggest that he is mistaken, based on an analysis of the role of the Chief Good.

Cephalus begins *The Republic* by asserting that wealth can offer old age the solace of having lived a just life. Money made it easier for him to tell the truth, pay his debts, and do his civic duty by sacrificing to the gods. It is immediately shown that he cannot universalize this criterion of justice, that is, he is unwilling to apply it to hypothetical situations drawn from real life. For example, he agrees that one should not return a borrowed weapon to a friend who has gone mad and also that there are exceptions to truth telling. The subtlety of Plato's sense of humor is on exhibit in that Cephalus, undeterred by the fact that his criterion of justice lies in ruins, goes off to act on it by sacrificing to the gods (*Republic*, I, 331). Cephalus represents a prephilosophical member of the older generation of Plato's day, a typical decent person who unthinkingly answers the question, What is justice? by giving examples from the code of an Athenian gentleman. Setting aside its other defects, such a method, citing examples from the conventions of one's time, could provide a criterion in accord with true justice only by an astonishing piece of luck. It is as if we asked a medieval knight what justice was, and he said, "Taking only one tenth of my serf's crops, fighting duels whenever challenged, and defending the honor of my lady."

Polemarchus, who is Cephalus's son and heir, becomes heir to the argument. He says that justice is giving each person his or her due. To avoid the implication that one should return a weapon to a friend gone mad, he adds that what is due to one's friends is the beneficial and what is due to one's enemies is the harmful. This is translated into benefiting the good and harming the wicked because a wicked friend would be no friend at all. But this criterion is nonoperational until we know who is really good and who is really evil. It also raises the question of whether it is ever right to harm anyone, even the wicked, particularly if that will worsen their character (*Republic*, I, 331–335). Polemarchus did not intend his criterion of justice to degenerate into the punitive, Old Testament concept of an eye for an eye, a tooth for a tooth, but he was betrayed by its empty generality. His method, the opposite of that of Cephalus, is equally defective. The assumption is that an ideal of justice is defective if it cannot be used to order a human society because that is the job of justice. Just as you cannot do that by listing examples of supposed just acts, which will always omit areas of human behavior we wish to regulate, you cannot do it by leaping prematurely to a concept so broad that it is nonoperational. Polemarchus's definition leaves open the question, To whom is due what? That question can be answered only by a psychology that classifies people and a sociology that classifies social roles, so that the proper person can be matched with the proper role, plus a criterion of goodness that ensures you are contemplating a good rather than a debased human society.

Thrasymachus offers the first definition of justice with a serious claim to be operational, one so powerful that it threatens to marginalize Plato's own. He bases it on the methodology of modern social science, the methodologies of cross-cultural anthropology and comparative politics. He has surveyed a variety of human societies, including democracies and tyrannies, and found no ethical principles in common. However, he can offer an empirical generalization: they were all ordered by the struggle for power. This struggle divides society into winners and losers, and the winners use the legal code to define as "right" for the losers what is in their own interest. There is no true right or wrong operating at all, of course. It is just that the rulers have the power to label the weak "wrongdoers" if they break the law (*Republic*, I, 338–339).

Thrasymachus presents Plato with a dual challenge: if reason defined as the scientific method is the only road to knowledge, it discloses no ethical truth; and even if there were such a thing as true justice, it would be purely academic. In the real world, politics is the ordering principle of human society, and ethics plays no role. So-called justice is rule in the interest of the stronger. It is no more or less than the principle of might makes right.

Initially, Plato uses ordinary non-truth-test arguments against Thrasymachus. Thrasymachus is shown to be unwilling to face up to some of the consequences of his principles in practice. Many political actors, Hitler, for example, were skilled at winning power but ruled in a way destructive of their own interests. Is anyone really bound to help them destroy themselves and often the rest of society with them? Thrasymachus responds that his ideal ruler would know not only how to achieve power but also how to use it in his or her own interest. So power is not enough; it must be accompanied by knowledge or wisdom, if only the amoral wisdom of enlightened self-interest. If the ruler must be knowledgeable, that suggests analogies with other occupations and their peculiar skills. Thrasymachus is forced to admit that the art of government, whether rulers are self-interested or not, involves knowing how to benefit someone other than oneself. For example, a doctor or a ship's captain, whether venal or not, must know how to cure illness or how to get the best out of a crew and navigate (*Republic*, I, 339–342).

Thrasymachus grants that all arts involve something beyond self-interest, namely, knowledge of how to perfect something or benefit someone, but he suggests an analogy of his own. The shepherd must know how to keep sheep healthy and how to fatten them, but the motive is solely to exploit them for the shepherd's own benefit. This analogy looks telling but, as soon becomes clear, contains a fatal weakness: the shepherd rules animals. Plato mounts a devastating counterattack. No human group can function without an ethical code within the group, even if its purpose is to exploit those who fall outside the group. Even a band of thieves needs honor among thieves. If everyone's hand were turned against everyone else, they could not even divide the booty without fatal conflict, which means that they would be completely dysfunctional (*Republic*, I, 343 & 351–352). It is not accidental that real-world tyrants have always made idealistic appeals, Hitler that Germany had a mission to save Western civilization from contamination by inferior races, Stalin that he was the engine of a historical process that would create a classless and humane society. No tyrant can rule without helpers. He or she needs a band of thieves, including some true believers, and the ruling elite cannot compel the masses without some degree of voluntary compliance. Thrasymachus claimed ethics was purely academic. Perhaps ethics alone cannot order a human society, but neither can politics. Politics requires ethics at least as a supplementary principle. Perhaps we can rule animals without ethics but not human beings.

At this point, Glaucon and Adeimantus jump into the debate. They are young Greeks and, unlike Cephalus, they cannot simply accept traditional mores. They feel genuinely torn between Plato's idealism and Thrasymachus's self-interested nihilism. Glaucon bluntly tells Plato that thus far morality seems no better than honor among thieves, a morality so debased it is hardly worthy of the name. Thieves need a code to exploit others, and perhaps that is all people really want to do. However, they realize that a war of all against all leads to a Hobbesian state of nature, a state of anarchy dangerous for all. Therefore, they adopt a so-called moral code that reduces exploitation to an acceptable level, but it is simply a game of let's pretend. No one is really committed to moral principles; everyone looks upon them as a necessary but unwelcome check on the real business of life, which is pursuit of self-interest. Glaucon drives the point home with the fable of the ring, the ring of Gyges that made the wearer invisible and therefore invulnerable. If only we had the ring, we could steal and kill and rape at will; lacking it, we must join others in the loathed mutual security pact that is morality. Fortunately, there are simpletons who take morality seriously and forgo more than their share of advantage. Glaucon demands of Plato an account of what justice really is and how it perfects human nature irrespective of real-world consequences (*Republic*, II, 358–361; VII, 538).

Adeimantus remarks that even the Greek gods seem to set no value on justice except insofar as it produces rewards in this world or the next. The fate of justice cut loose from knowledge of justice is pathetic. The cowardly and weak will use it to censure the strong, whom they would imitate if only they could, an anticipation of Nietzsche's account of herd morality. Adeimantus echoes Glaucon's demand that Plato show that justice is good as a perfection of human nature and show what is really right or wrong as distinct from mere opinion or appearance (*Republic*, II, 363 & 366–367).

Plato responds by a radical shift in the mode of argument. He begins to sketch an ideal society with the hope that justice will emerge in the process. Behind the detail there lies an overall objective. Plato is attempting to give a direct answer to one of Thrasymachus's main challenges: show me that ethics can organize a society without the aid of politics. Recall that Plato and Thrasymachus accept one thesis in common, that insofar as the struggle for power participates in organizing a human society, it dilutes ethics with the principle of might makes right. If that principle is to be banished, as surely it must in an ideal society, all sources of the struggle for power must be eliminated. One obvious source would be disputes within the ruling class, which focuses our attention on a promissory note Plato must redeem. Throughout his sketch of his ideal society, we are asked to assume that there is some method that generates unity of opinion about the good. The ruling class, the philosopher kings, have a monopoly of this knowledge; it is their distinguishing characteristic. Sooner or later, Plato must describe and defend his method of gaining ethical truth (*Republic*, VI, 506).

The first step toward the elimination of the struggle for power is an educational system that decides to whom is due what. The educational system serves as an apolitical institution that selects the ruling elite and allocates people to their social roles. All citizens go into it on a basis of equality. There is total social mobility from one generation to another, parental status counting for nothing, and equal opportunity for male and female, gender counting for nothing. At all levels, the citizens are assessed for both intellectual ability and virtue. Those few capable of learning the difficult science of dialectic, which confers knowledge of the good, plus possessing love of the good and courage become philosopher kings. A larger number not capable of dialectic but passionate in their love of good, when the philosophers expose them to it, and preeminent in courage become auxiliaries, an administrative cadre who staff the army and police. Those with practical talents become the mass of people who carry on the economic functions of the state. All classes must possess temperance, the willingness to accept that proven merit should determine one's social role, although this is preeminently the virtue of the masses (*Republic*, III, 400–402 & 412–413; IV, 423–424 & 428–432; V, 454–456; VII, 535–540).

Respect for proven merit will permeate society only if people internalize the appropriate mores. This brings us to the myth of the metals, not a lie or piece of propaganda but an anthropological concept, an anticipation of the role of cultural patterns and myths and heroes in conditioning people. All classes accept it, even the philosopher kings, who accept only the truth, although they alone could give a rational account of the concept of justice that lies behind it, the concept that the myth plants in the masses through the nonrational process of acculturation. The myth says that different people have different metals mixed with their characters, some gold, some silver, some bronze, that the philosopher kings will perceive which metal predominates as people go through the educational system, and that people must be assigned to their social roles accordingly (*Republic*, III, 414–415). The myth describes the only mores that set politics aside in favor of merit as a title to rule. The cultural patterns, myths, and heroes of all other societies lead straight to the struggle for power because they induce a competitive ethos. In democracy, worship of the common man leads to a popularity contest, for how else can you determine who is most popular? Militarist mores, identifying the good person with the good soldier, lead to a test of strength, for the best general is the one who can defeat the others. The love of money leads to the robber baron–dominated politics of late-nineteenth-century America, because the essence of competitive capitalism is using your wealth to outbid others for goods, including the prize of high office.

The next step toward the elimination of the struggle for power is to solve the problem of recognition. The masses may be predisposed to accept the rule of the best, but since they themselves lack knowledge of the good, how can they possibly recognize who possesses that knowledge and who has the virtuous character that justifies trust? Part of the genius of *The Republic* is that it gives the masses simple signs accessible to all. The fact that their rulers never dispute about the good is a sign of knowledge. In theory, it could be a conspiracy of silence that conceals differences of opinion from the masses, but their own children join the ranks of the philosopher kings, and such a conspiracy would be difficult in practice. The way of life of the rulers, the guardian class composed of the philosopher kings and their auxiliaries, is a visible demonstration that they are not motivated by greed or nepotism. The masses enjoy private property and family life, but their rulers have all things in common and a life-style Spartan compared to that of their subjects. The rulers are forbidden to be under the same roof with gold and silver, they live communally and dine on plain fare, they wear plain clothes without jewelry or ornamentation. They beget children at mating festivals with the nuclear family so undermined that no ruler thinks of any particular child as peculiarly his or her own (*Republic*, III, 416–417; V, 457–463). The moment a ruler moves into a mansion, opens up a Swiss bank account, treats a young person as son or daughter, the masses know they have been betrayed.

The community of property and family also eliminates greed and nepotism as things that might corrupt the rulers, and it helps bond them together. Small size contributes to the unity of the whole society, because there are none of the social divisions that make politics inevitable in a mass society that is always many "cities" pretending to be one. The rulers ensure that there are no extremes of wealth, so that there is not a "city" of the rich and a "city" of the poor. Small size also contributes to solving the problem of recognition. In a city-state of perhaps 100,000 people, the members of each age cohort going through the educational system know one another personally, and all know which among them stands out as gifted, courageous, generous, honest (*Republic*, III, 416; IV, 420–423; V, 463–465; VIII, 551).

All of this would not suffice to eliminate the struggle for power if the lust for power were innate in human nature. Plato tells us that life is not worth living unless people have a proper job or social role. Those who do find fulfillment and develop a sense of inner worth. Those who do not lack self-esteem and become hollow people who seek in the applause of others that good opinion they lack of themselves. Therefore, they begin to compete for power and the artificial prestige it brings (*Republic*, III, 406–407; VII, 521). In other words, the lust for power is not innate, it is a form of mental illness society creates when people are taught to despise or cannot find meaningful work. The resemblance to the psychology of Erich Fromm is striking. In his analysis of post-Renaissance people Fromm describes them as having freedom from traditional social constraints but, thanks to the worthless roles provided by mass society, lacking freedom to create a valued self. Therefore, they develop the pathology of aggression (Fromm, 1941). Such hypotheses must be tested empirically, but no one should dismiss Plato's prescientific psychology as primitive. He offers the image of a chariot in which the driver uses an obedient lead horse to control another wayward horse; that is, cool reason may know the good but cannot control the passions without a passionate ally, without a spirit that loves the good and greets evil with moral indignation (*Phaedrus*, 253–254; *Timaeus*, 70; *Republic*, IV, 440–442; IX, 589). Freudians recognize in this an anticipation of ego, superego, and id, just as they find familiar Plato's analysis of the dream-work. Plato tells us that when we sleep, reason and the better passions (spirit) lose control over the baser passions, and, therefore, in our dreams nothing is too shameful, whether sexual intercourse with a mother or beast, whether murder or sacrilege (*Republic*, IX, 571–572).

When we review all that has been done to eliminate politics in the ideal society, we discover a working model of justice. Justice is the myth of the metals operationalized, the principle of each person performing an appropriate social role, rather than aspiring to a role unmatched by his or her proven worth (*Republic*, IV, 432–434). Those who belittle Plato's ideal are blind to the many facets that emerge when it operates as the organizing principle of a human society. It guarantees to all people the right to an education that diagnoses and perfects their unique talents, plus a work role that conveys a sense of self-esteem, saving them from the neuroses of megalomania and the lust for power. It forbids privilege and sexism and all other criteria irrelevant to merit. It eliminates conflict of interest from those who hold office and gives the masses a potent checklist they can use to hold their rulers to account. Best of all, it eliminates all traces of might makes right and serves as a pattern laid up in heaven to rank actual societies in terms of what corrupts them. Society becomes more corrupt as the struggle for power becomes more brutal, ranging from rich versus poor, to the mob versus the forces of reaction, and finally to the tyrant versus everyone else (*Republic* VIII, 547–570; IX, 571–576 & 592).

Plato's concept of justice has been elaborated, but it has not been shown to be in accord with ethical truth. He has answered Thrasymachus's second challenge: show me a society that uses ethics to replace politics. However, he has not yet addressed Thrasymachus's first challenge: show me a nonscientific road to knowledge of good and evil. It is time for Plato to redeem his promissory note.

He tells us that his sketch of his society was not mere personal invention. It was a word-picture of an ideal society whose perfection can only be approximated by an existing state. That ideal society is ordered by absolute justice, whose opposite is absolute injustice, and it is one rather than many. The material world creates a multiplicity of imperfect societies that are a blend of justice and injustice. Knowledge of the ideal society, all knowledge, must be knowledge of a universal that exists in a real world. The visible world is a mix of the real and the unreal and gives rise only to opinion. The philosopher kings must look to the world of eternal, unchanging, absolute realities, and there they will find the eternal and immutable truth. They will find a model, perceive its every aspect, and become artists. They will paint on the canvas of an actual society, having wiped it clean, a copy of the model they have come to know (*Republic*, V, 472–473 & 476–479; VI, 484–485 & 500–501). Well, then, we gain knowledge of justice by perceiving the ordering principle of the perfect state of human society, which exists in a real world beyond the visible world. Clearly Plato's epistemology, his theory of knowledge, is based on his metaphysics, his theory of being. The latter must be summarized before we can comprehend the former.

I will attempt to summarize Plato's metaphysics, as he formulated it at the time of *The Republic*, in seven steps:

1. There exist in our minds general ideas not reducible to sense-images, one for each class of particulars.

2. There exists independently of our minds a physical universe that is the external source of our sense-images.

3. There exists independently of our minds a World of Forms that is the external source of our general ideals.

4. The Forms compare favorably with physical objects. The two are perfect and imperfect, real and a compromise with the unreal, one and many, eternal and changing, respectively.

5. The Forms structure the physical universe but cannot make it perfect or eternal because of its material composition.

6. There exists a Chief Good, a Form of the Good, related to the particular Forms much as they are related to sense particulars.

7. The content of the Chief Good is unknown, but it is the ultimate source of knowledge and transcends even justice, beauty, and truth.

As Russell (1912, chap. 9) says, Plato begins his metaphysics with a problem of logic. Despite their differences, we put a multiplicity of particular things into a single class and call them all the same name; for example, we put large and small chairs, brown and blue chairs into the single class "chair." It is our ability to classify things that allows us to distinguish one kind of thing from another, for example, to distinguish chairs from tables. How is that logically possible? The two chairs that differ from one another most must still have more in common than either does with a table. What they have in common is that they meet the criteria set by a general idea of chair existent in our minds, whether we are reflectively aware of it or not. It cannot be reduced to a sense-image of a chair because then its boundaries would be too narrow to include all the particulars that fall within its class. For example, every sense-image of a chair has a particular color, say, blue, and certainly a thing does not have to be blue to be a chair. Or it has a particular height, say, four feet tall, that would exclude from the class chair all chairs larger or smaller than that. The logic of the argument dictates that there cannot be more than one general idea of chair. If there were several, we would still call that diverse group the same name, "general ideas of chair," which implies that there is an idea truly broad enough to cover them all. Or alternatively, how would two general ideas of chair differ? If they are distinguishable from one another, one must have a characteristic the other lacks. But if we call them both "general ideas of chair," that difference must be irrelevant to being a chair (*Republic*, X, 596–597).

All classes possess a general idea, not just chairs and tables and beds, but also clouds and giraffes and human societies, triangles and things equal and things unequal (relations like larger than or heavier than), things beautiful or true or just. Any thing or relation or quality we can distinguish from all else falls under a general idea, which is to say that the Doctrine of Ideas (or Forms) has a *linguistic* role. The ideas are what modern philosophers call universals, and they clarify the meaning of certain words in sentences like "chairs are so expensive, but I would like to replace my easy chair." Clearly the first use of the word chair in that sentence refers to a whole class, while the second is like a proper name and singles out a particular chair for our attention. We may think we can evade positing a general idea or universal for each class of particulars. Can we not say that all chairs have a function in common that distinguishes them from tables, namely, they are devised to be sat on? However, sitting on a hard desk chair is different from sinking into a soft easy chair, so now we have a new class of differing particulars, all of which we call the same name, "sitting on a chair." Can we not simply say that all chairs resemble one another in a way that they do not resemble tables? But two similar desk chairs resemble one another much more than either does an upholstered easy chair. So now we have two differing resemblances, both of which we call "resemblance between chairs." A general idea surfaces no matter what we do.

Plato is a realist about the external existence of the physical universe, that is, he does not take seriously the possibility that the universe is a set of experiences existent only in our minds. In the simile of the sun, he assumes there are external objects of sight from which we get our visual images thanks to the light the sun provides, external sources of sound, and so forth. He also posits an external World of Forms from which our mind's eye gets the general ideas on a one-to-one basis, the general idea of chair from apprehending the Form of Chair, the general idea of human society from apprehending the Form of Human Society, and so forth (*Republic*, VI, 507–509).

Plato's argument for the external existence of the Forms is presented in earlier dialogues such as *The Meno* (82–85) and *The Phaedo* (73–77). He contends that there is no alternative explanation of how we happen to possess certain kinds of knowledge. When we learn geometry, we "recollect" concepts like square and number and ratio that are not part of what our sense experience has provided since our birth in the physical universe. People use these concepts to assess physical relations; for example, they say that two pieces of wood are almost equal, which implies a concept of perfect equality not found in the physical world. Probably they get these concepts between incarnations when their minds are detached from their bodies and dwell in the World of Forms (*Phaedrus*, 247–250; *Republic*, X, 611 & 614–620). If our passive capacity to be aware of the general ideas implies an origin beyond the physical universe, certainly human beings trapped in a body do not possess the active capacity to generate general ideas. Only a god might be able to do so (*Republic*, X, 596–597). Having eliminated an internal origin and an external physical origin, the existence of the general ideas in our minds implies an external nonphysical origin. They must come to us from a nonphysical realm.

The fact that only the Forms are perfect and physical things are always imperfect has wider implications. Only the general idea of chair captures the carpenter's ideal design (all physical chairs will have one leg a millimeter too long, will lack perfect stability). Precisely by being perfect, only the general idea captures the essence of what a chair really is. Actual chairs are a compromise between that and the opposite of what a chair really is, for it is no part of being a chair to be unbalanced and unstable. Similarly, only the concept of a straight line is of something perfectly straight, so only it captures what a straight line really is, the shortest distance between two points. All lines drawn on the blackboard are irregular and a compromise between what a straight line really is and its opposite, a crooked line. Perfection and reality or being are interrelated; imperfection and the unreal or not-being are also interrelated. The former belong to the World of Forms and the latter to the physical world.

The proof that each class has only one general idea also shows that the ideas are eternal. For an idea to change, it would have to be distinguishable at two times: at time two it would have to have a characteristic it lacked at time one, but if it were truly the general idea of, say, straight line at time one, no characteristic could be added or subtracted. Any change in the concept "shortest distance between two points" would mean it was not a concept of straight line at all. Physical "straight lines" made of chalk are always changing and decaying because they are material. They can be many because there are many ways of deviating from perfect straightness (*Republic*, V, 476 & 479; VI, 508 & 510–511; X, 597).

The Forms have a causal influence on the physical universe. God or gods may create the Forms but they do not seem to create matter, which, without the influence of the Forms, would be mere formless chaos. Human agents use the Forms, as when a carpenter copies the Form of Chair or a philosopher king paints a picture of the Form of Human Society, but they are also the originals of things beyond human agency like plants and animals and the heavens (*Republic*, VI, 501 & 510; X, 597). In *The Republic*, a divine agent is posited, for example, a maker of the heavens who used numbers and perfect figures to impose order and make the planets and stars as perfect as such things can be (*Republic*, VII, 529–530). Matter cannot take the Forms perfectly. It is as if someone took a perfect star-shaped mold and pressed it on dough to make a multiplicity of star-shaped cookies. Thanks to the dough sticking to the mold, sometimes one point of the star would be rounded off, sometimes another, each cookie differing because of its peculiar deviation from perfection but all belonging to the same class. In *The Phaedo* the Forms appear to have their own causal potency; for example, fire attempts to impose the Form of Heat on snow, which cannot accommodate it and therefore perishes (*Phaedo*, 103–105). This would imply that the influence of the Forms in shaping the physical universe need not have had a literal start in time. They may have exercised their causal pull on matter from all eternity, matter continually decaying and being reshaped by the influence of various Forms.

The Timaeus complicates the scenario of divine creation by mixing the influence of the Forms with virtually every cosmological myth current in Plato's day plus primitive Greek physiology. Admittedly, we are continually told that what is being said is conjecture only. Perhaps it is best to be content with this: the physical world is a realm of endless flux or becoming because it is a compromise between two opposite influences, the Forms pulling it toward being or changeless perfection, matter pulling it toward formless chaos (*Republic*, V, 478–479; X, 609 & 611). I shall call the influence of the Forms in shaping the physical universe the *metaphysical* role of the Doctrine of Forms.

The logic of Plato's argument drives him to posit a Form of Forms often translated as the Chief Good. Logic forced us to posit a general idea for each class of differing particulars, and now we have a new class of differing entities we can distinguish from all else, the class of Forms. Just as there must be a general idea of chair, there must be a general idea of what it is to be a Form, an idea derived from an externally existing Form of Forms, and there can be only one such. This exhausts all levels of existence in that the Chief Good, being one and unique, presents us with no new class of differing things all called by the same name. Just as a particular Form validates the credentials of its particulars, just as the general idea of chair sets a criterion all physical chairs must meet, so the Chief Good validates the credentials of particular Forms, vouches that they have the reality and perfection needed to enter the World of Forms. It is an absolute criterion of perfection broad enough to cover all the different kinds of perfection that exist in the World of Forms (the beauty of a painting, the truth of geometry, the justice of a perfect human society), so it is broader than mere moral perfection. Unless understood, the term Chief Good can deceive by suggesting moral goodness. The Form of Forms would be better translated as Absolute Perfection (*Republic*, VI, 508–509; VII, 533–534).

At the time of *The Republic*, Plato claimed at best a dim awareness of the content of the Chief Good. The hope held out is that just as we might prepare our eyes to see the sun by looking at its reflection in pools of water, so we might prepare our minds to directly apprehend the Chief Good by focusing on the Forms as reflections of the Chief Good (*Republic*, VI, 505–506; VII, 517–518 & 532–533). Presumably it would be a kind of divine harmony, catching the design of a beautiful painting, the coherence of mathematics, the harmony justice confers on social classes. This completes our account of Plato's metaphysics, so we proceed to the divided line, which conveys his epistemology or theory of truth.

The divided line has four levels, each conferring a higher understanding on the road to truth (*Republic*, VI, 511). The best way to appreciate the ascent is to take something up the divided line, and Plato's frequent references suggest geometry. I will go beyond the text to supply details of my own invention, taking solace in the fact that this is mere illustration. We will be on firmer ground when we ascend the divided line to knowledge of justice.

The first level of the divided line yields the lowest level of knowledge, called *illusion*. Here people focus on the physical universe and observe it unsystematically, often using what is closest to hand. Geometry on this level would work with crude physical things. For example, if you were laying out a tennis court, you might use wedges to square off the angles and cord to get the lines straight. You rise to *opinion* on the second level by observing systematically and making the best possible use of the physical universe. When the yearly Nile flood washed away property boundaries, the Egyptians, if they wanted to avoid disputes, had to survey accurately. They also wanted to build symmetrical pyramids, and they discovered a trick to square off the base. A slave stood at a certain point, a rope was passed to another slave 30 meters away, then passed to another slave 40 meters away, then passed back to the first slave and drawn taut. The result was a perfect right angle. The rope had, of course, delineated a 3-4-5 right triangle, thanks to the Pythagorean theorem that the sum of the squares of the lengths of the two legs (3×3 plus 4×4) equals the square of the length of the hypotenuse (5×5). The Egyptians could not state the theorem, much less prove it. Which is to say that they had to be content with the best geometry they could get when operating within the context of the visible world (*Republic*, VI, 510 & 515; VII, 527 & 531).

To ascend to *reason,* the sort of understanding mathematicians or scientists get when they do not question their methods or basic assumptions, you must go on to the third level of the divided line. This means leaving the world of sense behind and focusing the mind on the Forms, in this case the pure Forms of spatial entities and numbers. It is not just that only the general idea of a straight line is perfect and, therefore, that only the idea represents the shortest distance between two points. It is that physical representations of geometrical concepts cannot yield the basic axioms and postulates of geometry. Two lines drawn on a blackboard do not intersect at a point but rather in a small chunk of space like a miniature cube. Point is inherently a concept of the intellect. Here we have geometry as taught in secondary school: a deductive system that simply assumes its axioms and postulates and from them derives its propositions such as the Pythagorean theorem (*Republic*, VI, 510; VII, 516).

To attain real *knowledge* or truth, you must go on to the fourth level and solve epistemological problems about the foundations of the various specialized areas of "knowledge." I will illustrate the kind of problem I think a Platonist would envision. How is it that geometry, which measures purely conceptual entities, has so many applications to the physical universe, and why is it that it describes the physical universe almost but not quite accurately? When the Greeks tried to chart the heavens, the fact that their astronomy was earth-centered guaranteed at least some inaccuracy. Both of these epistemological problems find a simple and beautiful solution in Plato's metaphysics. Just as a material chair is an imperfect copy of the Form of Chair, so the physical universe is an imperfect copy of the pure

Forms of certain shapes and their relationships. Therefore, a geometrical description of the latter will have universal but imperfect application to the former. However, to be certain that our analysis of the relevant forms was valid, we would have to verify that our minds had focused on true Forms and not approximations. That means knowing the Chief Good, because it validates the credentials of Forms to qualify as such (*Republic*, VI, 505 & 508–511; VII, 516–518 & 528–530).

This has been speculation, not about the divided line, concerning which I have tried to remain faithful to Plato's account, but about the elevation of geometry from illusion to knowledge. But what is not speculation is that the divided line is the only road to truth, including the truth about justice. If that is so, and if Plato takes his own method seriously, and if *The Republic* is a search for absolute justice, then we must have been ascending the divided line from its very first page. Plato has given us a new pair of spectacles with which to read *The Republic*, so let us try them on and take *The Republic* up the divided line, specifying when it leaves one level for another.

Cephalus, sunk in illusion, is on the lowest level of the divided line. He defines justice purely by referring to physically present human societies, worse, only one such society, worse still, only one class from that society. Worst of all, he merely lists random examples of that class's moral code, namely, the code of an Athenian gentleman. We now have a deeper insight into his methodological mistake. It is not just that, like an unreflective medieval knight, he describes the peculiar mores of his time and place, the odds in favor of that time and place mirroring true justice being one in a thousand. Actually, his chances of success were zero. He tried to find the perfect state of human society by observing a society that was an imperfect copy. He is like someone who tries to capture the essence of a chair by pointing to a familiar rickety Victorian parlor chair, skeptical that a modern lawn chair was a chair at all. He is like someone who, impatient at being asked to define a straight line, gets up and chalks one on the blackboard.

Thrasymachus rose to the level of opinion by his use of the scientific method. Unlike Cephalus, who did not even try to describe the physical world accurately, Thrasymachus made systematic observations of all the physically present human societies he could find and made an accurate generalization: all of them to some degree are ordered by the struggle for power. Hitherto, we have criticized him only for failing to supplement this with another equally accurate generalization: all human societies supplement politics with ethics; all of them to some degree are ordered by a moral code, if only honor among thieves. Now we see that his methodology betrayed him on a far deeper level: what all actual human societies have in common is imperfection or defect; all of their ordering principles, despite a nod to justice, rely heavily on the principle of might makes right. The observational method, when focused blindly on the imperfect physical world, led Thrasymachus to what all people (even he) intuitively recognize as the opposite of justice. It is as if you tried to define a straight line by observing what all actual lines have in common, which is that none of them are quite straight. You would say that a straight line is not the shortest distance between two points, which is to say, you would be led straight to its opposite.

After Glaucon and Adeimantus demand to know the truth about justice, Plato has no choice but to ascend to the third level of the divided line and paint a word-picture of the ideal or perfect state of human society, which exists only in the World of Forms. Therefore, it is absolutely essential to transcend the physical world. But what we have learned in the physical world is absolutely essential to exploring the World of Forms. Witness the fate of Polemarchus, who offered us only his intuitions about justice. Thanks to the empirical method of Thrasymachus, we know the opposite of justice, and taking the opposite of that opposite leads us to justice itself, or at least a crude working hypothesis. We must ask ourselves, What is the opposite of "might makes right"? The answer is that "right makes might," or that proven merit justifies rule. Indeed, merit should allocate people to all social roles, which is the message of the myth of the metals. Moreover, we now have an operational strategy: whatever ethical principles eliminate the struggle for power must be at least an approach to true justice. The principles that pass this test are equal opportunity for all irrespective of birth or gender, wasting no person's talent, giving everyone work with dignity, no extremes of rich and poor, banishing conflict of interest from rule, and the dictum that justice must be seen to be done.

A rough approximation of the content of the Form of Human Society is not the ultimate aim. The full truth about justice is possible only on the fourth level, and that means that we must know the Chief Good. The Chief Good sets the criterion for entry into the World of Forms: an entity must be perfect of its kind, and (as we have seen) only one entity can meet that criterion. By dictating that the Form of Human Society shall contain the perfect state of human society, the Chief Good determines that justice will be found therein. By dictating that there can be only one Form of Human Society, the Chief Good creates the unity of opinion that constitutes knowledge, rather than the diversity of opinion that exists when knowledge is absent. All of this assumes that we know how to read the contents of the Forms. Plato has tried to describe the content of the Form of Human Society but, lacking knowledge of the Chief Good, he cannot hold his concept of it up to the light of the Chief Good. He cannot validate his concept against the criterion that must stamp the credentials of every putative Form.

Nonetheless, something has been achieved. The third and final role of the Doctrine of Forms, their *epistemological* role as givers of truth about the perfect state of things, stands revealed. That is enough to answer Thrasymachus's challenge to show him a nonscientific road to knowledge of good and evil. Our criterion of justice may be only an approximation, but still there is reason to believe we are not far from the truth. When we eliminated the struggle for power in favor of our criterion, a splendid society emerged, at least Plato thought so, and this can hardly have seemed to him an accident. Such a harmonious society simply must be far closer to the truth than Thrasymachus's ideal. After all, Thrasymachus endorsed the opposite of justice. All this suggests that while further progress toward knowledge of ethical truth may produce refinements in our criterion of justice, it will not substitute some radically new criterion. Our ideal has been sufficiently vindicated that we can tell all humankind, so long as we are honest about our reservations, that it is worthy of acceptance.

In sum, *The Republic* seems to have offered us a rough but workable truth-test, that is, a criterion of justice that has objective status. The formal criterion of how close a particular society comes to perfection is how close it comes to resembling the contents of its perfect Form. Various human societies should be ranked in terms of how closely they resemble the Form of Human Society. However, the truth-test is nonoperational until ascending the divided line has given us a description of the contents of the relevant Form. Plato's description of his ideal society, a society that eliminates the struggle for power by way of a meritocratic harmony, is held to be a reasonably accurate description. Athens (at its best) was closer to that ideal than Carthage (Kipling thought Carthage almost as vile as Manchester). Therefore, Athens was objectively more just, not merely more appealing to its citizens.

And then, with *The Parmenides*, everything starts to unravel. This is because of the various roles played by the Doctrine of Forms and how they are interrelated. They can serve as a road to ethical knowledge only if two prerequisites are met: we must be able to read the perfect state of things in the content of the general ideas; and there must be only one general idea for each class, otherwise there will be no unity of opinion about its perfect state. After all, if there were ten distinguishable general ideas of human society, each containing its own variant of its perfect state, the advocates of any one could not refute the advocates of the nine others. The second prerequisite can be met only if the general ideas are universals, because the argument that there was only one for each class was derived therefrom. The notion that there could be two general ideas of chair was deemed absurd, because if either idea covered all particular chairs, then whatever distinguished the second "general idea" from the first must be irrelevant. Plato's epistemology has an Achilles' heel: unless the general ideas can be both universals and contain the perfect state of things, unless these two roles are compatible, the case for ethical truth collapses. *The Parmenides* is frustrating in that the role of the ideas as perfect exemplars tends to be submerged. However, when the self-criticism is most acute, that role surfaces at least by implication.

The first question posed is whether there is a general idea for each class of thing, not just for abstract or mathematical relations and evaluative categories like beauty and goodness but also for concrete particulars like men, fire, and water, even hair, mud, and dirt. The young Socrates, young presumably to signal that the mature Plato would have had better answers to offer, says it would be absurd to posit general ideas or Forms for undignified things (*Parmenides*, 130). But why is that? There is no absurdity in positing universals for all classes. Certainly we can distinguish mud from hair, just as we can distinguish chairs from tables, so there must be a general idea of mud. What it is absurd to posit is this: a perfect state of mud.

The fact that classes of things can have general ideas without having a perfect state complicates Plato's epistemology. Until now, given a general idea, you simply describe its contents and thereby read off its perfect state. Now there is a prior question: How do we know it has a perfect state at all? It is certainly not obvious that human society possesses a true perfect state, that is, a perfect state independent of the many differing concepts of perfection people use when assessing it. It was only so long as every kind of thing appeared to have a perfect state that it seemed odd to dispute that human society had one. And what of relations? Two things that are not quite equal are not imperfectly equal, they are not equal at all. So here it seems absurd to say that there are particulars that are imperfect copies of the Form. The Forms now pose what I will call the first task of discrimination: How do we judge which Forms encompass the perfect only, which Forms both the perfect and the imperfect, which Forms the nonperfect in the sense that the word "perfect" does not even apply?

The next contention is that Plato, neither in *The Republic* nor in *The Phaedo*, has spelled out the precise relationship between a general idea and its particulars. The language used in those dialogues is subject to devastating criticism. To say that particular chairs become such by "partaking" of their general idea calls up the image of empty vessels that get filled by their general ideal. If so, each particular must contain either the whole idea or a part. The first is absurd because now particulars are virtually identical with their universals. The second is absurd because a criterion for a class, whose totality is necessary to delineate its class, cannot be divided into parts, each capable of delineating its class. To say that a general idea is "broad enough to cover" all of its differing particulars calls up another image. The general idea of human being becomes like a sail spread over all particular human beings, all of whom manage to stand under it. Since each particular person is standing under only his or her own particular part of the sail, this wording is no improvement on "partake" (*Parmenides*, 131).

The problem is compounded by what is called the "third man dilemma." We are impaled by that dilemma unless our account of the relationship between a general idea and its particulars clearly distinguishes that relationship from another, namely, the relationship its particulars bear to each other. In other words, particular chairs cannot be related to the idea in the same way they are related to one another. Their peculiar relationship with one another, all qualifying for the same name despite their differences, was what forced us to posit the idea of chair to delineate the class. If that same relationship holds between each particular and its idea, we must then posit an additional general idea of chair broad enough to cover the original idea plus its particulars, and so on ad infinitum. That is, the first chair (a particular) and the second chair (the initial idea) are joined by a third chair (covering the previous two), with a fourth chair (covering the previous three) on the horizon. The lesson is that we must not think of the idea of chair as if it itself possessed the characteristics of a chair. Identifying it with a perfect chair seems to imply that it does (*Parmenides*, 132).

The Republic and *The Phaedo* offer one more formulation of the relationship between a general idea and its particulars, namely, that the latter are "likenesses" or "copies" of the former. The particulars are imperfect copies of their general idea, which means they are like it to some degree and unlike it to some degree. If particular chairs are like the idea in whatever makes something a chair and unlike it in whatever is irrelevant to being a chair, that duplicates the relationship particular chairs bear to one another. A blue chair and a brown chair are unlike in color, which is irrelevant, but like in their chairness. Therefore, the concept of "likeness" entails, rather than avoids, the third man dilemma. It is stressed that all of these problems arise even if the general ideas exist in our minds only, rather than coming to us from an external World of Forms. This is true because the analysis has focused solely on the content of the general ideas, their nature as universals and perfect exemplars, rather than on their origins (*Parmenides*, 132–133).

Since we lack Plato's solution to these problems, let us ourselves attempt to clarify the relationship between a universal and its particulars. Crude physical analogies, particulars partaking as if they were consuming a pie, particulars standing under something, particulars being blurred copies or photographs of a universal—this sort of empirical imagery is useless. It is as bad as what goes on at the lower levels of the divided line. A universal is a criterion particulars must meet to enter its class. To be a chair, something must be manufactured, designed for the seated human form, made of material strong enough to supply support, and so forth. If we were to use any analogy, it would be of an entrance exam all candidates must pass to qualify for a class. This account of the relationship between a universal and its particulars answers many of the objections put. Candidates do not "partake" of the exam they pass, they do not devour the whole exam or a part of it. The exam does not "cover" the successful candidates; rather, it poses questions they must answer satisfactorily. Successful candidates are not related to the exam as they are related to one another, they are related to one another as members of the same class and to the exam as the criterion each of them met. Therefore, the third man dilemma does not arise.

This may seem to salvage the general ideas as true universals, but that is not the central problem, as we are soon reminded. There is a discussion about whether knowledge of the Forms and knowledge of the physical universe are compartmentalized, so that no one could know both; and that discussion emphasizes that the general ideas contain pure being and perfection, while physical things fall short of these (*Parmenides*, 133–134). The point is not developed, but the implications are potentially disastrous. We have said that if the general idea of chair were blue, it would set a criterion brown chairs could not pass, which would be absurd. Similarly, if the general idea of chair is perfect, all of the imperfect chairs in the physical universe would not be chairs at all. Identifying the content of the general ideas with the perfect state of things, in any simple sense, undermines them as universals. And yet both roles are essential for the case for ethical truth.

Clearly, if both roles are to be performed, the general ideas must be expanded to accommodate both perfect and imperfect particulars. A general idea provides the boundaries of a class, and perhaps those boundaries establish both an upper and a lower limit. For mud, there would be a moisture spectrum, the upper limit the point at which mud becomes so dry as to turn into dirt, the lower the point at which mud dissolves and becomes cloudy water. Neither limit would deserve to be called the perfect state of mud. For equality, the upper and lower limits would coincide. Things have to be perfectly equal to be equal at all, analogous to candidates having to score 100 percent to pass their exam. For chair, there would be a stability spectrum, the upper limit of which would be perfect stability, the lower limit that minimal level of stability beyond which something would be a broken or dismantled chair. Perhaps the upper limit would be labeled part of the perfect state of chair, although it might be argued that so long as a chair is very stable, perfect stability provides no extra advantage.

For human society, there would be a harmony spectrum, the upper limit that degree of harmony beyond which humans would have to turn into social insects, the lower that minimal level of cooperation beyond which you get anarchy or a state of nature. Plato might label the upper limit the perfect state of human society, hailing it as the point at which ethics has banished politics and maximum cooperation prevails. Such a concept of the general idea of human society looks as if it could salvage both of the roles required for Plato's case for ethical truth. The general idea would give all particular human societies, whether perfect or imperfect, a pass into its class, and it would also contain the perfect or just state of human society.

However, Plato's labeling would be gratuitous, because now where to

affix the label "perfect" within the harmony spectrum has become a legitimate matter for debate. In *The Republic*, it seemed that once we had learned
to read the content of a Form, we simply gave an exhaustive description,
and that was the thing's perfect state. Now we have another task of discrimination: within the contents of the Form of Human Society, how do we decide whether maximum harmony, or minimum harmony, or some point in
between constitutes its perfect state? Plato may opt for the upper limit, but
Thrasymachus might opt for the lower. He might well prefer the point at
which the struggle for power is mitigated no more than is necessary to keep
society from falling apart. He might opt for nothing more ambitious than a
mutual security pact or honor among thieves. An admirer of late-nineteenth-
century American capitalism might opt for some point in between.

Plato may have thought that equating the upper limit with true justice
was obvious, because only there is the principle of might makes right eliminated. But that is not obvious at all. It could be argued that some competition
is necessary for progress and that a total meritocracy freezes a society into
mediocrity. Witness *The Republic*'s lack of creative art, the fact that all but
a few are banned from thinking about anything new or interesting, the fact
that society is confined to the size of a city-state. Suddenly, Thrasymachus
gets a new life. Opinions about the perfect state of human society are only
that; no road to ethical truth exists to moderate between them. The Form of
Human Society pays a price for becoming a true universal. It is no longer a
pure criterion of perfection, capable of ranking particular societies into a hierarchy of perfection. Rather, it has become a mixture of the perfect and the
imperfect. Its contents must be assessed and labeled by each person, and to
do this, each person must apply a criterion external to its content, presumably a criterion based on individual commitment.

Leaving the Form of Human Society for the World of Forms in general,
that world now poses two tasks of discrimination: discrimination *between*
Forms to assess which are purely perfect (equality), which are nonperfect
(perhaps mud), which are a mix of perfect and imperfect (perhaps human
society); for the mixed group, discrimination *within* the contents of each
Form to assess where the label "perfect" should be affixed. Which brings us
to the Chief Good, the Form of Forms, the universal that sets the entrance
exam a candidate must pass to enter the World of Forms, Plato's criterion of
Absolute Perfection. A criterion of Absolute Perfection might perform both
tasks of discrimination: it might tell us which Forms have a claim to possess-

ing a perfect state, and within the Forms that do, where that perfect state resides. It is fascinating that Plato not only promises a solution to his problems (*Parmenides*, 135) but also promises us a dialogue called "The Philosopher" (*Sophist*, 217 & 268; *Statesman*, 257 & 311). The mark of a philosopher is, of course, knowledge of the Chief Good. There is a legend that Plato delivered a lecture on the Chief Good at his academy, perhaps a rough draft of "The Philosopher." The lecture, if there was such, is lost, and the promised dialogue either lost or never written.

Perhaps the dialogue was never written because the Chief Good cannot perform the set tasks. The price it pays to play the role of universal for the World of Forms is analogous to the price each Form pays for being a true universal for its particulars. The Chief Good is no longer pure or absolute perfection; rather, its contents must be expanded to accommodate everything found in the World of Forms, the perfect, the imperfect, and the nonperfect. Just as the Form of Human Society now needs help before it can rank particular societies into a hierarchy of perfection, so the Chief Good needs help before it can assess the contents of the Forms. Something else would have to assess where within its own heterogeneous content perfection resides. Since nothing lies beyond the Chief Good, no further help is possible. Once the Chief Good itself poses a task of discrimination, a task of finding the perfect within its contents, the game is over. Plato's case for ethical truth contains a contradiction that cannot be resolved.

The collapse of Plato's case for ethical truth strips the Forms of their epistemological role. However, their metaphysical role has also lost credibility. Perfect Forms might turn formless matter into an imperfect copy of themselves by leaving their imprint. Universals that admit both perfect and imperfect particulars into classes presuppose the existence of both; that is, entrance exams have nothing to do with creating the candidates who take them. Universals have no direct causal effect on the world of matter, they merely apply words to it and help us talk about it.

The problems posed in *The Parmenides* render inevitable the evolution of Plato into Aristotle. And yet this judgment seems impertinent. We are judging perhaps the greatest mind our civilization has ever produced. What a pity we do not have his answers as well as his courageous and uncompromising self-criticism.

3

Truth-Tests and Proofs

This chapter has a single purpose: to argue the improbability of a valid case
for objective status in ethics. Certainty is not possible for reasons forthcoming.
The argument will run as follows: first, I will try to show that the contradiction
in Plato's ethical truth-test is not unique; second, I will criticize moral
realism; third, I will suggest that proofs of ethical objectivity are flawed; and
finally, I will note a trend away from both truth-tests and proofs toward approaches
that offer our ideals something less than objective status. As a preface,
the concepts of truth-test and proof will be clarified and distinguished.

An ethical truth-test is supposed to have a neutrality that transcends the
partisan content of conflicting ideals and a direct relevance to the validity of
those ideals. These attributes allow it to act as a higher court of appeal. It
applies an overriding criterion of right and wrong that is supposed to be nonpartisan
and can, therefore, confer objectivity on the ideals approved. The
content of the Form of Human Society is supposed to supply a nonpartisan
criterion of perfection that can rank human societies as objectively more or
less just. Kant's categorical imperative, at least some of its formulations, tests
opposing maxims or principles of human behavior to determine which of
them are objectively right or wrong. Locke and Rousseau use the concept
of nature to determine what is natural (and, therefore, objectively right) and
what is unnatural (and, therefore, wrong). The ethical truth-tests our civilization
has produced all rest on some kind of transcendental metaphysics. They
all rest on a theory of being that posits something beyond the physical universe,
such as God or the World of Forms, or that asserts that the physical
universe contains something not revealed by science, such as the purposes of

nature or people as creatures whose essence escapes causality. Usually, some sort of case is made to show that these transcendental entities are morally relevant. The way in which ethical truth-tests operate as a higher court of appeal is analogous to how the scientific method operates as a test of the truth-status of competing scientific theories. Both are neutral, both are relevant, both hand down decisions that coerce reason. One affixes rational belief to assertions about what we ought to do, the other affixes rational belief to propositions that describe or theories that explain events.

Proofs that our humane ideals, or perhaps our opponents' antihumane ideals, possess objective status are quite different. They start from some nonmoral premise or premises, such as that all people value happiness, all are purposive agents, all exercise freedom, premises that are supposed to be certain or beyond dispute. They then purport to show that, in the light of these premises, eschewing humane ideals is self-contradictory. If that were true, the proof would lend humane ideals an unchallengeable objective status. Note that since the premises proofs use are nonmoral, they do not themselves constitute criteria of right and wrong. The premises are noncriterial propositions supposed to be peculiar in a certain way: when their truth is acknowledged, it becomes logically impossible to believe in anything save a particular morality. The fact that proofs do not posit some criterion of right and wrong, over and above the ideals they vindicate, will assume importance later when we exempt proofs from a "darker side," a taint that afflicts truth-tests. Proofs are as different from truth-tests as geometrical demonstrations are different from the scientific method.

Truth-tests and proofs do not, of course, exhaust all possibilities. There are many approaches to justifying ideals that promise something less than objective status, approaches I call substitutes for objectivity. Thus far, only one of these, my own, has been described. This chapter will provide a list of such, but for now, think of Marx. Marx rejected ethical objectivity, but as a substitute he argued that history was on the side of humane ideals.

The fact that Plato's truth-test is invalid does not show that others are invalid. Nonetheless, I believe that, upon examination, all the truth-tests the great minds of Western civilization have offered show the same kind of contradiction. That contradiction can be best understood by expanding our account of the attributes an ethical truth-test must possess. Three things make it plausible as a higher court of appeal. First, we have said that it must be an impartial court, one whose overriding criterion of what is really right and really wrong must be nonpartisan. This means that there must be nothing in the content of its criterion that would give either a humane person or Nietzsche good reason to reject its jurisdiction. Second, we have said that its overriding criterion must have moral relevance. Flipping a coin would be a nonpartisan test of whose ideals were to be endorsed, but the parties would hardly accept its verdict because of that. Third, there is another attribute hitherto implied but not stated. When the court hands down its verdict, its overriding criterion of moral rectitude really must dictate that verdict. The connection between the test applied and which ideals are endorsed must be clear.

There is a trade-off between the first and the third of these tasks of persuasion. On the one hand, the obvious way to make a truth-test nonpartisan is to ban substantive ideals from its content. If it contains a humane criterion like the greatest happiness of the greatest number, an obvious bias against antihumane ideals, Nietzsche would quite rightly claim that it was designed to give him a negative verdict. Then we would need another truth-test that was truly nonpartisan to vindicate the original truth-test, and so on ad infinitum. On the other hand, banning substantive ideals from its content handicaps a truth-test in terms of handing down a clear verdict. If it contains no substantive ideals whatsoever, will it not be a blank check whose verdicts look torturous and contrived? Historically, truth-tests that have delivered a clear verdict have not been nonpartisan, and truth-tests that were nonpartisan did not deliver a clear verdict. Whenever a truth-test appeared to be an exception to this, there was sleight of hand somewhere.

Plato's sleight of hand is masterful. *The Republic* conceals the partisan bias of his overriding test, the World of Forms, behind a language veil difficult to penetrate. He weaves an identity between general ideas and perfection. General ideas or universals look absolutely free from built-in bias yet somehow become perfect in a way specific enough to hand down verdicts. Geometry conditions our minds to be receptive. What could be more objective than the concept of a straight line, yet its perfection ranks all actual lines drawn on a blackboard without ambiguity. Once *The Parmenides* breaks the association between general idea and perfect state, the veil lifts. We realize that the Form of Human Society, to be nonpartisan (a true universal), must be broad enough to accommodate all the human societies that exist, Thrasymachus's tyranny as well as Plato's Republic; and that Plato's attempt to pin the label "perfect" on one of the societies the Form accommodates, his own roughly humane ideal society, was both partisan and arbitrary. This is to say that once the Form of Human Society becomes truly nonpartisan, its ability to deliver a verdict disappears.

Other truth-tests are less successful in concealing the contradiction at their core. The purposes of nature look neutral or nonpartisan only until they begin to hand down verdicts, humane verdicts in the case of Locke and Rousseau, antihumane verdicts in the case of the vulgar Social Darwinists. Then it becomes clear that all of these thinkers are reading their own biases into nature. Nature has no "purposes." All it has are patterns or trends that can be mistaken for such. As Mill in *On Nature* pointed out, these are so variegated that you can select out whatever you want. You can get the ethics of the Borgias, whose assassinations were nothing compared to the crimes nature perpetrates against the innocent, for example, earthquakes exterminating whole villages and nature red in tooth and claw presiding over random slaughter. Or you can get the high-minded political ethics of Locke, for whom the fact nature gave us free will shows that we are intended to consent to our form of government. As Mill says, clearly nature herself does not provide the verdicts; rather, we use our own preexisting ideals to pick and choose from nature, emphasizing whatever gives us the desired outcome.

Later Kant's categorical imperative will be critically analyzed. For now, I will say only that, contrary to his own prohibitions, Kant incorporated into its content a distinctively egalitarian concept of justice. This enhanced the capacity of the categorical imperative to render verdicts but undermined its claim to nonpartisan status.

The will of God as an ethical truth-test may appear to be an exception but actually teaches the same lesson. If God were an all-powerful Hitler, creator and master of the universe but vicious morally, no humane person would accept his or her will as an overriding test of moral rectitude, except perhaps through fear. Omnipotence does nothing to confer nonpartisan status. We are susceptible to the notion of God's will as a higher court of appeal because we assume God's benevolence, or, if you hold antihumane ideals, because you assume he or she is a vengeful God made of stern stuff. God may be our judge, but we judge God to satisfy ourselves that God is a worthy judge. Nature and God are the same: without our own preexisting ethic, we would find no ethic there.

This analysis may seem to betray a nonreligious psychology. What of those who assume that God possesses both omnipotence and omniscience, a perfect wisdom that extends to knowledge of good and evil and that imperfect creatures cannot imitate? They would trust God as they trust a judge who knows the law beyond their ken, a judge who will always render the correct verdict, perhaps beyond their understanding but still worthy of acceptance. Worthy of their acceptance even if the verdict flies in the face of those ideals to which they have a deep personal commitment. First, note that the connection between God's truth-test and its verdicts is now totally inscrutable, so even here the usual trade-off between nonpartisan status and plausible verdicts surfaces. But more fundamental, a logical prerequisite for faith in God's truth-test is the belief that it could, if only we understood it, show us how to combine nonpartisan status with plausible verdicts. But up to now, we have found no reason to believe such a thing is possible. All that remains is the old demeaning adage, "I believe it because it is absurd."

Leaving ethical truth-tests, providing a comprehensive critique of either moral realism or proofs (the other grounds for contending that humane ideals possess objective status) poses a dilemma. Plausible truth-tests have been invented only by our greatest minds—Plato, Kant, Rousseau, Locke—and therefore are few. Cases for moral realism and proofs are numerous, if only because they have been too unconvincing to enjoy more than a short life. Nielsen (1984, 59–60) catches the prevailing mood: the latest case for a supreme principle of morality, the denial of which is self-contradictory, awakens mainly a sense of this must be wrong, let us quickly identify the flaw, and get on to other things. But the lust for objectivity is such that each generation piles its own contribution on the heap inherited from the past.

An obvious solution would be an overall case against ethical objectivity so persuasive that no case for it could hope to succeed. John Mackie and Gilbert Harman have done an excellent job of rehearsing a wide range of general arguments against objectivity in ethics. But I believe this cannot save us the trouble of criticizing particular thinkers in detail. The general arguments used are convincing as conclusions stated after criticizing thinkers one by one; they are unconvincing as refutations stated prior to critique. Take two widely accepted arguments: that scientific theories can be tested against observations grounded in external reality, while ethical theories are tested against "observations" purely the product of individual psychologies

(Harman, 1977, 5–6); that moral status or what ought to be is never conse-
quential on the natural features of an ideal, for example, the fact that an ideal
is humane rather than cruel (Mackie, 1977, 41). The great thinkers were
great because they anticipated such objections. No one needed to tell Plato
that he had to make a case for an external moral reality (the World of Forms)
and show that the natural features of his ideal society (no struggle for power,
meritocratic classes) represented the perfect state of things (what ought to
be). Just as Plato deserved a personalized critique, so other thinkers deserve
the same courtesy.

In other words, the conclusion that there is no valid case for objective
status must be based on induction, that is, showing that every case ever offered has failed. Since that is not possible here, I will offer a second best: summarize Mackie's general arguments against ethical objectivity; offer a brief
critique of the mainstream of moral realism, that is, the view that we can at-
tach ethical objectivity to certain ideals because of some perceived property
those ideals possess; criticize a prominent classical proof and a prominent
contemporary one; and show that, like truth-tests, proofs contain a common
flaw, albeit different in kind. I will also recommend the common flaw as a
helpful guide. It cannot save the reader the trouble of making his or her critical examination of all the proofs going, but it may save time: look immediately for the common flaw, and refutation, I believe, will quickly follow.

Mackie (1977, 36–49 & 64–73) marshals these arguments. First, the
argument from relativity. It appears that people approve of monogamy because they participate in a monogamous way of life, rather than that they
participate in a monogamous way of life because of some shared perception
that monogamy is right. It is possible that all variations in moral codes reflect
distorted perceptions of objective values, but it seems unlikely. Second, the
argument from queerness. If there are objective values waiting to be com-
prehended, their property of being action-guiding makes them radically different from anything else in the universe. Third, every other claim to objectivity is based on a well-defined method of testing hypotheses, or inference,
or logical construction, or conceptual analysis. The ethical claim rests on
methods that are either poorly defined or clearly unable to support it. Fourth,
the core of this epistemological failure seems intractable. There is never a
clear connection between the natural properties of an action, say, the property of benefiting others altruistically, and its rightness. Fifth, it is easy to ex-

plain how people would come to believe in objective values even in their absence. Sixth, there is no meaningful bridge between "is" and moral "ought." For example, arguments based on performatory utterances always have an unstated moral premise. Take the notion that when we in fact make a promise we ought to keep it. This presupposes that we ought to respect the institution of promise-keeping.

Some of Mackie's arguments are derived from a critique of G. E. Moore. I will add my own critique, because Moore was the greatest of those who argued for the variant of moral realism called intuitionism. Moore's intuitionism is based on two contentions: that moral goodness is the name of a nonnatural property that certain states of affairs possess; that we can cognize which states of affairs possess goodness, just as we can see what physical objects possess the color yellow. This constitutes a case for humane ideals because Moore cognized that personal affection and aesthetic pleasure were the only great unmixed goods. That established, every human being is duty bound to attempt to create a society in which personal affection and delight in beauty are shared to the maximum possible degree. The good society will lack certain things. Moore had a very low opinion of lust; enjoying certain organic sensations and perceptions of states of the body is labeled a great evil in itself (Moore, 1903, secs. 113 & 125).

Both of Moore's contentions are false. As for the first, Moore realizes that the very concept of natural objects (states of affairs) possessing a non-natural property is unusual and must be defended. Natural objects are those that exist and can be experienced in the world of space and time. They are distinct from nonnatural objects like God or Plato's Forms that are supposed to exist in a realm that transcends the physical universe. This underlines the formidable nature of his task: anyone who said that a nonnatural object possessed a natural property, claimed that God was yellow, would be talking nonsense, but the opposite claim is supposed to be plausible. Moore discusses how to determine the status of a natural object's properties. A property is natural if its removal would destroy its object, for example, if all volume were removed from a sound, the sound would disappear. By implication, a property is nonnatural if its removal would leave its object unaltered. Goodness certainly passes this test: if we removed the notion of goodness from aesthetic pleasures, they would survive unaltered (Moore, 1903, secs. 25–26).

Moore's test for nonnatural properties is really a test for whether or not something belongs to an object, and the fact that goodness passes shows that goodness is no kind of property at all. Something is normally called a property only if it is related to an object in a way that affects the object's existential status. This is true even of secondary properties like color. Stripping an object of its color alters those features of its structure that reflect a certain wavelength of light. In contrast, being beautiful is not a property of a sunset at all, precisely because it is the same sunset whether anyone thinks it beautiful or not. Moore is free to use words as he likes. If he wishes, he can have an eccentric usage that calls things properties of objects even though they fail to alter those objects. But that is a dead end. It merely calls for a distinction between properties-sub-one and properties-sub-two, the former altering their object and the latter not. And these peculiar properties-sub-two are functionally related to their objects in a way identical to what the rest of us call assessments or labels. No matter how you assess an act of premeditated killing, label it wrong, label it right, or affix no label at all, it is still the same act, namely, a premeditated killing. Therefore, Moore's properties-sub-two do not function like a property that really belongs to a state of affairs, the kind of attribute that can be established to be really there or not. Rather, they function like a subjective assessment of a state of affairs that is there only if someone pastes on the label.

As for Moore's second contention, that we can cognize which states of affairs possess goodness, it raises the question of who we are. Imagine that Moore converted Nietzsche to his brand of moral realism, and Nietzsche took up cognizing, and cognized that personal affection and aesthetic pleasure possessed goodness only when enjoyed by the great, the fate of herd people being irrelevant. Moore (1903, sec. 45) grants that such disagreements would be unsatisfactory but says it is not unsatisfactory that he cannot resolve them. He uses an analogy with logic: logic cannot prove its own rules but still commands respect. The analogy is misplaced. If we are persuaded to use the rules of logic or the scientific method, we reach common conclusions. When Nietzsche is persuaded to use the method of cognizing, he reaches conclusions that are radically different. Once again, you can propose a method that behaves unlike all other methods of truth-finding, grant that it does, and still insist on calling it a method of establishing ethical truth. But you enter a familiar dead end. Your language cries out for a distinction between truth-finders-sub-one and truth-finders-sub-two, the former generating common conclusions (which is why they command respect) and the latter diverse conclusions (which is why they do not).

The subjectivity of Moore's cognizing is evidenced by its arbitrariness. Proper Victorians did not conceive of sex enjoyed for itself as good, but high-minded things like friendship and art were another matter. The later advocates of intuitionism, whatever their differences with Moore, did little to enhance its viability. Writing during the 1930s, confronted with the Great Depression, the rise of Hitler, the Italian invasion of Ethiopia, a world on the brink of war and chaos, they were not distracted from the central moral issues of the day: promise-keeping and the return of borrowed books. A plague of irresponsibility had swept Oxbridge: a book lent was as good as a book lost.

Contemporary moral realists discuss more significant issues and no longer use the term "nonnatural." Brink (1989) believes that moral facts are attached to certain actions, or people, or institutions, and calling them properties is acceptable, but only if they are designated "natural" properties. He provides no summary description of moral facts, but apparently a list would include not causing unnecessary suffering, not holding people responsible for doing what they could not have known to be wrong, that goodness deserves reward, that the turpitude of a crime should determine the severity of punishment, and that there should be a sphere of behavior that is other-regarding in the sense of benefiting others. Let us perform the same experiment we did with Moore, that is, let us assume that Brink converts Nietzsche to his total package of moral realism. It then turns out that Nietzsche's list of moral facts is radically different. His description of moral reality reveals that the benefits of other-regarding behavior and conjoining reward and punishment to deserts should be confined to supermen, with ordinary people valuable only as means to the purposes of the great. I believe that the test of all moral realists should be the same. Imagine that you have converted Nietzsche to every realist proposition going; given his and your radically different descriptions of morals facts, what separates you? If Nietzsche has become a true convert, not even inner certitude.

Worse, Nietzsche does not exhaust alternative descriptions of moral facts. Cattell would point to the fact that we are obliged to inflict great suffering, just so long as doing so helps humanity to liquidate itself in favor of a higher species. Sumner would point to the fact that any society is morally insipid if it does not give preeminence to the middle-class virtues of sobriety, hard work, and thrift. Contrast this situation with ordinary facts. Theories that attempt to explain our observations may differ radically, but our perception of facts is strikingly uniform. This was proven by falsification of the Worfian hypothesis. Benjamin Worf hypothesized that cultural differences fundamentally influence perception, for example, that different color vocabularies would mean cross-cultural differences in colors perceived. He was mistaken: even if a people have no word for orange, they can discriminate that color if offered sufficient incentives.

Without the uniformity concerning perception of facts that the human race enjoys and even shares with other species, it is doubtful we could even think of ourselves as inhabiting the same shared physical universe, as distinct from separate "realities" (Flynn, 1973, appendix). Just imagine a "world" in which I cut you, but I perceive a happy smile while you perceive tears and blood. Diversity in something as elemental as facts is a good reason for not talking about a reality. Diversity in appreciation of art keeps us from positing an aesthetic reality, diversity in senses of humor from positing a comic reality, diversity in taste from positing a good-candy reality. Brink recognizes the necessity of replacing the present disagreement about moral facts with progress toward moral unity. He does not hope for unity based on a valid ethical truth-test or proof. After all, such an achievement would itself confer objectivity and render cases for moral realism redundant. As I argued in chapter 1, nothing less than a truth-test or proof, neither my own approach, nor Rawls's approach, nor others mentioned later in this chapter, can rationally impose the necessary degree of unity. It is true that moral debate shows participants with diverse ideals scoring points off one another. But not one good argument owes anything to the presumption of a moral reality. Therefore, their soundness makes no case for a moral reality.

Brink cites Sturgeon, who argues that moral facts function as causes of historical events; for example, they influenced where slavery was first abolished, and they influenced Hitler's behavior. If this were true, if moral facts really play the kind of the causal role ordinary facts do, it would make one more friendly to moral realism. Sturgeon (1988, 237) asserts that the case depends on whether a certain set of claims (about what is really moral) can attract rational agreement. This assertion is necessary to avoid an absurdity: a variety of conflicting and equally valid causal explanations (his explanations, Hitler's, Nietzsche's) based on conflicting moral claims (his, Hitler's, and so on). However, whether you have an accurate grasp of moral facts is really important only if moral facts really do influence history. If they do not, we are left with nothing more than that the morals of historians may influence how they write history.

Sturgeon (1988, 250–251) captures the core of the issue in a single question. Would Hitler, assuming his psychology and world-view and so forth were unaltered, have done exactly as he did, even though Hitler did not constitute a case of moral depravity? Now if Hitler's depravity is a necessary causal factor, every competent historian must comment on it, and Sturgeon (1988, 244) praises those who do. Let us free our minds of all we know about Hitler (doing so is crucial to what follows) and see what contribution Hitler's depravity makes to causal explanation.

We read a passage in which a historian calls Hitler morally depraved. Does that describe a moral fact? If so, it describes a fact whose causal role is completely incomprehensible until other moral facts are described, and, more damning, after they are described it adds nothing whatsoever. In itself it conveys no more information than saying that ho-hum caused Hitler's behavior. Fortunately for the reader, the historian's next sentence describes another moral fact: it is wicked to dance on Sunday. Now we have some substance, we know why Hitler was morally depraved, but none of this takes us very deeply into Hitler's character or behavior. It would be better if Brink was writing about Hitler. Presumably he would describe his list of moral facts, such as it is wrong to cause unnecessary suffering and it is wrong to target other-regarding behavior to too restricted a group. At least these moral facts focus us on things like Hitler's cruelty and his love of Germany and his hatred of Jews. But then we read a third historian and find something peculiar. His or her list of moral facts is less sensible than Brink's. It adds things like extroversion is morally remiss and having an average IQ is morally remiss. But despite their absurdity, these additions pay a dividend: they focus us on a wider range of relevant personal traits.

In other words, there is an imperfect correlation between the quality of the moral facts described and success in identifying the relevant causes of Hitler's behavior. The reason is clear: moral facts get their causal potency only insofar as they correspond one to one with relevant personal traits. Their causal role is no different from the role that might be played by astrological facts. The fact that Hitler was a Pisces might focus a historian on his ambition, his extroversion, his rashness. It is true that astrological facts would not consistently correlate with relevant personal traits, but then neither does a sound description of moral facts (witness Brink). Moral facts simply do not behave like ordinary facts. Ordinary facts cause effects in a simple and direct way; moral facts gain whatever influence they have only by enhancing a historian's competence in psychology. When historians write history, the psychological competence is appreciated, whatever its source, but we hope those who believe in astrology will set that aside. When historians write history, I hope that they will set their ethics aside. I do not want to read about how often Hitler danced on Sunday or how morally depraved someone thinks he was. Moral judgments may be appreciated for their own sake, of course. Humane historians might condemn personal traits of Hitler that would illuminate my own assessment of his behavior. Most welcome, but the history itself is no better for that.

Moral realism has its own history, and it is a history of a school of thought in decay. Changing the name of moral facts from nonnatural to natural properties leaves their existential status unaltered: they are still ghostly things that cling to certain natural entities, and they are called facts only in an effort to objectify them. Whatever the defects of Moore and his cognizing, he attempted to give moral realism its own method of determining just what was really right and really wrong. Contemporary moral realism is essentially parasitic. Brink and Sturgeon agree that its viability depends on the prospect of resolving at least the most acute moral disputes. They depend on Rawls for this (more on Rawls in a moment), which is to say that moral realism is at the mercy of an epistemology with no logical link to its metaphysics.

Having stated a case against those who claim objectivity from perception of moral properties or facts, it is time to address those who offer proofs. The greatest thinker of the nineteenth century to offer a proof was John Stuart Mill. In chapter 4 of *Utilitarianism*, he attempts to show that everyone should espouse the greatest happiness of the greatest number as the sole test of whether actions are right or wrong. The proof has four steps: the test of what is good is what people actually desire as an end; each and every person desires only one thing as an end, his or her own happiness, all else being desired as a means to that end; therefore, for each person the only good thing is his or her own happiness; therefore, for all people collectively, the only good is the general happiness.

I will put two objections. First, the conclusion of the proof lacks plausibility. It asserts that the general happiness is the sole moral good, in the sense that it is the sole good people value as an end. In rebuttal: if some people would accept a loss in the general happiness for a gain in something else, they must value that other thing as an end at least as much as the general happiness. I will use an example I thought I got from Bertrand Russell, but Russell experts tell me I did not. Imagine that psychology discovers that sadistic pleasures are the most intense possible and also discovers a way of conditioning everyone to be a sadist. A machine is invented that can give everyone the illusion of torturing innocent people; the people are imaginary but they are believed to be real, otherwise it would spoil the fun. This would be a utilitarian heaven; everyone possesses maximum happiness, not one real person suffers pain. It would not be difficult, I think, to find some among us who would accept a lower level of general happiness in return for a gain in human dignity. Better some preventable unhappiness than a human race so degraded in character.

Second, the proof in itself is invalid. The crucial step from you valuing your happiness and I valuing my happiness to everyone valuing the happiness of all is illogical, unless a connecting proposition is provided. Imagine a world of misers: you value money in your pocket and I value money in my pocket, and we are told that this entails all misers valuing money in everyone's pocket, without any distinction between mine and thine. No one would be convinced without a connecting proposition, something like, every one of you will gain from maximizing the general wealth. Similarly, Mill's proof would gain plausibility if stated in this way: each person values his or her own happiness; each and every person enjoys the happiness of others just as much as his or her own; therefore, each and every person values the happiness of all. The intermediate proposition is so obviously necessary, and so obviously false when stated, that we must ask what nullified Mill's critical judgment. The attraction of getting all human beings within the circle of moral concern, of course. But note the attraction of the vehicle: all people need do to qualify is be capable of pleasure and pain and value their own happiness; they certainly do not need to possess any unusual trait, say, creative genius, to merit admission; they do not even need to be altruistic rather than selfish.

The proof's flaw is a leap to all people being worthy of moral concern without any discussion of what people merit. The penalty of being aware of the leap is having to confront Nietzsche and ask yourself whether you really have any good arguments against him. And then the abyss of humane ideals lacking objective status opens at your feet. For a twentieth-century proof, and a far more subtle proof, I have selected one offered by my old professor, Alan Gewirth. His detailed argument for humane-egalitarian ideals has attracted much critical attention (Gewirth, 1978; Regis, 1984).

There are five steps.

Step 1. Human beings are purposive agents.

Step 2. Freedom and well-being are practically necessary to playing my role as a purposive agent.

Step 3. Therefore, I must assert the proposition, "I must have freedom and well-being." This is simply a recognition of causal necessity on my part. Having accepted that having freedom and well-being is necessary to operationalizing my role as a purposive agent, how can I deny the causal link between the two?

Step 4. Therefore, I must assert the proposition, "I have a right to freedom and well-being," which is equivalent to saying, "Others ought to refrain from interfering with my freedom and well-being." This is a recognition of logical necessity on my part. Having accepted that others must not interfere with my freedom and well-being, how can I refrain from the rights-claim that they ought not, when the very function of "ought not" is to forbid certain behavior? To refrain from that rights-claim is to grant it is permissible for others to interfere (Gewirth, 1984, 206).

Step 5. Logical consistency dictates that I universalize my last utterance by asserting that all rational or purposive agents have a right to freedom and well-being, that is, they ought not to interfere with one another. This step, at long last, provides a full-fledged moral principle (Gewirth, 1978, 147). It gives us something that both uses the moral ought and is other-regarding. All human beings must recognize one another as fellow members of a community of moral concern.

I believe that Step 4 of this proof is invalid because it makes a rights-claim without giving reasons. It tells other people that they ought (in a moral sense) to refrain from interfering with my freedom and well-being while giving them no reasons for such benevolence. As I argued in chapter 1, any non-benevolent person who accepted humane advice without reasons, who accepted such advice simply because I gave it, would be behaving irrationally. And it is hardly rational of me to treat others as irrational when I know them to be rational. At Step 5, Gewirth's argument depends on my awareness of the rationality of others. It seems odd that I apply my knowledge of this at Step 5 and yet ignore my knowledge of their rationality at Step 4. It is, of course, not accidental that no reasons are given for the rights-claim. To do so would be to open the Pandora's box of their status, whether they were partisan or nonpartisan reasons. The absence of reasons means that the rights-claim must be withdrawn. Therefore, there is nothing left to universalize into the egalitarian moral principle of Step 5.

As an assertion whose function is to influence the behavior of a population of rational agents, what is said at Step 4 is no better than using a ritual phrase like "abracadabra." Making a rights-claim unsupplemented by reasons is actually inconsistent with my playing my role as a rational purposive agent. An obvious rebuttal: better to accept one such violation of my role than to fail to make a claim essential to the preservation of my role. So the claim that others ought not to interfere with my freedom and well-being wins the rationality stakes. However, this rebuttal rests on an assumption that is false, because making such a rights-claim has no effect whatsoever on preserving my role as a purposive agent. Gewirth recognizes this and never argues that the transition from Step 3 to Step 4 can be made by appealing to causal considerations. My making and accepting a rights-claim, that others ought not interfere with my freedom and well-being, is a private act not affecting the outside world. No audience is posited to overhear me and either applaud or jeer and react either by forbearance or interference. Gewirth bases the transition not on practical necessity but on logical necessity, that is, on his assumptions about the logic of the moral ought. But he is mistaken: the logic of the moral ought is such that it cannot carry the burden of an unsupplemented rights-claim.

Leaving Step 4, I wish to backtrack to Step 3. Step 3 does appeal to practical or causal necessity. It says that a rational person, a person who recognizes that freedom and well-being are essential to his or her playing the role of a purposive agent, will then say, "I must have freedom and well-being." Let us test this against the reactions of two kinds of people. First, there are herd people who endorse the great purposes of a superman and recognize that those purposes are incompatible with their making rights-claims. These people have not totally abandoned their role as purposive agents, of course. Even slaves are not reduced to the nonpurposiveness of an animal; so long as they remain alive, they have a rational plan for dressing themselves, preparing their food, making love, and so forth. They have undertaken a voluntary and purposive sacrifice of rights-claims out of moral principle. Is that truly an abrogation of their role as purposive agents, or would forbidding them such a sacrifice not be an even greater violation of that role? After all, people sacrifice their lives on moral principle, and this sacrifice is far less.

Second, there are supermen who espouse a rights-criterion such that to qualify for rights someone must be a creative genius. Since they themselves still merit rights, they have made no personal sacrifice at all. It is true that the supermen, thanks to their elitist principles, have refused to grant herd men rights. But, *at this point in the argument*, each person is merely protecting his or her own role as a purposive agent. True, at the conclusion of the proof it is forbidden to deny the rights of others. However, that assumes that the preliminary steps are valid enough to proceed to the conclusion. The conclusion is arrived at by universalizing a rights-claim that is supposed to be common to all. But now, at Step 3, we have a variety of rights-claims, based on diverse moral principles, all of which can be universalized with logical consistency. Those with egalitarian principles will praise everyone who accords rights to everyone. Supermen will praise both supermen and herd men who restrict rights to supermen. Once Step 3 is modified, universalizing leads to new and multiple conclusions. Gewirth can always save his proof by legislating a protective rule: no one is allowed to formulate rights-claims in terms of their own moral principles at preliminary steps, because moral principles are forbidden until the proof is over. This seems a very arbitrary rule.

At one point, Gewirth defends what is operationally equivalent to a ban on using moral principles. He considers the possibility that a person might say that his or her unsupplemented rights-claim to freedom and well-being should or could be supplemented. He imagines an agent possessed of traits (lacked by others) who espouses those traits as a necessary criterion to having rights and who rejects the criterion of merely being a purposive agent as insufficient (Gewirth, 1978, 125–126). His reply is to reiterate that there is a necessary connection, in a causal sense, between freedom and reason and my playing my role as a purposive agent. And he adds that the supplementary elitist criterion for having rights lacks such a necessary connection and that no rational case for such a connection can be made. This reply ignores the fact that if I am allowed to apply my moral principles, whatever necessary connections exist are overridden by the assessment that I am unworthy of having a right to freedom and well-being unless I can meet the supplementary criterion. Gewirth cannot understand why any actual agent would accept such a criterion. The answer is that my principles demand it. Once again, Step 3 works only if the application of moral principles is forbidden at that step.

Really, Gewirth's proof comes down to this: if a purposive agent cannot assess something in terms of his or her moral principles because that thing is prudentially essential (actually, of course, it is not even as prudentially essential as self-preservation); and if a purposive agent can make an unconditional rights-claim whose whole point is to bind others without asking why it binds others; then it follows that, having made an unconditional rights-claim for oneself, universalizability requires recognizing its validity for everyone (Step 5). Stripping the diverse principles people hold of their normal role, assessing self-interest and rights-claims, ends in unity.

Gewirth's proof and Mill's proof have a common flaw. Its core is the vehicle used to include all people within the circle of moral concern. That vehicle is always something that reduces people to a common denominator, such as valuing happiness or being purposive agents, and it functions to distract us from the differences often used to rank people by merit. Awareness of this provides a pair of spectacles, so we can scan proofs, focus immediately on the flaw, and attain quick refutation. For practice, scan Kant's derivation of the third formulation of the categorical imperative (chapter 4), the step that levels all people thanks to their freedom, or James's version of the "tolerance school fallacy" (chapter 9), the step that levels all human demands thanks to lack of an absolute standard for ranking them.

Awareness of the common flaw proofs share can also save time by revealing the potential of a particular justification of humane ideals. Take John Rawls (1972) and his theory of justice as first presented over twenty-five years ago. Hare (1973, 145) accused Rawls of believing that his theory conferred objective status on an egalitarian concept of justice. I think the passage Hare cites merely claims impartiality, claims that Rawls's concept of justice is egalitarian in the sense of favoring no person over another. Indeed, I know of few who share Hare's interpretation. However, Rawls cannot patent his arguments, and some may believe that he proved more than he claimed. Our critical spectacles allow us to quickly determine whether or not his theory could possibly qualify as a proof of the objective status of humane ideals.

The theory posits people in an original position, that is, people not yet conceived and not yet reared in a particular place at a particular time. Therefore, they have no particular genetic endowment, or personal traits, or social status, and, indeed, a veil of ignorance forbids them knowledge of any particularity they may eventually attain. They calculate what would serve their interests and, not surprisingly, decide in favor of social arrangements that protect even the most unfortunate from misery, social arrangements with a strong humane-egalitarian flavor.

Our spectacles focus us on the original position as a leveler. In stripping people of differences in genetic potential and developed talent, it obliterates the distinction between the great (whom Nietzsche thought merited concern for their fate) and the herd (who merit no concern). Or, alternately, being ignorant of whether you are great or ordinary is simply a way of legislating that difference irrelevant. Every human being has been transformed into an everyman who therefore takes every man's interests into account. Nietzsche would, first, reiterate that the difference between the great and the ordinary is all-important for those with antihumane and elitist ideals and, second, point out that the original position covertly gives all human beings a ticket of admission into the circle of moral concern without regard to merit. Rawls's theory would be bankrupt as a proof. It would be no better than positing a calculating machine that made no distinction between the interests of human beings and animals. This is too easy a road to the objective status of animal rights.

The common flaw attributed to proofs differs from that attributed to ethical truth-tests. This is because they are two distinct generalizations drawn from critical analysis of two different sets of data. I hope it is clear that these flaws are not held to be necessary truths. If someone ever does formulate a valid truth-test, it will by definition solve the problem of having both a nonpartisan content and sufficient specificity to hand down plausible decisions. If someone invents a valid proof, it will give nonarbitrary reasons for attaching little or no significance to individual differences, at least in terms of classifying people as worthy or unworthy of moral concern. Nothing said here can determine the future. Someday objective status in ethics may be vindicated, and then it will make sense to use an all-embracing moral ought. However, when an enterprise has been pursued by our best minds for over two thousand years with such unhappy results, perhaps we should invest our philosophical capital elsewhere.

Given the track record of truth-test and proofs, it is understandable that other approaches to the problem of justification have emerged. None of these offer objective status. Rather, they all appeal to some clearly valuable thing and purport to show that some ideals correlate with it while others do not.

The list begins with Aristotle. Setting aside Aristotle's teleology, what remains is a contention that roughly humane ideals characterize people whose personalities and temperaments and faculties had developed along an optimum road, namely, men of practical wisdom. This is equivalent to saying that humane ideals characterize people who enjoy psychological health (Flynn, 1973) and leads directly to Erich Fromm (1941, 1955). Marx offers us the comfort that history is on our side as a substitute for objectivity, Nietzsche claims good taste is on his side, Sumner and Cattell appeal to progress. Tawney (1920) appeals to the fact that only social democracy rationalizes property rights, Oakeshott (1962) to the notion that tradition is the only competent political tutor, Popper (1945) to the fact that science flourishes only in an open or nontotalitarian society, Gauthier (1986) and Kavka (1986) to the notion that the individual's true interests usually dictate adherence to fairness and the pursuit of the common good. Thinkers like Toulmin and Nielsen, at least at one time, attempted to show that elitists lack a moral point of view, that is, would have to try to live bereft of any morality whatsoever.

There is one nonobjectivist approach that calls for detailed comment because, suitably revised, it might be a close relative of my own. John Rawls (1985) and Kai Nielsen (1994) have recently championed an approach to justification called wide reflective equilibrium. Nielsen sees a trend in pluralist constitutional democracies toward achieving a liberal-left consensus about justice. He believes that modernization makes the trend likely but not inevitable; for example, it could be reversed by economic scarcity or deteriorating educational systems. However, at present, this trend can be furthered by philosophers promoting a rational scrutiny of conflicting ideals along these lines: seeking coherence between our considered moral convictions and our moral principles; relating these to general social theory, theory of moral development, theory of the role of morality in society, a scientific account of human nature, and a wide range of factual considerations. The objective is a rational consensus, rational within the context of what is known at a particular time in a particular evolving constitutional democracy, that will marginalize racism, sexism, and class elitism, perhaps even negotiate common ground with Nietzsche, and provide a cooperative basis for humane-egalitarian-tolerant social arrangements. This process is supposed to render irrelevant the metaphysical, epistemological, and ethical theory preoccupations of traditional philosophy, which is deemed fortunate, because the inevitable lack of agreement on these is divisive in a pluralist society.

For this approach to be acceptable, four alterations or clarifications are necessary. First, the antiphilosophical rhetoric should be dropped. Since ideals are to be tested against science and facts, all of the metaphysical and epistemological presuppositions of doing science must be confronted. After this method of justification has been used to vindicate humane ideals, we will have to answer the usual questions about what status they have, what language it makes sense to use to talk about them, which is to say, all of the traditional problems of ethical theory raised in this book will have to be confronted. Second, it should be made clear that while we all hope that history is on our side, that it will provide a social setting in which people will espouse humane ideals and appreciate whatever rationality they possess, it is the rational enterprise alone that counts as a justification. Even if history for some reason secured the domination of humane-egalitarian-tolerant ideals, were those ideals as rationally indefensible as classical racism, they would hardly have been vindicated.

Third, the fact that any actual social consensus will always be protective of falsehoods, not just truths, should be acknowledged. The emerging American liberal-left consensus is no exception. It regards as indecent questioning beliefs no sane person can hold. Blacks are said to suffer from great environmental handicaps when below average achievement is explained, and yet blacks are supposed to emerge from that environment without crippling intellectual or characterological deficiencies (Flynn, 1980, 210–212). There are supposed to be no intellectual group differences that are of genetic origin, something unlikely to be true of the huge gap between Jewish and Chinese Americans in visuospatial skills (Flynn, 1991, 120–123 & 140). There is supposed to be no tension between raising wages, by legislation or collective bargaining, and job creation. Unemployment is supposed to be the major cause of crime. I am a part of the Left and am conducting no vendetta; a list at least as long could be compiled for the Right. The point is that no social process is ever really very good at truth-testing, and no social trend will ever replace the lonely individual as the assessor of truth. Fourth, a summary point: Does not wide reflective equilibrium, when relieved of excess baggage, really come down to something fairly simple? Every one of us should test conflicting ideals in the light of all we know to be true at the moment. Perhaps we can show that humane ideals do not require sweeping the truths of social or biological science under the carpet while antihumane ones do. To show that, we will have to come down from the heights and get our minds dirty by using social science to refute our antihumane opponents in detail.

If that is what wide reflective equilibrium is all about, this book operationalizes wide reflective equilibrium, which is not to say that I believe that its success (such as it is) lends humane ideals the objective status that moral realists and many others assume. Moreover, until the approach is reformulated as above, I prefer to say that I am operationalizing an agenda for moral debate implicit in the early discussion of justice in Plato's *Republic*. Alternately, I can derive it by critical analysis of those who used the concept of a moral point of view as a justification. We will soon undertake that analysis. But first, we have something to learn from a great objectivist thinker, the only moral philosopher who could be considered a rival of Plato.

4

Kant and Sister Simplice

Kant dominates this chapter because analyzing Kant introduces a new thesis: that ethical truth-tests have a darker side. Truth-tests, more subtle and exciting than proofs, have a powerful attraction that has little to do with a sober assessment of their validity. Perhaps we can bring this to an end. I believe that even if a particular truth-test were valid, even if it were to vindicate humane ideals, it would distort them in the process of vindicating them. It would strip humane ideals of their capacity to generate humane reasons for the goodness of acts. This is a necessary consequence of truth-tests: the fact that they elevate a nonpartisan criterion of right and wrong above humane ideals necessitates the downgrading of humane ideals. Proofs do not have a darker side. Recall that the premise from which each of them begins is not some kind of overriding criterion of moral rectitude. Rather, it is a nonmoral assertion (all people value happiness, all people are purposive agents) in the light of which eschewing humane ideals is supposed to be contradictory. A proof of the objective status of humane ideals would no more alter their substance than geometrical proofs alter the substance of geometrical propositions. If they worked, proofs would be pure gain.

Therefore, our thesis is limited to ethical truth-tests. It imposes two tasks: showing what viable truth-tests would logically entail and dramatizing their darker side by showing how the categorical imperative distorts Kant's moral reasoning.

Recall what an ethical truth-test must do if it is to qualify as a higher court of appeal. If both the humane and the antihumane are to accept its jurisdiction, it must use an overriding criterion of moral rectitude that is

nonpartisan, which is to say that its content cannot be either prohumane or ✓
antihumane but, rather, must be nonhumane. Once again, the humane will
rightly reject its jurisdiction if the principle of might makes right dominates
its content; their opponents will rightly do so if the greatest happiness principle, or some other humane-egalitarian ideal, dominates its content. Thus
the appeal of criteria that appear to transcend the dichotomy between humane and antihumane ideals, the contents of a Form, the will of God, the
purposes of nature, and so forth.

When the truth-test or higher court hands down a decision, its criterion
of moral rectitude generates its reasons for calling acts right or wrong. Acts
(or societies) are morally right (or just) because they match the perfect harmony of the Form of Human Society, accord with the will of God, accord
with the world's prehuman design, operationalize what presocial instincts
would dictate. Assume that the court decides in favor of humane ideals and
our antihumane opponents are all laid low. They must then give up their
distinctive reasons for calling acts right or wrong. They can no longer give
reasons such as acts are good when they extract the revenge due the injured
party, discard the weak in favor of the strong, elevate supermen and subju-
gate herd men. Instead they must discard these in favor of the court's nonhumane reasons. We have won our one big victory. *Our opponents* ought to
adopt humane ideals because humane acts meet the court's nonhumane cri- ✓
terion of moral rectitude. *All humankind* ought to behave humanely because
humane acts meet the court's nonhumane criterion of moral rectitude. *We*
ought to behave humanely because humane acts meet the court's nonhumane
criterion of moral rectitude. And suddenly we realize that the higher court,
the very truth-test that gave us our one big victory, has extracted an appalling
price.

Having endorsed the court's nonhumane criterion of moral rectitude, we
have committed ourselves to conceding the obsolescence of all humane criteria of morality. When we and our opponents accepted the court's jurisdiction,
we both agreed to accept not only its decisions but also its criterion and reasons for making its decisions. Having won, we tell our opponents they must
give up their most cherished ideals and acknowledge that ours are worthy of
their acceptance, purely because of the court's nonhumane reasons. Surely we
must follow suit and acknowledge that our ideals are worthy of *our* acceptance, purely because of the court's nonhumane reasons. We can hardly

expect our opponents to take the reasons we urge on them seriously if we do not. But do we really want that? Certainly, what we really want is to call acts morally right precisely because they are humane. We want to praise people for their compassion, their struggle to benefit others, their desire for humane consequences, not because their behavior is in accord with perfect harmony or the purposes of untouched nature or the instincts of presocial human beings. What the truth-test has done is nothing less than this: it has stripped our ideals of their capacity to generate reasons, it has forbidden us to give distinctively humane reasons for the moral rectitude of acts.

Those who welcome truth-tests without reservation ignore their darker side by a piece of intellectual dishonesty. When the decision is handed down, they force the court's nonhuman reasons on to their opponents, but then they revert to using their own distinctively humane reasons when pondering moral questions. The court's criterion of moral rectitude is treated like a best room, opened only on Sundays for visitors, then shut up the rest of the week for ordinary living. This dishonesty breaks the agreement we made with our opponents. If we studiously ignore the court in our own moral reasoning, our opponents have every right to do the same. Our one big victory must be forfeited.

It is instructive to note why ethical truth-tests have a darker side when resolving disputes about basic ideals, while the truth-test of science has no such darker side when resolving disputes about competing factual hypotheses. A hypothesis differs from a moral ideal in a crucial respect that has to do with the specification of reasons. A hypothesis merely tells us something is the case. It does not specify the kind of reasons that lead us to accept that what it says is true; only the scientific method does that. Therefore, when we use science to resolve a dispute about competing hypotheses, science poses no complications; it does not replace an old criterion of reasons for calling something true with a new one. A person's basic ideals are different. They do give us our reasons for calling acts right or wrong, and, therefore, anything that imposes different reasons, the nonpartisan reasons necessary to defeat our opponents, replaces our old humane criterion with a new nonhumane one. It is as if a scientific hypothesis suggested a truth-test and we could vindicate it only by applying some new and overriding truth-test.

It may be argued that a hypothesis does suggest a truth-test in a sense. If one person says, "All swans are white," and another says, "At least one swan is black," the hypotheses themselves seem to specify what must be done to test them; that is, we must go out and look at swans. However, note that here the conflicting hypotheses specify one and the same truth-test, while conflicting moral ideals, say, a humane and a Nietzschean ideal, specify two quite distinct criteria for calling acts morally right. So the moral dispute logically entails an overriding criterion to resolve it, while the factual dispute does not.

Some technical terms may help. Offering nonhumane reasons for the acceptance of our moral ideals reduces our humane criteria from *testing criteria* of morality to mere *grading criteria*. Take the case of ranking wines. The real test of a wine's quality is the delectable taste sensation it arouses, plus certain medical considerations such as its not making us sick or attacking some bodily organ. However, a wine maker does not want every bottle tasted before it is sold, and, fortunately, we have discovered certain things that are correlates with a wine's quality; that is, we have discovered that wine tastes best if it has aged a certain length of time or has a certain color or (more recently) has a certain chemical composition. We use these things as grading criteria: rather than tasting every bottle, we grade wine by age and color and so forth. Similarly with ranking apples. The real test of quality is taste plus nutritional value, but we have discovered certain correlates of quality: Granny Smiths taste better than Golden Delicious, ripe apples taste better than unripe, and so forth. So we use these as grading criteria: rather than biting into every apple, we rank apples in terms of brand, size, color, lack of worms. However, such grading criteria are purely derivative. The testing criteria are the real tests of quality, and the grading criteria are merely easily discernible aspects (which is why they are so useful in grading) of whatever passes the tests.

Using a truth-test to vindicate humane ideals puts our humane criteria of moral rectitude in exactly the position of grading criteria. The fact that an act is humane is no longer the test of its moral goodness: it becomes a mere correlate, a mere aspect of the thing that passes the overriding test, and it has no value except insofar as it passes that test. We are forced to say that just as redness or large size in apples is good only because it passes a taste-test, so humane acts are morally good only because they pass an overriding test. We are forced to say that just as redness is worth nothing in itself, so acts are worth nothing simply because they are humane. And yet, if we are honest with ourselves, we will admit that it is the humane character of an act that excites our moral admiration. Take a family who lied to the Gestapo at the risk of their lives to save a Jew with whom they had no personal tie. Certainly we admire them precisely because they were humane and not because of something else.

The will of God may seem an exception to the rule, a kind of truth-test that may replace humane reasons for calling acts right or wrong with new reasons, but new reasons to which no believer would object. But that is because, as we have already seen, we tend to assume that God's overriding criterion of moral rectitude is similar to our own. The humane posit a benevolent God, the not so humane a stern God, a dichotomy caught in two favorite quotations: "your God is my notion of the devil" and "a God all mercy is a God without justice." Reasons for calling acts right or wrong that equate with our own reasons are not really new reasons. Actually, a believer should appreciate, rather than reject, the drift of our analysis. When a truth-test reduces our own criterion of morality to mere grading criteria, it threatens the integrity of the very thing we want to defend, our ideals as creators of moral reasons. It is as if a believer could prove the existence of God only at the price of establishing the existence of something that created God, only by downgrading God to the status of a created creature. Certainly no believer would purchase a rational advantage over unbelievers at that price. I hold my basic ideals as dear as a believer does his or her God, and I am unwilling to see them nullified as the creators of reasons.

This kind of abstract analysis lacks vitality until rendered concrete by example. Therefore, I move on to show how Kant's use of the categorical imperative as an overriding criterion of moral rectitude distorts his moral reasoning. Those who wish a fuller and more balanced discussion of Kant can find it elsewhere (Flynn, 1979). Following Paton (1967, 129–131), I will distinguish five formulations of the categorical imperative. My own analysis supplements his and argues that those five formulations belong to three types.

The first formulation (Paton's I) tells us that for something to qualify as a moral principle, we must be willing to accept it as a universal law. The fourth formulation (Paton's III) tells us that we must be willing to make it into a universal law. The alternative wordings signal that the formulations have different derivations, but it is their application that concerns me. Since they test principles in exactly the same way and validate exactly the same principles, I will ignore the fourth formulation in favor of the first and label the first an overriding criterion of *the realm of the moral*. The second formulation (Paton's I A) tells us that principles must qualify as universal laws of nature, the third (Paton's II) that principles must treat people never simply as means but always as ends as well. These formulations apply different tests to validate principles, and, therefore, neither can be ignored in favor of the other. However, they are alike in that both are overriding criteria of *moral rectitude*, which is why they are grouped together. The fifth formulation (Paton's III A) tells us to always act as if we were a citizen of a universal kingdom of ends. This formulation does not test principles at all; rather, it refers to the ideal society that would exist if all people lived by the principles passed by the other formulations. Since it does not itself function as any kind of overriding test, I regretfully set it aside.

The distinction between criteria of the realm of the moral and criteria of moral rectitude is important, both now and later. The latter separates the morally right from the morally wrong, the former the moral from the nonmoral. Take a group of our antihumane opponents, say, Social Darwinists who lack any compassion for the weak. Assuming that they had principles that took priority over their desires, that they had some notion of justice, that they tried to render their principles logically coherent, and so forth, I would not call them nonmoral. Rather than accusing them of having no morality at all, I would say that they had an antihumane morality. After all, they label things right and wrong, they just do so according to principles or ideals that I reject. In other words, I believe the realm of the moral is inhabited by a variety of people who hold conflicting criteria of moral rectitude. Which is to say that my criterion of the realm of the moral reserves the term "nonmoral" for people who have no other-regarding principles at all, for example, the classical egoist.

Some would claim that I have drawn the boundaries of the realm of the moral too broadly and that some or all of those who hold antihumane ideals can be expelled. But whether the boundaries should be broad or narrow, the distinction between criteria of realm and criteria of rectitude is the same. As for its importance, when we are trying to vindicate certain ideals, these two different kinds of criteria offer different victories and extract different prices. As shown, using an overriding criterion of rectitude promises total victory but has a darker side. The realm of the moral approach lacks the darker side precisely because it promises less. Assume we could expel all of the advocates of antihumane ideals from the realm of the moral. Even so, they need not concede that they ought to accept humane ideals: they would be left with a choice between accepting humane ideals and wearing the label nonmoral. The latter option may appear unpalatable, but the choice is there.

While this kind of victory over our opponents is less than total, that fact is mitigated somewhat by the absence of a darker side. The test that overrides cherished criteria of moral rectitude, both humane and antihumane, is not a new criterion of moral rectitude but one different in kind. It merely imposes reasons for calling things moral or not moral, it leaves undisturbed our humane ideals as the source of our reasons for calling acts right or wrong. We are still free to say that acts are morally right because they are humane; we need not forfeit that in favor of giving nonhumane reasons for their rightness. This approach, the realm of the moral approach, was fully developed only in our time. Nonetheless, the distinction between realm and rectitude is directly relevant to my analysis of Kant. If I am to use him to exemplify the darker side of ethical truth-tests, I must isolate just when he uses the categorical imperative as an overriding criterion of *moral rectitude* to vindicate his ideals. And this means defending my classification of the various formulations of the categorical imperative.

Kant believed that the various formulations of the categorical imperative all reflect an underlying unity, so he does not classify them by type. My classification is based on how the various formulations actually function when used to validate moral principles, because then criteria of realm and rectitude show different patterns. The latter exhibits a pattern that is straightforward and direct. An overriding criterion of moral rectitude is supposed to be a nonpartisan test of what is really right and really wrong. If a principle passes that test, what it recommends is objectively right, and that is that. However, an overriding criterion of the realm of the moral exhibits a pattern that is by necessity indirect. It is not enough that one of your principles passes such a test. That merely shows that it is moral as distinct from nonmoral, which leaves open the possibility that competing principles are also moral. Therefore, you must go on to show that all competing principles, Social Darwinist and Nietzschean principles, cannot pass the test; that is, you must show that your principle is the sole occupant of the realm of the moral. This is what gives using a criterion of realm its distinctive pattern: not only passing your principle but also excluding, and thereby discrediting, alternative principles.

This brings us back to the first formulation of the categorical imperative. Kant argues that benevolence, or promoting the happiness of others, cannot be part of the content of the categorical imperative. He sees that benevolence would infect the content of the categorical imperative with a humane bias and thereby undermine its nonpartisan status (*Critique of Practical Reason*, AK. V, 34–36 & 118; *Groundwork*, AK. IV, 427 & 442–444). However, he wants to use the categorical imperative to validate the principle of benevolence and tries to use the first formulation (universal law) to do so. The argument: when in need, even a selfish person wills that others give him help; were the principle of refusing help out of selfish motives a universal law, everyone would be entitled to refuse him help; therefore, he cannot will that the principle of selfishness should be a universal law (*Metaphysics of Morals*, AK. VI, 453). As to how this justifies the principle of benevolence, Kant says, "The reason why I should promote the happiness of others is . . . solely because a maxim which excludes this cannot be present in one and the same volition as a universal law" (*Groundwork*, AK. IV, 441). In sum, when a selfish person tries to will selfishness as a universal law, his or her will is hopelessly divided against itself. He wills both that others offer help and that others are entitled to withhold help. The conclusion: since all alternatives to benevolence flunk the test of universalizability, benevolence alone has a claim to be a moral principle.

A brief digression on the validity of Kant's argument in favor of benevolence. The assumption behind the first formulation of the categorical imperative is sound enough. If we espouse something as a moral principle, we must universalize it in the sense of wanting a world in which everyone, not just ourselves, acts on it. But there are two difficulties. First, no doubt selfish people in need find it unpalatable to grant that others are entitled to withhold help. On the other hand, surely no selfish person wants to be bound to always help other people on the innumerable occasions when they are in need. So a selfish person's will is going to be divided against itself no matter whether he or she rejects benevolence or espouses benevolence. Second, Kant's argument is incomplete. There are nonselfish alternatives to the principle of benevolence, such as the antihumane ideals of Nietzsche and the Social Darwinists, and Kant has done nothing to show they flunk the test of universalizability. This is understandable since he never encountered them. We will discuss how far universalizability can be pushed against thinkers like Nietzsche and Sumner when we put our own case against them.

Our concern is the pattern of argument that emerges when Kant applies the first formulation. It matches the realmish pattern perfectly: your principle passes the test, all alternative principles are supposed to fail and therefore can be excluded from the realm of the moral, which indirectly validates your principle as sole remaining occupant of the realm of the moral. When Kant applies the second formulation of the categorical imperative, live in accordance with nature (*Metaphysics of Morals*, AK. VI, 419–420), and the third formulation, treat people never simply as means but also as ends (*Metaphysics of Morals*, AK. VI, 331–332), a quite different pattern emerges. It matches the rectitude pattern: a principle that passes the test qualifies as morally right without further ado; whatever flunks the test is morally wrong without further ado. The method could not be more straightforward and direct. In the *Metaphysics of Morals*, the section entitled "The Elements of Ethics," Kant quickly disposes of case after case. The use of the second formulation as an overriding test is signaled whenever he speaks of man as a physical or natural being and of nature's aims or purposes. The third formulation is signaled when he speaks of man as an end in himself, as more than a means or thing, as capable of self-legislation, as valuable because of the humanity in his own person.

Here is the rectitude pattern at work. Suicide is wrong because nature "aims at the preservation of the individual" and because "to dispose of one's self as a mere means to an end of one's own liking is to degrade humanity in one's person." Sexual perversion is wrong because "sexual love aims at the preservation of the . . . species" and because man thereby "uses himself as a means for the gratification of an animal drive." Drunkenness and gluttony are wrong because nature aims at the preservation of our powers and our capacity for the enjoyment of life. A man should not lie because it is "directly contrary to the natural purposiveness of his capacity to communicate his thoughts" and because he thereby uses himself as a mere "talking machine" free from the limits set by a purpose. Self-esteem is right and servility wrong because each man should prize himself as an end in himself. Each man ought to develop his capacities and powers, both of mind and body, so as to be fit to pursue "the end of his existence" (his role as a being capable of self-legislation). Each of us ought to become a useful member of society out of respect for "the worth of humanity in his own person." We should respect our fellow man because "man can be used by no one (neither by others nor even by himself) merely as a means but must always be used at the same time as an end." Moreover, our duty to respect others entails a wide range of more specific duties. We must not inflict cruel and unusual punishments on criminals, or demand that others fawn on us and treat us as superior creatures, or spread scandal, or hold up others to ridicule (*Metaphysics of Morals*, AK. VI, 420–430, 434–435, 444–446, & 462–468).

When Kant uses the purposes of nature as an overriding criterion of moral rectitude, he does no better than Locke or Rousseau. He compromises its nonpartisan status by reading into nature whatever content he needs to get decisions in favor of his own principles. Nature aims at self-preservation so as to condemn suicide but not to endorse a lie that might save one's life. Nature aims at enhancing our capacity for enjoyment so as to condemn alcoholism but not to endorse the pleasures of unorthodox sex. Kant had little choice: it was hardly viable to keep the purposes of nature nonpartisan and get no verdicts; therefore, he gets verdicts by rendering their content partisan. Kant's use of the concept of people as ends in themselves as an overriding test of moral rectitude also involves a trade-off between nonpartisan status and plausible verdicts. To understand how, we must clarify both the meaning and status of the concept of people as ends. And since that concept is the core of the third formulation of the categorical imperative, we must analyze the derivation of the third formulation.

When Kant introduces the third formulation, he gives a cryptic summary of its derivation, and it is illuminating to compare that to the elaborations that follow. The summary consists of three propositions. First, I must conceive of myself as an end in myself because I am a rational being. Second, all others must be conceived as ends in themselves on the same grounds. Third, I must, therefore, treat everyone (including myself) never simply as means but also as ends (*Groundwork*, AK. IV, 429–430). Eventually, these propositions are elaborated as follows (Flynn, 1979, 299–301; 1986, 441–444).

First, I possess practical reason; that is, unlike an animal, I ponder and assess alternative courses of action. As a rational creature, I am committed to the use of my reason and must presuppose whatever preconditions are necessary for its operation. That means I must presuppose both my negative and positive freedom. If ever I thought of myself as determined when contemplating an act (waited for a cause to determine my decision), then the process of pondering alternatives would grind to a halt. It would be a sort of cognitive suicide, and I would be literally immobilized. However, freedom from determination is not enough; that would merely be the random freedom of a Mexican jumping bean bounding aimlessly about. For choice to be directed by reason, I must be free to choose in accord with rationally imposed principles or against them. The only rationally defensible test of principles is the categorical imperative, so it turns mere negative freedom into positive freedom (*Groundwork*, AK. IV, 431–434 & 446–447).

Second, just as I must presuppose my own negative and positive freedom as concomitants of my rationality, so I must presuppose them in others, for certainly they also possess practical reason (*Groundwork*, AK. IV, 447–449).

Third, negative and positive freedom entail that all human beings are moral agents, creatures capable of choosing either right (what accords with the categorical imperative) or wrong (what conflicts with it) and deserving of praise or blame. Therefore, every person has a right to justice, to be rewarded if praiseworthy, to be punished only if blameworthy. That is the essence of people being treated as ends in themselves. We can treat submoral creatures as means only: it is permissible to discard a worn-out shoe or to leave unpunished a dog who has bitten someone. Only moral creatures add moral value to the universe, and we must cherish this attribute, not only in others but also in our own person. Suicide means subtracting something from the sum total of moral value, exterminating a creature capable of choosing rightly in accord with objective moral law (*Groundwork*, AK. IV, 434–436; *Metaphysics of Morals*, AK. VI, 331–332, 434–436, & 441).

The third formulation of the categorical imperative is really an egalitarian concept of justice: all people should be allocated rewards and penalties strictly according to their deserts. Kant feels free to elevate this concept to the status of a truth-test because he believes it to be objective, something that will not compromise the categorical imperative's nonpartisan status. Benevolence, until validated by the categorical imperative, is based on mere subjective sentiment. But just treatment is derived from the undeniable fact that all people possess practical reason. Kant's truth-test now has a substantive content that renders its decisions more plausible. The third formulation really does seem to condemn arbitrary treatment of human beings, really does seem to condemn suicide. This is not to say that there is a clear connection between its content and all of its applications. It is not at all clear why unorthodox sex, accompanied by mutual consent, treats someone as a means only rather than as an end as well.

Nietzsche would not find it difficult to refute Kant's claim for objectivity on behalf of his concept of justice. The fact that certain creatures are free may be a prerequisite for assessing them in terms of praise or blame, but that fact does not impose itself as a sufficient condition. Nietzsche argues that before you admit a creature into your circle of moral concern, you must value that creature enough so that it counts. Some value ordinary people who have no more to offer than their freedom, others despise them and value only those with creative genius. It is a matter of subjective sentiment. Kant himself says that you must banish criteria based on subjective sentiment from the content of the categorical imperative. Therefore, he has bought enhanced plausibility of its decisions at the cost of compromising its nonpartisan status.

Kant's truth-tests, the overriding criteria of moral rectitude enshrined in the second and third formulations, have a profound effect on his moral reasoning. Even if he has no valid case for the objectivity of his concept of justice, the fact remains that he has put it into the content of the third formulation. And this means we must adapt our model of what truth-tests entail. Insofar as truth-tests banish humane ideals from their content so as to attain nonpartisan status, they substitute their own alien reasons for calling acts right or wrong for our humane reasons. By banishing humane ideals like benevolence, Kant has impoverished his reasoning from a humane point of view. However, by making an exception of justice, he has salvaged *it* as a source of reasons. Let us take up these two points, first by detailing just how Kant salvaged justice as a source of reasons and second by showing how, despite this, his moral reasoning is impoverished.

Recall that proofs of humane ideals have no darker side. Kant's derivation of the third formulation is essentially a proof. Indeed, its starting point, that all men have practical reason, is the same as Gewirth's starting point, that all human beings are purposive agents. It is an interesting commentary on the logic of proofs that despite a common premise, the two diverge thereafter. Now imagine that Kant had gone beyond attempting to prove the objective status of a roughly egalitarian concept of justice and had also attempted to prove the objective status of benevolence. In that case, Kant might have relied solely on proofs, and his justification of humane ideals would not have compromised them, that is, would not have compromised their role of generating reasons for the rightness of acts.

But unfortunately, Kant did not choose to rely solely on proofs. He takes his concept of justice, sets it alongside the purposes of nature, and appoints both to a higher court of appeal. And sadly, this is a higher court from which benevolence has been excluded. So while justice and nature both sit on the bench and can generate reasons for the rightness of acts, benevolence cannot. Later, we will illustrate the effect of the ban on benevolence concerning his moral reasoning by analyzing his discussions of lying and treatment of animals. But first, let us illustrate the effect of justice sitting in judgment on benevolence. This emerges clearly in Kant's discussion of punishment, and that discussion reveals something new and disturbing: justice must take priority over benevolence whenever the two conflict.

Setting aside for the moment whether Kant must favor justice over benevolence, his discussion of punishment leaves no doubt that he does do so: "He (the criminal) must be found to be deserving of punishment before any consideration is given to the utility of the punishment for himself or for his fellow citizens. The law concerning punishment is a categorical imperative, and woe to him who rummages around in the winding paths of a theory of happiness looking for some advantage to be gained by releasing the criminal from punishment or by reducing the amount of it" (*Metaphysics of Morals*, AK. VI, 331). The striking thing about this passage is not that it is always wrong to punish the innocent because of utilitarian considerations, though even this might be disputed, but the notion that it is always wrong to mitigate the punishment of the guilty out of humane considerations. Kant implies that any modification of the principle of treating someone according to his or his deserts is illegitimate, even if done for the good of the criminal or even if the survival of a whole people is at stake. We must not compromise this principle, because "a human being can never be manipulated merely as a means to the purposes of someone else," an obvious reference to the third formulation (*Metaphysics of Morals*, AK. VI, 331–332).

I believe that Kant's priorities are dictated by his views on objectivity, his belief that justice possesses the objectivity to qualify as a truth-test but that benevolence would infect a truth-test with subjectivity. Only after benevolence has passed the categorical imperative is it binding on all rational creatures. Kant never doubts that it tests out. It passes the first formulation, as we have seen (*Groundwork*, AK. IV, 423 & 441; *Metaphysics of Morals*, AK. VI, 393, 451, & 453), and apparently nature intends the goods of the world to benefit everyone (*Lectures on Ethics*, Infield, 1930, 192–193), and treating people as ends is said to entail a genuine concern for their welfare

(*Groundwork*, AK. IV, 430; *Metaphysics of Morals*, AK. VI, 395). None-theless, benevolence must test out. Certainly, whenever a test conflicts with something valid only insofar as it tests out, the test must prevail. Which is to say that justice must take priority over benevolence.

Kant may well exaggerate the frequency of conflicts between justice and benevolence. When he says that not even one innocent person should be sac-rificed to save a whole people from extermination, it could be argued that most of the people under threat are also innocent of wrongdoing. Sacrificing only one innocent person would surely be a lesser injustice than sacrificing many innocent people. However, sooner or later, the demands of justice and benevolence will conflict, or at least any humanist will think so who has not completely abandoned the notion of matching rewards and punishments to deserts. And when such situations do occur, the very logic of the categorical imperative dictates something very serious. Those who hold humane ideals lose the freedom to balance justice against benevolence in accord with their ideals, favoring justice when the loss in terms of human happiness is accept-able, favoring benevolence when the sacrifice would be too great. Take the problem of how to treat the Germans at the end of World War II. We could have given an absolute priority to justice, that is, we could have done liter-ally everything we could to punish every German who cooperated in any un-necessary way with the Hitler regime. We could have punished millions. But most of us were unwilling to add that much to the sum total of human mis-ery. So we tried to strike a balance: prosecution of the worst offenders, relief to mitigate the lot of the rest.

When Kant elevates justice to the level of a truth-test, he does succeed in altering the price that truth-tests normally extract. But humanists will find even this new price highly objectionable. When one humane ideal is elevated, the rest are left on the wrong side of the test/test out dichotomy and thus downgraded within a hierarchy of humane ideals. Kant may have preferred justice to take automatic priority over benevolence, but I want more flexibil-ity than that. I want to weigh them against one another when they conflict, rather than have "objectivity" do my weighing for me. Moral judgments in which we really believe are replaced by moral judgments we reject or, at least, would reject did not objectivity ram them down our throats. Our cherished ideals, which we want so much to be vindicated, have been dis-torted in the very process of being vindicated. This threat to our ideals transcends Kant. The notion that justice is somehow prior to benevolence has surfaced periodically throughout the history of Western thought, all the way from Plato to Rawls.

In his famous essay "On a Supposed Right to Lie from Benevolent Motives," Kant defends an assertion he made on a previous occasion. He had said that it was a *crime* to tell a benevolent lie; for example, to lie to a murderer who asked us whether a friend, of whom he was in pursuit, had taken refuge in our house. He does not even discuss whether it is *morally remiss* to tell a benevolent lie. Presumably, this is because his earlier works have already shown that lying is always wrong with only trivial qualifications (*Metaphysics of Morals*, AK. VI, 429–433). Lying flunks the first formulation of the categorical imperative because it cannot be universalized without contradiction. Its purpose is to deceive, but in a world in which everyone lied to deceive, no one would trust anyone's word, so its purpose would be frustrated (*Groundwork*, AK. IV, 403 & 422). Lying flunks the second formulation because the natural purpose of our ability to communicate is to convey our thoughts accurately (*Metaphysics of Morals*, AK. VI, 429–430). Lying flunks the third formulation because it reduces my physical being to a mere means and uses another (the hearer) as a means to my own ends (*Groundwork*, AK. IV, 429; *Metaphysics of Morals*, AK. VI, 429–430). Since the question of the morality of lying has been settled, the only question left is whether a benevolent lie can be a crime punishable by law.

Kant argues that lying to a murderer about whether a friend has taken refuge in my home may well qualify as a crime. To be a crime, it must meet three conditions: be morally wrong, which has already been shown; be unjust, which it is, because any lie threatens all rights based on faith in contracts; inflict a direct injury, which is clearly possible. What if, unknown to me, my friend had left my house, and, thanks to my lie, the murderer encountered him? Then I would be an accessory to murder ("On Benevolent Lies," Abbott, 1927, 361–363). It seems natural to respond by saying that if we told the truth and our friend was murdered thanks to that, we would be accessories in an even more culpable sense. However, this misses Kant's point: considerations about culpability under the law arise only if an act is morally wrong, and truthfulness is never wrong ("On Benevolent Lies," Abbott, 1927, 364–365). Something must both inflict an injury and be wrong to be a crime.

Paton (1954) argues that Kant's rigorism in forbidding exceptions to truthfulness was idiosyncratic. He claims that the content of the categorical imperative does not really forbid all exceptions, for example, that a principle like "I will lie when this is the only way to save a life" could pass. He supplies no details, but no doubt he is correct. As for the first formulation, if everyone told the truth almost all of the time and lied only in exceptional cases, this would not undermine trust in everyone's word, so the exceptions would accomplish their purpose of deception. As for the second, one can make the purposes of nature generate any principle one chooses. Rather than assuming that communication has the purpose of conveying our thoughts, we could assume it has the social purpose of helping people to live together harmoniously. Therefore, a benevolent lie that avoided a murder would further the purposes of nature. As for the third, rather than saying that lying to murderers uses them as a means to my ends, we could say that murderers who demand information necessary to commit their crimes use me as a means to their ends.

However, there is one problem Kant's apologists cannot solve. They can search the categorical imperative and find a variety of reasons for calling benevolent lying right, but they can never call benevolent lying right because it is benevolent. Therefore, humanists will always feel a profound disgust when they watch the categorical imperative operating as a truth-test. I will try to dramatize this point by recourse to a great humanist. In *Les Misérables*, Victor Hugo introduces us to Sister Simplice and prepares us for a moving climax. Sister Simplice has always believed that lying was an absolute form of evil and took her name after Simplice of Sicily, who was martyred rather than lie about her place of birth. Hugo shows her resisting the temptation to tell lies out of kindness. She meets Jean Valjean and recognizes his essential goodness. Finally, she is approached by Javert, who seeks to arrest Jean Valjean for a trivial offense and restore him to the horrors of the galleys. Sister Simplice has never told a lie in her life, but to save Jean Valjean she "lied twice in succession, without hesitation, promptly, as a person does when sacrificing herself." Hugo adds, "O sainted maid! You left this world many years ago; you have rejoined your sisters, the virgins, and your brothers, the angels, in the light; may this lie be counted to your credit in paradise."

Victor Hugo wanted to say that a benevolent lie was right because it was benevolent. It is hard to see him settling for something else. At last, we see the darker side of the categorical imperative fully revealed. As a truth-test, it has sucked up all relevant reasons for calling acts right or wrong within itself, as it must. If there were valid reasons outside the categorical imperative, it would have competition as a test of principles, and its authority would not be beyond dispute. When benevolence was banished from the content of the categorical imperative because of its subjectivity, one of our most cherished ideals was stripped of its power to generate reasons for the moral rectitude of acts: benevolent acts can be right, but never because they are benevolent.

Moreover, the categorical imperative does more than cheat us of the reasons we want to give. Look at the sort of reasons it puts into our mouths: that it is right to tell a benevolent lie because this is in accord with the "natural purpose" of communication. Paton (1967, 172) provides another example when he searches the categorical imperative for something that would allow for a right to commit suicide, at least in some circumstances. He argues that suicide could be justified if pain is so unendurable or insanity so certain that there is no longer any hope of "manifesting moral worth." I doubt that whether or not someone suffering hopelessly still has the capacity to manifest moral worth, for example, whether they are sufficiently compos mentis to interrupt their agony to be polite to the nurses, would loom large in anyone's mind, save that it has a foothold in the third formulation. Reasons of this sort strike a false note; they seem simply beside the point from a humane point of view. Who would care to give them, if the prospect of "objectivity" did not lend them an artificial allure?

Let us return to Victor Hugo and imagine he had added a tag on the story of Sister Simplice. She tells her lie, Javert leaves, and she says to Jean Valjean, "I can see that you are surprised. But over the last few months, I have been thinking about teleology and now believe that the natural purpose of communication is not to convey our thoughts accurately, or at least not in every instance." Or she says, "It recently occurred to me that when you give people false information, it is not simply a matter of your using them as a means. When they ask you for information you hate to give, they are using you as a means. At any rate, be reassured that I did not allow any thought of benevolence to enter in while I thought this question out." My point is that humanism is not simply a set of conclusions about what is right; it has its reasons. If we are honest, we will admit that the categorical imperative thrusts upon us a whole range of reasons we do not really care about, to the detriment of reasons about which we really do. The latter may seem "subjective," but they are our own.

I have emphasized that Kant had no right to incorporate justice into the content of the categorical imperative. But given that as a fait accompli, he could have improved his reasoning about lying by exploiting the advantage thereby conferred. For example, he could have said it would be right to lie to a murderer who seeks an innocent victim because the latter has done nothing to deserve losing his or her life. Or he could have said that it would be right to lie to Javert because Jean Valjean had done nothing to deserve the terrible punishment he would suffer if apprehended.

A partisan concept of justice certainly gives better reasons than the nonpartisan reasons suggested by the purposes of nature. Nonetheless, even an egalitarian concept of justice can never do the work of benevolence. A man near death asks why his son has not arrived. In fact, his son boarded a flight the previous evening, and we have received word that he was killed in a plane crash. We decide to lie and tell the father that the flight has been delayed, wanting to spare him a crushing blow, wanting to spare him the knowledge that not only is his life at an end but his son's life as well. In such a case, I doubt that any of us would want to cast about looking for a rationale in terms of justice. I doubt that any of us would review our knowledge of the man's past life so as to assess whether or not he deserved to be spared the pain in question. Such a thing would seem bizarre or even disgusting. We would lie to him out of benevolence; we would think it wrong to inflict so much pain to achieve so trivial a result in terms of truth. Which is to say that we would reason in terms of utilitarian considerations and would feel crippled to have such considerations excluded.

At this point, I wish to make quite clear that I am no utilitarian. Not only do I reject Mill's proof, but my basic ideals go well beyond the greatest happiness principle. Sometimes other humane ideals should take priority over benevolence, not only justice but also things like the pursuit of truth and the creation of beauty. I suspect a familiar temptation lies behind utilitarianism. The justice road to objectivity may have tempted many, but the utilitarian road has always beckoned some. After all, happiness looks so measurable. Certainly something like this is needed to explain thinkers who impoverished humane ideals by trying to subsume them all under happiness.

However, precisely because benevolence is one of my ideals, I want no absolute ban against giving utilitarian reasons for the moral rectitude of acts.

Kant's discussion of the treatment of animals provides an exception to my analysis. For once, benevolence is more than something that tests out, it plays the role of testing a moral principle. And yet I believe that this exception does more than anything said thus far to reveal the darker side of the categorical imperative.

Although Kant clearly wanted to vindicate the principle of kindness to animals, he could extract no decision in its favor from the various formulations of the categorical imperative. The third formulation was particularly troublesome. Kant's argument for it holds that human beings are valuable because they are free and that rationality is a prerequisite for freedom. Animals, being nonrational, are no more than things, and their presence adds no moral value to the universe (*Groundwork*, AK. IV, 428; *Lectures on Ethics*, Infield, 1930, 121–122). He never turns to the second formulation, presumably because in his day it was commonly believed that nature intended animals to be used by people as they saw fit. As for universalizability, or the first formulation, sadists who wish to harm animals for pleasure need not grant that animals are entitled to harm them for pleasure, because animals are not entitled to anything. Thus far, cruelty seems an open option. Kant's solution is in effect to use benevolence as a test of principles about the treatment of animals. He argues that cruelty to animals will decrease our compassion for them, which will reduce our compassion for people, which will weaken a predisposition serviceable to morality. Kant says that "he who is cruel to animals becomes hard also in his dealings with men" and that "tender feelings towards dumb animals develop humane feelings towards mankind" (*Metaphysics of Morals*, AK. VI, 443; *Lectures on Ethics*, Infield, 1930, 240).

This leaves much to be desired from a humane point of view. Even if people who enjoyed being cruel to animals could show that this had no effect on their being kind to people, I would condemn them on moral grounds. Which underlines a point already made, that no one ideal, not even benevolence, can supply all the reasons humanists will want to use to call acts right or wrong. However, at present, our main point is not the limitations of benevolence but our need for it as one source of reasons. And for once, Kant has used it as a test of moral principles. But what allowed him to do so, what allowed him to ignore his ban on benevolence as a test? The fact that the categorical imperative could say nothing useful to resolve an important moral question. Principles are supposed to be tested by the categorical imperative, not by principles like benevolence that would infect an overriding test with subjectivity. But if the categorical imperative itself proves irrelevant, then Kant is free to treat a question as if it were merely a matter of means to an end, merely a matter of how to get people to act on a principle that has received a pass. The principle of benevolence has earned a pass, kindness to animals encourages benevolent behavior, and that is that (Broadie & Pybus, 1974).

This exception to the ban on utilitarian considerations reveals a paradox at the heart of Kant's truth-test. The categorical imperative becomes acceptable to humanists only to the extent that it cannot do its job. Imagine that the categorical imperative proved inadequate to settle all moral questions with one exception: it did vindicate the rightness of benevolent acts. Then benevolence would be the sole consideration relevant to all subsequent moral questions. However, even then, humanists could not be happy with its role: benevolence would have the job of grading all other moral principles, but still, it could not provide reasons for why acts were right or wrong. When asked whether acts were right because they were benevolent, we would have to say no. We would have to say that the real reasons that benevolent acts were right is because they accord with the purposes of nature or because they can be subsumed under justice. We would have to refer to the overriding tests of moral rectitude that the principle of benevolence had passed, the truth-tests that had lent it objectivity. Even with its role reduced to the absolute minimum, just so long as it had any role at all, the categorical imperative would extract its irreducible price.

TRANSITION
AN AGENDA

5

Morality and Moral Debate

Philosophy unaided cannot provide a defense of humane-egalitarian ideals. Neither truth-tests nor proofs nor moral realism can give us valid arguments against our antihumane opponents. However, philosophical analysis can lead us toward something better.

This chapter is a transitional chapter. It offers an agenda for moral debate composed of seven items. The items are crucial: no one who is serious about their ideals, whether humane or antihumane, can refuse to defend their ideals against the challenges the items pose. When they do so, they suddenly find that they are at the mercy of logic and social science. Therefore, this agenda allows us to transcend the limitations of philosophy by revealing the potency of social science. Its items were derived from a critique of a modern variant of the realm of the moral approach, one developed by S. E. Toulmin and Kai Nielsen. These two thinkers developed that approach in the 1950s, and readers should consult their recent works to appreciate their life-long contributions to the central problems of ethics (Jonsen & Toulmin, 1988; Nielsen, 1985, 1989).

The tasks described provide this chapter with a beginning, a middle, and an end. First, it shows why it is futile to attempt to expel our antihumane opponents from the realm of the moral. Second, it suggests that a debate about moral principles is a better option and itemizes the necessary agenda. Finally, it shows why both the humane and the antihumane find it too costly to ignore that agenda.

Toulmin (1950) tried to expel the antihumane from the realm of the moral by positing two rules of ethical inference. People were reasoning morally only if they assessed acts in terms of an accepted principle or social practice and if they assessed social practices in terms of general fecundity, that is, alleviating suffering with equity. As we saw under Kant, this kind of realmish approach is different from using a truth-test. Certain formulations of the categorical imperative tested conflicting moral principles and determined which were really right and which were really wrong; they were ethical truth-tests. Other formulations determined that certain principles (benevolence) were moral principles and that others (selfishness) simply did not deserve to be called moral. That approach, casting your opponents outside the realm of the moral, has the disadvantage that it leaves them with a choice. They can either adopt your principles or simply grant that they have no moral principles at all. However, most of our opponents would find that choice unpleasant. Even Nietzsche believed that supermen owed justice to one another. No one would like to raise a child without making appeals to right and wrong. In addition, using criteria of the realm of the moral lacks the darker side of truth-tests: recall that they do not use an alien criterion of right and wrong to override our own cherished criteria.

That said, Toulmin no less than Plato must convince us that he is using something nonpartisan, something Nietzsche is obliged to respect because its content is not loaded against him. The content of Toulmin's second rule of ethical inference is that you must assess principles in terms of whether they alleviate suffering with equity. This is so patently humane-egalitarian in content that it can be taken seriously only if Nietzsche's obvious objections to it can be answered. Toulmin never confronts Nietzsche or any other serious antihumane opponent. The overwhelming consensus of scholars was that his rules were simply partisan rules. Toulmin sets out criteria that are merely "the dominant ones at present" (Mackie, 1951, 116); he eliminates other modes of reasoning by "arbitrary fiat" (Sacksteader, 1951–1952, 218); his criteria are really "criteria accepted among a certain class or groups of people, e.g., those at Cambridge" (Dykstra, 1955, 465); he ties the evaluative meaning of ethical to a "particular criterion" (Nakhnikian, 1959, 67); and he is actually "expressing a moral preference" (Wadia, 1965, 91).

Toulmin's sins of omission are not peculiar to himself. One searches in vain through the indexes of most books written by contemporary moral philosophers to find a Nietzsche entry. He is the specter at the feast; everyone wants to exorcise him, but few want to acknowledge his presence, much less argue against him. This conspiracy of silence suggests that were he confronted things might begin to unravel. The rules of moral reasoning, the moral points of view, the moral facts, the "we" this and the "we" that (for example, "we" always know that unnecessary suffering is wrong and that every human being counts in the moral equation)—perhaps all of these things would be revealed as merely humane-egalitarian ideals in disguise.

Kai Nielsen has always stood out as a hard-minded exception. He believed that Toulmin's rules could be defended by analyzing the characteristic functions of moral discourse. However, he acknowledged the fact that any account of those functions that disadvantaged the antihumane would be challenged by the antihumane; that is, they would argue for their own competing accounts. Nielsen believed there was a method that could resolve such a debate. Operationally, Nielsen's method consists of two steps. First, take stock of certain usages and concepts we all know preanalytically to be central to ethics: usages such as advising people how to live, laying down rules for dealing with conflicting interests or demands, allocating praise and blame; concepts such as universalizability, justice as fairness, happiness, and sympathy. Second, show that all accounts but one conflict with the central usages and concepts of ethics (Nielsen, 1957a, 99–100; 1957b, 243–244; 1958, 16–17).

Nielsen asserts that any account of the functions of moral discourse that omits guiding conduct toward maximization of the happiness of humankind is defective. As for alternative accounts, he posits one worthy of Nietzsche (guide conduct to produce superior people who use all others as means), and it is not difficult to posit accounts on behalf of Sumner (reward middle-class virtue) and Cattell (promote the evolution of human beings into a higher species). In my opinion, Nielsen does not show that his account is uniquely viable; indeed, his arguments against Nietzsche clearly fail (Flynn, 1976). Some fail because Nietzsche can provide rebuttals that are unanswerable, as chapter 7 on Nietzsche will show. Other arguments look more promising. They appear to fail, not so much because they are inherently weak but because they have not been pushed far enough. Those arguments have something in common: every one of them calls for a more systematic application of modern social science.

However, if further argument could discredit all antihumane accounts of the realm of the moral, would that not leave a humane-egalitarian account the only one viable and thereby salvage the realm of the moral approach? In my view, it would not. My case rests on an analysis of the pattern of argument that realmish thinkers have used to defend their humane accounts.

Toulmin refers to the role of ethics in organizing a human society and the need for something more than enlightened self-interest. Nielsen's arguments include accusing our opponents of falsifying facts about human nature, ignoring the demands of justice, being unwilling to stand by their moral principles with logical consistency, being unwilling to face up to the consequences of what their principles entail in practice. Suddenly, we realize that these arguments are familiar. They are the arguments Plato and Thrasymachus used against one another in the early pages of *The Republic*, the debate they carried on before Glaucon and Adeimantus intervened and demanded an ethical truth-test. They are the kind of arguments people have always used when they want to discredit one another's moral principles. This suggests that if Nielsen had won his debate about competing accounts of the realm of the moral, he could have used the very same arguments to win a debate about competing moral principles. Take the Nietzschean account: the functions of moral discourse are to guide conduct so as to produce superior people who use the rest of humankind simply as means. The substance is the same whether we call it an account of the functions of moral discourse or a fundamental moral principle. Certainly, if it forces Nietzsche to falsify facts, or into logical incoherence, or into hiding from its consequences, it is discredited in either case.

The whole point of the realm of the moral approach is to help us rout our antihumane opponents. But to use it, we must argue for our own account of that realm. Let us imagine the optimum result; that is, we argue down every one of our opponents and show that their accounts are nonviable. Now we can use the realm of the moral approach, but only because we have already won the debate. We cannot use it when we need it (before we have won), and we can use it only when we no longer need it (after we have won). Moreover, in arguing about accounts, we have not come up with anything really new, we argue just as we would if we were arguing about moral principles. So we might just as well stick to arguing about moral principles and forget about various accounts of the "function of ethics," or "moral reasoning," or the "moral point of view." In vindicating the realm of the moral approach, we have proved it useless.

This assumes that persisting with realmish concepts will not produce any really new pattern of argument in the future. I cannot prove such a thing, I can only give my reasons for being pessimistic. Any new proponent of the realm of the moral approach must argue for a criterion narrow enough to expel our antihumane opponents, a criterion like "the function of ethics is to maximize happiness with equity." When we argue for something like that, we are arguing for something whose content is just as narrow as a moral principle, at least as narrow as our basic ideals or first principles. I suspect that such a debate is very much determined by the content of what is being debated, same content, same opponents, same arguments likely to be effective against those opponents. Therefore, I suspect that this approach will never do more than affix a new and strange label. Its sole consequence will be to persuade us to stop calling moral debates "debates about moral principles" and take up calling them "debates about who really has moral principles." So what is the point? Therefore, a shift of method. I will list seven items from an age-old agenda, the kind of agenda that has governed moral debate right from the start (Plato) to the present (*The Bell Curve*), governed it because it is implicit in the cut and thrust of the arguments people actually use.

The agenda for moral debate asserts a right to interrogation. Everyone committed to certain basic ideals has a right to ask his or her opponents whether they

1. have ideals that take priority over their desires, ideals that give them their reasons for labeling acts right or wrong, so that they have an obligation to perform those acts subject only to a plea of moral weakness;

2. have a criterion as to what creatures are significant enough to qualify for the circle of moral concern, qualify for just treatment and consideration of their welfare and interests (the circle of moral concern may include anything from all living creatures to a fragment of humankind);

3. have a criterion of justice that, at least within the circle of moral concern, allocates boons and ills according to merits or deserts;

4. are willing to universalize all of the above: whenever they label something or someone as right, or worthy of regard, or just, they must be willing to give reasons until they reach their basic ideals or first

principles, and then they must stand by those principles with logical
consistency;

5. are willing to face up to the consequences their ideals entail when put
   into practice;

6. are willing to show that their ideals can serve as the ordering principle of a human society;

7. are willing to show that their ideals do not require them to falsify or
   evade any of the truths revealed by science, usually social science, but
   biological and even natural science can be relevant.

Each item on the agenda carries two kinds of price, the price we forfeit
if we refuse to argue over that item, and the prices we may incur if we do argue over that item. The former are too heavy for any participant in moral
debate to be willing to forfeit, which is why the agenda structures moral debate. The latter always differ from the former because they are peculiar to
the content of the ideals that are being attacked or defended. I will argue
that humane-egalitarian ideals can be defended over all seven items and
emerge unscathed, while antihumane ideals sooner or later encounter an
item that extracts a demoralizing price.

I know of no moral or political advocate of historical importance,
whether humane or antihumane, who has not accepted every item on this
agenda. Nietzsche is often called an amoralist. However, Nietzsche put ideals
like the creation of beauty above desire, he had a criterion that certified supermen alone as worthy of regard, he believed in justice as fairness for supermen,
he would be willing to praise anyone, herd man or superman, who promoted
the hegemony of supermen, he did not flinch from the suffering his ideals
entailed, he thought his ideals could be used to order a cosmopolitan Europe,
and so forth. There is one group of people who can evade the agenda without
paying a crushing price. They do so by rejecting the first and second items;
that is, they have rejected all ideals or concern for others that transcend enlightened self-interest. Therefore, they have chosen a path that gives them
nothing to defend in moral debate. However, such people are happy to defend themselves on their own terms, and this makes it more difficult, rather
than less difficult, to find arguments against them. The problem they pose
will be acknowledged in the final chapter.

In order to show that the price of forfeiting an item differs in kind from the prices incurred by debating that item, I will proceed item by item, beginning with the third. For each, I will try to define the price of forfeiting it (labeled "first price") and then give one example of a price someone incurred, or might incur, by arguing over it (labeled "second price"). The latter will be multiplied and clarified when we offer detailed criticism of antihumane ideals in the light of our agenda.

The price of having no criterion of justice is that you must tell people, even those you value highly, that you are indifferent as to whether they suffer arbitrarily (first price). Sumner's criterion of justice forced him to espouse a motivational psychology that is false (second price). The price of refusing to give logically consistent reasons for your moral assessments is that you must ask people to accept your ideals without comprehending them. For example, imagine that you praise the military virtues one day and refuse to praise someone who practices them the next. People then have the right to refuse to espouse your ideals on the grounds that they are baffled as to just what kind of conduct your ideals recommend (first price). When racists attempt to be consistent about their ideals, they are often trapped into declaring that certain personal traits are irrelevant to assessing people. Those same traits are ones that no one, including racists, would omit when assessing people (second price).

Those who will not face up to the consequences of their ideals pay the heaviest possible price. They can be told that, with full knowledge, they would prefer failure in converting others to their ideals to success (first price). Recent critics of humane-egalitarian ideals argue that our ideals in practice would produce a class hierarchy we would loathe (second price). Having no coherent scenario as to how your ideals could order a human society forces you to endorse the early Rousseau, that is, advocate that people should live like animals dispersed in the forest (first price). (Rousseau tried to mitigate this price: he pointed out how few animals died during the Lisbon earthquake.) Nietzsche could not have used his ideals to order a society without choosing between the two ideals he cherished most (second price). Finally, if you grant that evading the truths of science is a prerequisite for accepting your ideals, you give all rational human beings a good reason not to accept them (first price). The examples already offered show how various ideologues can come to grief thanks to this item (incur second prices). This is because when you submit to scientific truth, it is most likely to inflict wounds when either social consequences or social dynamics are debated. Note the contention that social science can show that egalitarian ideals in practice entail anti-egalitarian consequences. Also the contention that social science can show that one of Nietzsche's most cherished ideals would rob the other of any part in ordering a human society.

✓ Indeed, social science plus logic give our agenda its unity. The discussion of prices shows that while its items are set out one by one, they often interact when ideologues actually debate them, and the connecting thread is almost always logic and social science. Before applying these formidable tools to moral debate, one last clarification. This method of defending humane-egalitarian ideals, assuming our ideals do prevail, has no darker side. It posits no *ethical* truth-test, the peculiar *kind* of truth-test that uses an overriding criterion of moral rectitude. Therefore, it imposes no overriding criterion that replaces our own partisan reasons for calling acts right or wrong with so-called objective reasons.

As usual, the absence of a darker side limits the scope of the victory our ideals can hope to win. No matter how effectively we use our agenda to wound our antihumane opponents, we will never find ourselves giving them a reason for accepting humane ideals. The best our agenda can do is force them to confront a series of choices. For example, consider opponents whose ideals were proved to be counterproductive in practice. First, they can go on advocating their ideals, despite admitting that these ideals would produce consequences they are unwilling to accept, hardly psychologically viable. Second, they can try to revise their ideals, hoping that the new versions will both eliminate the unwelcome consequences and still be attractive to themselves, attractive enough so as to leave their commitment intact. Third, they can abandon their ideals for no ideals and become creatures of self-interest. Fourth, they can embrace eroscentrism, that is, recognize moral obligations only or primarily within the circle of their loved ones, an option that will be described in chapter 10. Fifth, they can search their hearts to try to find a commitment to some new ideal. These may be unpleasant and perhaps even demoralizing choices. But there is nothing here that entails the kind of rational ought Plato or Kant could impose, a rational ought that tells all humankind they must accept the moral oughts embedded in humane ideals.

In sum, our agenda offers not objectivity but a substitute for objectivity. This entails certain concessions. I concede that our opponents can refuse to argue over our agenda, and in doing so they commit no logical mistake. Let them; the prices they forfeit thereby suffice. I concede that our agenda cannot offer humane ideals one big victory. Rather, it commits us to an endless and open-ended debate. We must sweat to load down each and every opponent with price after price until collectively these are enough to sink them, and we must sweat to defend our own ideals so as to exempt them from similar prices. Still, all along we have been searching for a method that could both provide a nonpartisan criterion and hand down plausible decisions. Social science plus logic give us something nonpartisan; they can hand down plausible decisions and levy fines costly enough to be potent. What kind of decisions remains to be seen.

PART TWO

THE POTENCY
OF SOCIAL SCIENCE

6

Race and Class

The common characteristic of our antihumane opponents is that they favor a part of humanity at the expense of the rest. The favored groups vary. They have been selected by criteria as diverse as superior versus inferior race, upper versus lower class, fit versus unfit, exhibiting creative genius versus being ordinary. They differ in size from a few to a significant minority of humankind. They differ in status from being merely morally superior to being the sole locus of moral concern. They differ in prerogatives from having the right to treat all others as animals to having an obligation to offer the unfit nonpunitive options. Sometimes the favored group is a real group with a supposed positive correlation with merit, sometimes it is an ideal group defined by merit, sometimes competition for entry is open to all at least in theory, sometimes millions are barred by color or accident of birth.

The case made for the status of the favored group usually includes a theory of social dynamics and a theory of social or biological change. I will call the total case an antihumane ideology. The term "ideology" is not used pejoratively. Everyone, humane or antihumane, ought to have a plausible theory of social dynamics and social change. Modern antihumane ideologues, with the possible exception of Cattell, do not claim objectivity for their ideals, but they all offer substitutes, that is, something that makes a commitment to humane ideals look forbiddingly unattractive. They castigate humane-egalitarians as people who ignore the role of race in humanity's rise from savagery to civilization, who encourage viciousness, who constitute the main impediment to the perfection of the human species, whose egalitarianism is a symptom of "soul superstition," and so forth.

I will offer a critique of the following antihumane ideologies or ideologues: classical racism; William Graham Sumner as a reputed Social Darwinist; Raymond B. Cattell as a true Social Darwinist; and Nietzsche as the
presence who, above all, has destroyed the peace of mind of those committed to humane-egalitarian ideals.

RACISM AND BOOK REVIEWS

Classical racism posits a hierarchy of racial or ethnic groups and proposes
that group membership outweighs any individual differences within groups.
It can be refuted by forcing its proponents to choose between two options.
Either they must assert that people of a certain appearance (colored black) or
lineage (born Jewish) are to be despised or feared or exploited simply because
of their appearance or lineage, or they must assert that such people merit such
treatment because their appearance or lineage is correlated with certain personal traits. An item on our agenda, namely, logical consistency or the rule
of universalizability, can be used to show that the first option is nonviable.
The second option forces the racist to assert propositions that can be falsified
by evidence.

Take racists who say that people ought to be exterminated simply because they are Jewish or because they are black. Following R. M. Hare
(1963), we can ask what they would say if we found a document showing
that they had a Jewish grandparent, or what they would say if their own
skin turned black, perhaps because we sneaked a pill into their food or because of some pollutant in the water supply. Logical consistency would then
demand either that they grant that they should be exterminated, or that they
find a morally relevant distinction that can serve as an escape clause. Let us
focus on the former. They cannot endorse their own demise because this
carries too high a price to be acceptable. It is important to be clear about
the nature of that price, if only because Hare made the mistake of calling
those who would accept their own demise "fanatics." This provoked the response that those who have the courage to die for their ideals could just as
easily be called "dedicated," followed by reminders that Nazis and other
racists have been proud to lay down their lives to prevent a so-called superior race from being dominated by a so-called inferior race.

This response overlooks what I take to have been Hare's point: these
racists are not dying for their ideals; rather, they are dying for a "principle"

in which they do not really believe. They are dying for the notion that color nullifies personal traits as criteria for assessing human beings. After all, the Nazis admired their fellow Germans not simply because they were white but primarily because they were supposed to be more creative, courageous, commanding, and so forth than the rest of us. Changing skin color leaves all of those personal traits intact, and endorsing the demise of such a splendid group flies in the face of what Nazism was all about, namely, a wonderful world ruled by the master race. Just imagine a Nazi orator telling a German audience that they deserve to be dominated by Africans simply because the two groups had exchanged skin colors. However, the specific example must not cloud the general point. The real price logic has forced racists to pay is that they must classify as irrelevant all the personal traits people, including racists themselves, actually use to assess one another. Granted that a textbook racist who pays this price cannot be convicted of logical inconsistency. But no real-world racists will ever pay it because they realize full well that it renders their ideology completely nonviable.

One example from everyday life will prove the point. Imagine two book reviewers. The first tells readers on Monday to buy one novel because it has a white cover but to avoid another because it has a black cover, and then on Tuesday tells them to do the reverse because second printings have reversed the colors. The second says that a novel is worth reading today because the bookbinder has no Jewish grandparents but not worth reading tomorrow because the binder of the new edition has at least one Jewish grandparent. Even Nazis would give up on book reviewers of that sort and start reading one who deigned to discuss plot, character, dialogue, style. If racists grant that it is absurd to ignore the traits of fictional characters when nothing is at stake except a good read, will they seriously contend that we can ignore the traits of real people, where the stakes are life and death and the future course of history?

The absurdity of ignoring personal traits is why all real-world racists do not condemn people on color alone. Rather, they choose the option of asserting correlations between color or lineage and certain personal traits. In classical racism, this takes the form of condemning all members of the despised group irrespective of individual differences within the group. All blacks are said to be inferior to all whites because all blacks are stupid, permanently immature, prone to rape. Falsification of classical racism by evidence follows automatically. We can point to thousands of counterexamples, the thousands of blacks of genius or talent from Saint Augustine and Victor Hugo to Paul Robeson and Thomas Sowell. The last word belongs to Frederick Law Olmsted. When traveling through the antebellum American South, he heard laws against educating blacks defended on the grounds that blacks could no more learn to read or write than animals and maniacs. Olmsted (1969) asked, Why, then, were there no laws forbidding people to teach animals and maniacs to read and write?

None of this is to deny the facts of racist psychology: a racist may well hate Jewish ethnicity or black skin as such. However, even on the psychological level, our analysis works. The racist's intense loathing of blacks impels him or her to ascribe loathed traits to black people. The stronger the hatred, the more impossible to say, "I loathe blacks, but I must admit many of them are wiser, more creative, more courageous, more generous, more admirable than myself." Hatred of color for its own sake tends to liquidate color as a criterion of human worth.

More important, sheer hatred of color would be a quirk unproductive of a racial ideology. Booth Tarkington speaks of a Frenchman who went berserk every time he heard the word "camel." Interesting psychologically, but not much ideological potential. Marx did not just write love letters to the working class, and for the same reason no racist just runs through the streets shouting, "I hate the color black." Racists want an ideology that organizes the world, one that explains history and sets a political agenda. Hitler used Jewish traits to illuminate the defeat of Germany in the First World War, the Russian revolution, the Bolshevik domination of Russia. Once one sees that Nordics are born rulers, Alpines perfect slaves, Irish childish and unstable, Slavs beings who think with the spinal cord rather than the brain, Jews no more than Alpine Slavs, much becomes clear. Hitler did not neglect blacks. He was not impressed that a few could be educated to practice a profession. They are born half-apes, and the same effort expended on the intelligent races would bring all of the latter to the same achievements a thousand times sooner (Hitler, 1943, 285–286, 301–302, 325, & 430; Dawidowicz, 1976, 121–122; Prange, 1944, 71–79).

Our refutation of classical racism has one piece of unfinished business. When we confronted racists with the possibility of a pill that would blacken their skin and asked whether they would then sentence themselves to death along with all other blacks, we said they could attempt to find a morally relevant distinction as an escape clause. What are the possibilities? They might modify their criterion of who deserves to be exterminated by saying that one must be born black. But then we could speak of putting a pill in the food of all pregnant German women so that all German children would be born black. This leaves the classical racist with something rather pathetic, modifications that aim at nothing more than giving his or her child an escape clause. For example, a particular German mother might concede that all Germans born black should be exterminated, except a child born at exactly 9:32 A.M. on 1 August 1999 and baptized Adolf, which just happens to be the time of birth and baptismal name of her child. Once again, there is no logical inconsistency in "committing oneself" to that kind of criterion of human worth. But no real-world racist could do it: no one who truly cherishes an ideal can bear to see it trivialized to that extent, much less perpetrate the deed themselves.

These evasions will not appear to be real possibilities if we view them in the context that generates them. They are attempts to salvage sheer standalone blackness as the sole criterion of human worth; they are essentially damage-control strategies brought into play when that criterion is threatened. Therefore, they make sense only if salvaging such a criterion really makes sense. As we have seen, that makes no sense at all. Refusing to give blackness a larger significance, refusing to correlate it with despised human traits would reduce racial ideology to an aversion to certain colors. It would rob blackness of the profound social significance that real-world racists believe skin color has. No racist really believes that he or she merely has a personal quirk about the color black. They believe that humanity needs to be warned against a group that appears human but is not fully human, a people who will debase one's grandchildren if allowed to mate with one's children. Academics in the study can play games with racist criteria to try to evade the rule of universalizability because they do not take those criteria seriously. Someone who does take them seriously cannot honestly choose to do so. Imagine that we humanists felt tension about whether our humane ideals allowed us to punish Hitler for punishment's sake and, therefore, as an escape, said we could punish people whose first and last names started with A and H and whose names together numbered eleven letters. To trivialize our ideals in that way would be impossible if we were really serious about them.

This analysis of racist attempts to evade the rule of universalizability allows us to answer certain more general criticisms of that rule. Some claim that it has a fatal weakness: it says that people must make the same assessments about similar situations or find a morally relevant difference. Yet it supplies no criterion of what constitutes a morally relevant difference, which appears to open the door to endless evasions. We now see that this criticism mistakes where the burden of clarification lies. Recall why no ideologue refuses to argue over this item on our agenda. If you praise the military virtues one day and refuse to praise someone who practices them the next, you cannot expect others to adopt your ideals as long as you leave them baffled as to what conduct your ideals recommend. If you espouse sheer blackness as a criterion of human worth one day and imply that it is significant only as a correlate of traits the next, we can politely say that once you are clear about your own criteria we will pay attention. If we say humane ideals forbid punishment for punishment's sake one day and punish someone for punishment's sake the next, others can ask us to make up our minds. The rule of universalizability has no obligation to anticipate the thousands of refinements people make when they attempt to render their moral systems coherent. It is ideologues who want to be taken seriously who must introduce these refinements, hoping to salvage logical consistency. And when they do, when they argue over this item, some of them encounter a devastating price: for classical racists, it is that they must either deny the relevance of personal traits to human worth or face overwhelming falsification.

All of this assumes that debate over our agenda is conducted with interior honesty and according to the rules of reason and evidence. An actual debate in front of the Hitler Youth may simply get a rational person howled down. It is not actual debate that determines whether our ideals can be reconciled with reason and reality; rather, it is an ideal debate, one that can and should take place in the privacy of our own minds. That ideal debate is what philosophy is all about. Getting people to take that ideal debate seriously is the business of the psychology of persuasion. Once again, the latter directs our attention to Martin Luther King Jr. and his techniques for making whites face up to the truth about blacks, which may or may not succeed. However, the fact that we cannot always convince the irrational of the irrationality of their ideals is no more relevant, in the light of truth, than the fact that we cannot convince a stone. To my demand for an ideal debate, it may be objected that I also demand that the participants stick to defending the ideals of actual real-world ideologues. There is no true contradiction here. It is merely a matter of using reason to force real-world people to face a choice: between standing by the ideals in which they really believe or abandoning reality by resorting to trivialized ideals in which they do not believe. The choice is up to them. But what imposes the choice is reason operating in the context of an ideal debate.

We leave classical racism behind to confront a spectrum. At one end there are close relatives of the classical racist who are filled with race hate but who recognize, however rarely and grudgingly, the existence of outstanding individuals among the despised group. At the other there are antiracists who may be well-meaning but attempt to make the genetic equality of all groups an undiscussable dogma. The first needs no refutation because their claims, like those of classical racism, always outrage evidence. The second can be dismissed quickly because they hide behind arguments too invalid to have a long life expectancy. The usual ones are that the concept of race is not biologically respectable, that all human groups share most of their genes, that the concept of intelligence is culturally relative, and that current theories of intelligence have not given an adequate pretheory definition of the term. Brief rebuttals: the races investigated are defined sociologically; despite their similarity, human groups show enough genetic variation to cause statistical differences for other traits, like the occurrence of sickle-cell anemia, so why not intelligence; black parents want their children to excel in the kind of intelligence that pays dividends in America or England or France, not in some pre-industrial society; even the hardest sciences do not give elaborate pretheory definitions of their key concepts, for example, Newton did not wait to refine the concept of celestial influence before embedding it in his theory of gravitation.

Finally, there are those who do scientific studies of group differences, some of whom, despite being free of personal bias, reach conclusions that one racial group has on average a genetic advantage over another. These scientists should not be classified as racist at all because they seek the truth, and the truth cannot be racist. In recent years, the debate over whether the fifteen-point IQ advantage of American whites over American blacks is partially genetic or entirely environmental has provoked much bitterness. Jensen has tentatively asserted that about two thirds of it is genetic, that is, that a ten-point gap would persist given equal environments, which would mean that the upper 25 percent of blacks and the upper 50 percent of whites would overlap. This conclusion is unwelcome, although note that it is enough to deal a fatal blow to classical racism. The fact that it is unwelcome should not be held against Jensen. If Jensen is correct, he has done us a favor by forcing us to face a facet of reality in that certainly, no one who holds humane ideals wants to pursue those ideals in anything except the real world. Chapter 8 will show that our ideals are quite capable of offering justice to both black and white, whatever the origin of group differences.

That said, it must also be said that certain truths about reality can have unpleasant consequences. This one would be a blow to black pride. In addition, most people use group membership to assess other people in everyday life, reserving exhaustive investigation of people as individuals for a few intimates. Therefore, scientific evidence of racial differences unfavorable to blacks implies that the use of racial profiles, profiles that make life difficult for blacks, will be with us for a long time. Enough is at stake so that the evidence should be clear before either a genetic or an environmental hypothesis is accepted. I cannot in a paragraph summarize my twenty years of research that adds plausibility to an environmental hypothesis (Flynn, 1980, 1987a, 1987c, 1989, 1990, 1991, 1992a, 1992b; see Flynn, 1999, for an overview). But as an inducement to those tempted to explore the literature, I will say something about the implications of the so-called Flynn effect, that is, the phenomenon of massive IQ gains over time.

Jensen notes that genetic differences are a factor in individual IQ differences, both within white America and within black America. He believes that no unique and potent environmental variable operates between the races and, therefore, argues that genetic factors probably play a role in explaining the IQ gap between black and white. However, the present generation outscores the last generation on IQ tests, registering gains of nine to eighteen points, depending on the kind of test. No doubt genetic factors operate within both generations, but the large between-generation IQ gap is entirely environmental, so IQ gaps the size of the black/white gap can certainly be caused by environmental factors. Jensen argues that if the same factors operate within and between the races, a purely environmental explanation of the racial IQ gap would put the average black American environment below 99 percent of white environments, hardly plausible. However, American IQ gains show that blacks match the mean IQ of whites after a fifty-year lag. Therefore, a purely environmental explanation of the racial IQ gap need posit only that the average black environment of, say, 1995 equals the average white environment of 1945, quite plausible. Jensen believes that between-group IQ differences can be equated with intelligence differences. However, twenty nations show huge IQ gains over time, sometimes totaling over twenty points, even over forty points. These are far too large to be equated with intelligence gains (Flynn, 1984, 1987b, 1987d, 1994, 1998, 1999).

Equating IQ gains over time with intelligence gains would imply that our ancestors were functioning like those with IQs of 70 to 80 in our own generation, or that we were functioning like those with IQs of 120 to 130 in their generation. It would imply that some 65 to 90 percent of English at the turn of the century were too limited to understand the rules of cricket (Irish take note) or that the average Dutch male in 1982 was at the ninetieth percentile of his father's generation for intelligence. Clearly these implications are false. The lesson is that IQ tests cannot bridge the cultural distance nations travel over time, often over no more than a decade. For example, the Netherlands covered enough cultural distance between 1972 and 1982 to nullify the correlation between IQ and intelligence. What, then, of the cultural distance that separates American whites and American blacks?

THE MARX OF THE MIDDLE CLASSES

William Graham Sumner was the greatest of those whom their contemporaries called Social Darwinists. They drew upon the vocabulary of evolution to defend their ideals. Sumner's favored group was the middle class of late-nineteenth-century America. He used biological terms plus his social theories to give historical importance to middle-class virtues and to justify the fate of the "unfit" who lived in poverty. He recognized that nineteenth-century capitalism had its flaws but believed that it had replaced military competition for scarce resources with economic competition, a competition that both maximized humanity's control over nature and was essential for human progress. So long as special interest groups did not succeed in using government to extract unearned benefits, it came as close as any system could to rewarding virtue with success and punishing vice with failure (Persons, 1963, 49–56, 84, 93–97, & 139; Keller & Davie, 1969, II, 153–154).

The middle-class virtues Sumner praises are hard work, self-denial, frugality, and temperance. The weak who need public assistance are "nasty, shiftless, criminal, whining, crawling, and good for nothing people." The successful are consistently described as the fit and, at least in Sumner's early writings, include millionaires and captains of industry, who have merely developed middle-class virtues par excellence. The unsuccessful are described as unfit, indeed, as "worthless," and any aid to them is a shift of capital from the deserving to the undeserving, whether it takes the form of progressive taxation, welfare, or even voluntary contributions to public charities. The rare deserving case should be the object of private charity given to someone you know personally. Ideally, the unfit would disappear. People who wish to marry would undergo state inspection and approval, in defiance of the fantastic notion that the liberty to marry has nothing to do with whether we live in the "house of have" or the "house of want" (Sumner, 1883, 157–160; Persons, 1963, 23–24, 72, 77–82, 93, 118, 134, 157, & 166; Keller & Davie, 1969, I, 277–278 & 373).

Sumner's rejection of militarism and imperialism was totally sincere and found expression in his classic essay, "America's Conquest by Spain." In this essay, written after the Spanish-American War of 1898, Sumner lamented the irony that while America had won military victory, Spain had won the contest of ideas. America had gone to war to liberate the Spanish colonies. At the close of the war, she had annexed the "freed" colonies herself, and Spain's imperial psychology permeated the minds of America's leaders, who had begun to preach that America had a "manifest destiny" to rule over other peoples.

Sumner (1940) was also a pioneer sociologist. Following in the footsteps of Voltaire and Marx, he analyzed history not as the result of what general or army had won a battle but in terms of social forces. The English revolution was reversed because it tried to reconstruct the mores of the English people. The French revolution was not reversed because economic change foreshadowed the new mores that the revolution served. Power is determined by possession of capital, and the only power is economic power (Davie, 1940, 87, cited in Dougherty, 1983). His sophistication is revealed in his legendary analysis of why most prostitutes in Boston were Anglicans. The Anglican ministers of Boston were alarmed and feared that, despite their best efforts to preach virtue, some inducement to vice had crept into their sermons. Sumner pointed out that the orphanages of Boston were run by the Anglican Church and that most prostitutes were the graduates of impersonal institutions like orphanages. Sumner placed particular emphasis on the family as the vehicle of human progress that fosters virtue from generation to generation. It is the most important factor in the child's development: the home through attention, patient training, and encouragement weaves a "tissue of unconscious habit," and a child neglected at home is corrupted by that neglect. Any attempt by society to raise children in a nonfamily environment reduces human beings to swine (Persons, 1963, 90–91; Keller & Davie, 1969, I, 253, 277–278, & 406; II, 72–73)

Sumner knew that analogies between the social and organic worlds had no substantive significance (Davie, 1940, 84). He borrows little more from evolutionary biology than the terms "fit" and "unfit," plus the notion that humanity must work hard to win the "struggle for existence." Nonetheless, comparing his thought to an evolutionary model poses two interesting questions.

First, biological evolution is open-ended in the sense that the fit are simply those who survive to reproduce as a result of natural selection. There are no characteristics or traits that have any intrinsic worth, and no trend can be condemned because it extinguishes a trait we admire. Primates in trees develop keen eyesight; cave fish consigned to eternal darkness go blind. Therefore, we have a right to ask Sumner a question. Does he welcome whatever characterological traits unameliorated capitalism favors, or does he value capitalism because it favors certain traits? The answer, of course, is the latter. No one values a historical outcome blindly; everyone has an ideal human being, and history is applauded on the assumption it progresses toward it. Marx would have felt differently about the dialectic if it took us toward eternal class exploitation. Sumner's ideal person is the frugal, temperate, hard-working family man who puts something aside each month in a savings account. He reveals his hand when he says that even if these traits were not needed to amass capital, any utopia whose inhabitants lacked such virtues would have a population "insipid and characterless" (Sumner, 1883, 78–79). Second, species evolve because certain traits are blindly favored by a certain environment. Sumner the sociologist recognizes that character is molded by a wide range of environmental influences. Whether Sumner the moralist does is another matter.

As we have seen, Sumner places strong emphasis on justice as fairness and the thesis that late-nineteenth-century capitalism rewards virtue and punishes vice. Comparison with Nietzsche and classical racism shows that

Sumner's emphasis on fairness, both in principle and practice, is not accidental. Nietzsche's favored group contained extraordinary people of creative genius, and, therefore, so far as relations between supermen and herd men are concerned, his criterion of justice is rewarding merit or excellence. Sumner's favored group consists of very ordinary people, and, therefore, that option is not open to him. He must espouse a concept of justice as rewarding desert or virtue, rewarding those who have chosen to be hard-working, frugal, and temperate rather than lazy, spendthrift, and alcoholic. The classical racist has heavy penalties in store for his despised group and, therefore, needs to offer the favored group potent reassurance that they will not be demoted. Race is ideal reassurance in that, rare and hypothetical situations aside, white cannot become black. Sumner also endorsed heavy penalties, but his favored and despised groups are classes, and people can be demoted from one class to another. While he can give no absolute assurance to members of the middle class that they will not go under, he needs to give them whatever reassurance he can. Therefore, the message is that the system is fair, so fair that the truly virtuous among the middle class need not be concerned. In other words, two equations operate here: the less extraordinary the favored group, the more emphasis on justice as rewarding desert rather than justice as rewarding merit; the greater the penalties levied on the despised group, the more reassurance needed that members of the favored group are secure.

Three items on our agenda will focus our critique of Sumner: the demand for logical consistency, in his case, logical consistency between his ethics and his sociology; whether his allocation of rewards and penalties can pass his own criterion of justice; and whether he has faced up to the consequences of his admired social system. Concretely, these constitute one question of value and two of fact: Do the unsuccessful really deserve their fate? Who wins under capitalism? Who loses?

The tension between Sumner's ethics and Sumner's sociology is almost total. Recall his emphasis on the family as the vehicle that transmits virtue or vice from generation to generation. Children do not choose their parents, they are the "unconscious" recipients of the habits their parents choose to bestow, and this character formation predates the choices they will eventually make. Therefore, even assuming the present generation was sorted according to its deserts, the next generation will be sorted by parental influence rather than its deserts. The penalties suffered by the present generation for its wickedness intensify the tension. Parents weak in virtue will have a hard time raising a virtuous child under any circumstances, but when their task is complicated by poverty, the outcome is even less likely to be favorable. Justice for the present generation equals injustice for the next. In fact, the equation really extends to the present generation as well: thus far, we have treated them as a collection of uncaused first causes who were captains of their fate, but they too were once children molded by parents who were either virtuous and enjoyed the advantage of affluence or vicious and handicapped by poverty. Sumner has no solution to a perennial problem of those with a punitive attitude toward the poor: how to leave wicked parents unrewarded for their vice without penalizing the innocent child.

The best hope of giving children justice as fairness is to try to give them all environments of reasonable quality and allocate benefits to virtue only above that level. This entails forgetting about what the parent deserves until that level is reached: the children of the poor will need assistance so that they enjoy, as far as possible, an undemoralized home, adequate health care, adequate education, and so forth. The form this assistance takes is a question of means to ends. However, a word about those who wish to enhance the power of the parent over the fate of the child, for example, those who want to give parents education and health vouchers and who oppose welfare agencies and state schools as an unwarranted interference with parental prerogatives. They above all must reject Sumner's attitude toward the poor. They cannot both castigate poverty as proof of viciousness and endow poor parents with the altruism and wisdom to make market choices beneficial to their children. There are those who reject Sumner's accusation that the poor are vicious but who accept his conclusion that the poor are genetically inferior. If they really want to thin out the ranks of the unfit, they must endorse alleviating poverty. As Hofstadter (1959, 96) points out, the poor reproduce very efficiently, and making them poorer still increases rather than diminishes their reproductive rates. Sumner recommends forbidding them to marry, presumably because he suffers from the delusion that this would stop them from breeding.

Sumner could relieve the tension between his ethics and his sociology by jettisoning the latter. However, this would carry an unacceptable price, a sort of cognitive suicide. If he reverted to a prescientific approach to human behavior, he would have to sink to the level of the Boston divines: no sophisticated analysis of why prostitutes were Anglicans, no sophisticated account of child development, no sophisticated history of the English and French revolutions. To his credit, he persisted with his social science. Can that social science come to his rescue and suggest a solution to the above tension?

It can only if we take one of Sumner's arguments out of its original context. Sumner concedes that inheritance is unjust because it gives some an undeserved head start in life. However, he then defends it as the lesser of two evils based on a theory of motivation. Love of children and concern for their welfare is our strongest motive to work and save; it above all engenders self-respect, fuels ambition, and drives us to conquer limiting conditions (Persons, 1963, 89–90; Sumner, 1883, 72–73). Therefore, abolishing inheritance would erode the motive to work: without the prospect of handing capital on to their children, parents would be tempted into sloth, and society would suffer. As it stands, the argument does not do much to discredit liberal/left policies on taxing inheritance: usually the moderate inheritances most people hand on to their children are exempted from tax; huge inheritances may well kill the incentive of heirs to work and, therefore, taxing those might encourage the work ethic; even if money inheritances were abolished, people would still work hard to provide their children with their most precious inheritance, the effects of being raised in a good environment.

However, we are not so much interested in the argument in its original context as in taking it out of that context and generalizing it. It then might read: poverty inflicts a grave injustice on children; but, alleviating their lot would mean parents need not worry about the possibility that their children would suffer from extreme privation; therefore, this would undermine the primary motive to work; therefore, grave injustice to children is the lesser of two evils.

I want to stress that it is I who have created this argument by giving a specific debating point general applicability. Sumner might well reject a theory of motivation so simplistic. It takes no account of parents desperately trying to fight their way out of poverty for the sake of their children whose morale is broken by crushing circumstance. For them, a helping hand from the welfare state might make all the difference. Some realistic hope of success, rather than the hopelessness of watching their marriage being undermined by unemployment, rather than seeing their children ill or ignorant or corrupted by peers without prospect of remedy, is a powerful motive to keep trying. Moreover, a significant part of American society is so well off that its members need not fear poverty. If they are lazy, the case for their virtue is undermined; if they are hard-working, the theory that fear of poverty is a necessary motive is falsified. An ad hoc hypothesis is possible, namely, that the upper classes work for positive incentives while the lower class can respond only to negative incentives. This is challenged by societies in which unemployment rates fluctuate from high to low despite a well-developed welfare state. At least in those societies working-class people seek work even though they are protected from poverty. The chief ideological role of the positive versus negative incentives hypothesis is to justify tax cuts for the rich while enacting welfare cuts for the poor.

Who were the winners under nineteenth-century American capitalism, and what traits did they actually exhibit? Veblen (1899) describes hollow men seeking prestige by conspicuous display and wasteful consumption of material goods. Like Kwakiutl at a potlatch, they put their rivals to shame by outspending them, a million spent on a coming-out party for a daughter, thousands on a fur coat for a dog, culminating in the proverbial lighting of a cigar with a five-dollar bill. Worse, the mores of the millionaires and captains of industry infected the middle class. No house big enough, wives and children turned into possessions for display, the husband who boasts that his wife does not have to work, the wife accepting that role, the devaluation of work thanks to the ideal of being a member of an affluent leisure class, the worker hiding his blue collar from his family, the millions longing only for retirement and idleness. Tawney (1920) sums up the soul of the acquisitive society: to gain much without giving respected, to give without gaining despised. As the economy evolved, the captains of industry gave the middle class new marching orders: impulse buying, self-indulgence, and life on a mountain of debt. None of this is very close to the Calvinist virtues Sumner so admired. Veblen and Tawney describe only some features of the social landscape, of course, but they were social realities that Sumner's balance sheet omitted. They are still with us today.

Who were the losers? Sumner seeks to reassure the successful that they will never join the failures, but the reassurance amounts to little more than rhetoric. The system favors virtue and punishes vice, failures are negligent, idle, and extravagant, paupers are shiftless or criminal, any slum dweller can by modest effort make his or her way to where conditions are easier, culminating in this: "In general, there is no man who is honest and industrious who cannot put himself in a way to maintain himself and his family, misfortune apart, in a condition of substantial comfort" (Persons, 1963, 84, 118, 134, & 158–159).

The reality was somewhat different. Sumner wrote these words in the late nineteenth century, a time when the lives of millions were blighted by a cycle of boom and bust. The recession of 1894 was particularly severe: Eugene Debs describes his dismay at watching children fighting over garbage in his hometown of Terre Haute, Indiana. During the 1930s, the Great Depression plus the Dust Bowl, the great drought that struck the American prairie states, sent people to the wall who had been industrious and thrifty all their lives, many of them impeccably middle class. In 1931, 70 percent of the farmers of Oklahoma were unable to pay the interest on their mortgages; in 1933, unemployment reached a peak of fifteen million. Today, the erosion of marriage has created a single-mother poverty trap, and the white middle class is not exempt. In 1991 a white woman of average ability and from an average socioeconomic background, raising children while separated, divorced, or never married, had a 33 percent chance of living in poverty. The rate for all single mothers was worse at 36 percent, but note how little protection middle-class women actually derive from their status. The effects on American children are profound: 22 percent of all American children under the age of fifteen are being raised in homes below the poverty line (Shannon, 1960, 6–10, 16–34, & 72–92; Herrnstein and Murray, 1994, 137–139).

It is sometimes asserted that white America is approaching an affluence that leaves its members only temporarily in poverty; that is, poverty may blight people's lives for a few years, but they will escape soon enough. This ignores the fact that the years when one raises children are a bad time to be poor and that becoming poor in old age may mean being liberated only by death. No one has the same optimism about the underclass of black Americans or about most of the earth's inhabitants who do, after all, live outside America. You do not have to go to the Third World to find middle-class people reduced to poverty and despair. The thousands still wearing their white collars as they sleep and beg in the streets of Tokyo are a heartrending spectacle.

Poverty is still real and inflicts heavy penalties. These penalties are all the more heavy thanks to those who share Sumner's perspective. I refer to his tendency to neglect social trends beyond any individual's control and to assume that a person's traits are virtually the sole determinant of his or her fate. Why is this assumption so persistent? We can only speculate. Perhaps it is because people perceive other people being ranked by their personal traits at any given time and, therefore, tend to exaggerate the potency of traits over time. For example, in America, black single mothers suffer poverty above all, so to avoid poverty, black women must compete to marry black men who have steady work. Naturally, intelligent, educated black women have a competitive advantage that creates a hierarchy for these traits. This creates a correlation between admired traits and economic success, and while the correlation is by no means perfect, it is highly visible.

However, the potency of personal traits at a particular time does not entail a potency that persists from one time to another. The most important thing that alters over time is the dividing line for success or failure, and this line is not determined by the individual's personal traits but by larger social forces. Let us compare 1960 and 1990. During those years, two trends had a powerful impact: the proportion of black men with steady jobs declined from three quarters to about half, and, thanks to a sexual revolution that has affected all races and classes, men became less likely to marry a pregnant partner. Therefore, the number of black women who had children by men unlikely to be permanent partners doubled from 25 to 50 percent. When social forces of this sort double the number of black women living in poverty, personal traits will not prevent many of yesterday's successes from becoming today's failures. However, the trends at work, or at least the way in which the trends determine the fate of so many individuals, are not highly visible. So long as there is a social hierarchy in which personal traits count, so long as there is a competition for scarce goods, and so long as we are hypnotized by who loses at a particular time, we will exaggerate the causal potency of personal traits (Flynn, 1991, 135–136 & 141).

William Graham Sumner tried to turn classes into separate species characterized respectively by virtue and vice. Class may rank people into a hierarchy that has a rough correlation with socially valued traits, but it does not operationalize justice, and no class has a monopoly on virtue. The successful may recite a litany of stability and reassurance, but class traits alter, and history, that elephant, has a way of trampling class divisions. The colonel's lady and Rosie O'Grady are sisters under the skin.

7

Superpeople and Supermen

Cattell and Nietzsche introduce a new perspective. They look beyond ordinary people toward extraordinary people, whether of the present or the future. Cattell has an affection for the virtuous middle classes, but they, like the rest of us, are to sacrifice themselves on the altar of evolutionary progress. Nietzsche loathes the exaggerated claims racists make for some pedestrian group of people and yearns for a group whose excellence cannot be exaggerated. We will examine Cattell and Nietzsche and then draw some summary conclusions about why antihumane ideologues are vulnerable to critique.

THE ONLY TRUE SOCIAL DARWINIST

Raymond B. Cattell made landmark contributions to the theory of intelligence. However, his heart lay in the advocacy of an evolutionary ethics he called "Beyondism." Sadly, the latter cheated him of recognition for the former. Shortly before his recent death, the decision to give him an award for lifetime achievement in psychology was vetoed by those who think it always wrong to reward the wicked.

Cattell rejected the school called Social Darwinism because of its emphasis on individual rather than group survival. The differences go deeper than that. In fact, he is the only moralist to embrace the substance, as distinct from the language, of evolutionary biology. He has a single ideal: organizing all humanity to liquidate itself in favor of a higher species at maximum speed. The so-called Social Darwinists merely borrowed labels from evolutionary biology and affixed them to social classes or social processes under the misapprehension that if they could find analogies between their ideal society and evolution, the scientific status of the latter would confer some kind of objectivity on the former. Needless to say, this is false. It is no more sensible than using the oval orbits of the planets as a reason for advising people to run about in circles. Sumner recognized this, although that did not keep him from using terms like "fit" and "unfit."

Cattell (1972, 1987) believes that the history of the universe suggests only one goal worthy of universal admiration. That goal is the evolution of higher and higher species, that is, species more and more aware of their environment and more and more in control of their environment. We are the highest species produced on earth thus far, and we should strive to turn ourselves into a higher species still. Human beings should treat themselves like animals being bred for certain traits. There should be a World Federation of Nations with its own World Research Center that will put two principles into practice.

First, if new species are to evolve, there must be a multiplicity of genetic plus cultural variants within humanity. Fortunately, there exist religious, national, social, and physical differences that create aversion, and if we have the good sense to foster these, "dislike of the stranger" may cause each human group to isolate itself for breeding purposes. Someday we will want a controlled increase in the mutation rate to produce new gene forms. Nuclear power as an accidental source of radiation is not undesirable, and even nuclear war might have a credit side. Fewer than fifty thousand people with one good university library could begin with a clean slate and repopulate the globe with variant groups on a carefully planned basis. Cattell says that Hobart, home of the University of Tasmania, would do. The academic staff at Hobart point out that he never visited their university library.

Second, there must be competition that selects both between and within human groups for the desired traits of intelligence and scientific advance. Competition between nations, whether economic or military, will normally favor better genes for intelligence and better cultures, those that allow intelligence to be applied to the solution of moral, social, political, economic, and scientific problems. Special ethical controls are needed to keep war from being counterproductive; for example, it would be wrong to allow populous Arab nations to exterminate "the Israelites," whose expansion may be a permanent cultural and genetic gain. Failed groups must go to the wall.

It is clearly wrong to give foreign aid or famine relief if its effect is to preserve sick societies. Some fifty years ago, Cattell (1938, 94) concluded that although the Negro race had endearing qualities of humor and religiosity, these traits hardly compensated for its lack of mental capacity. However, American blacks should be treated humanely: they should be confined to adapted reserves and asylums and phased out by way of a reduced birth rate. His later works say that his experimental groups would not be existent races but, rather, races of the future. He entrusts the task of deciding which groups are "moribund" to the World Research Center. For failed groups, the humane alternative to starvation or slaughter remains the same: aid and protection contingent on accepting a geometrical rate of population reduction, a process he calls "genthanasia."

Cattell emphasizes the threat of a recent historical development: the rise of utilitarianism and the possibility of a Hedonic Pact. Evolutionary progress requires an intense competition between societies, including the threat of war. Evolutionary progress requires self-inflicted suffering and deprivation within societies, so that failed ethnic groups and individuals can be eliminated. How can these preconditions be preserved if the utilitarians prevail and the nations of the world negotiate a Hedonic Pact: some kind of pernicious agreement to cooperate and minimize suffering and maximize happiness.

Cattell made only a few converts and hardly ranks with racism or Sumner or Nietzsche in terms of historical importance. But he is of great philosophical interest because he poses a difficult problem of refutation. It is not difficult to put objections to his plans for realizing his goal, but what of the goal itself? Most antihumane ideologues endorse a variety of ideals, Calvinist virtue plus American capitalism, meritocracy plus a caste society, and, therefore, we can ask whether one of their ideals conflicts with another when both are operationalized. Most antihumane ideologues admire an existing group and, therefore, make claims about the virtues of their chosen people that can be falsified by evidence. Cattell is different. He has one goal only, and it focuses on a group to be manufactured to certain specifications. The radically mono-idealistic character of his ethics nullifies the potency of many items on our agenda for moral debate. Nonetheless, our agenda offers one item that retains its potency, namely, the rule of universalizability.

If all that matters is producing a higher species, one a quantum leap beyond our own in terms of intelligence and scientific expertise, it should make no difference who they are, or what they are, or where they are. Cattell says we should liquidate our own species in favor of a higher one. If a higher species visited earth and needed our space, would he say we ought to conspire in our own demise? There would be no biological continuity between humanity and them, but surely that is morally irrelevant. They would have done us the favor of providing a short cut to our goal: we could make way for them now rather than wait thousands of years to evolve into something like them. Ethics aside, it is hard to see why biological continuity between our species and another species should have any psychological appeal. Cattell hopes that the next ten thousand years will produce a dozen species so far removed from one another, and from ourselves, that they cannot mate successfully. We must face up to how different these creatures would be from ourselves. As Cattell himself remarks, the gap would be at least as great as between ourselves and a chimpanzee. Olaf Stapledon (1968) in his novel *Last and First Men*, written in 1931, confronts us with seventeen successor species evolving over two billion years: giants with fused toes, short-lived creatures without humor, big-brained creatures with vestigial bodies and without any emotion we would consider normal, creatures with life expectancies of 250,000 years, and so forth. No matter where they came from, outer space or terrestrial evolution, does anyone really want to sacrifice themselves to creatures of this sort? It is one thing to be kind to species at our mercy, another to be morally obliged to put ourselves at the mercy of an alien species.

If we must maximize intelligence, there is the option of creating artificial intelligence. Here there would be no biological substratum at all, but again that seems irrelevant, unless Cattell makes the fatal concession that he feels no psychological tie with inorganic entities. At least with them, we could minimize the risk to ourselves by following Isaac Asimov's laws and building into our creations an inhibition against taking human life. I present this option not so much as a realistic possibility but rather to pose the question of how much we would be willing to sacrifice for intelligence, assuming a total absence of psychological rapport with whatever is intelligent. Then there is the likelihood that our experiment with intelligence is not unique, that countless planets have already populated the universe with higher intelligences. Cattell grants this possibility but offers a rebuttal: Why have we not received any communications from outer space? Perhaps all other intelligent species have made the Hedonic Pact: they may have been too weak to do their duty

and traded away evolutionary and technological progress for universal cooperation and happiness. So our species may offer the universe its last chance.
One must weigh the probability of Cattell's explanation against a certainty:
the ten thousand years of suffering dictated by choosing his path. However,
it is far more important to note what he has conceded: the obligation he
wishes to impose is falsifiable. The first communication received from a
higher species (the very fact that we receive it will almost certainly betray
the presence of a higher species) will relieve us of our burden.

Cattell does not rest his case purely on the strength of his own moral
commitment. He has two self-justifying arguments. The first need not detain
us long because it is an appeal to the purposes of nature. As we have seen, nature or the universe has no goals, it merely shows trends, and we can evaluate
these as we wish. The trend Cattell cites is not even a consistent trend. It may
be that during a fragment of the universe's history, there has been a trend
toward the evolution of greater and greater intelligence. However, Cattell
himself believes that recent trends have been counterproductive. He says
that the last twelve thousand years show no trend to better brains and that
the last one hundred years have been a period of decline. Like all of those
who think they take a trend from nature, Cattell really picks and chooses. He
might say he picks the trend with the greater longevity, but longevity is irrelevant to quality. As Aristotle says, a white thing is no more perfectly white
because it has existed for an eternity rather than merely for an instant. And
in fact, favoring intelligence and environmental control is not even the universe's dominant trend in terms of longevity. Taking inorganic and organic
evolution as one continuous process, life takes a long time to appear, flickers
briefly, and then disappears, leaving countless eons in which it is absent.

Cattell's second argument is that unless we evolve into a higher species,
we may not have the intelligence to avoid catastrophes, such as the elimination of the human species by a meteor, or mutated bacteria, or radiation,
or pollution. He argues for a sense of emergency and maximum speed. The
recipe for maximum speed is suspect. To divert our attention away from cooperation to solve these problems within the limitations of our present species in order to foster a competition that might in ten thousand years deliver
a new species may not be a maximizing strategy. Moreover, would a brighter
species provide more solutions or more problems? The last quantum leap in

intelligence evolution produced made every catastrophe Cattell names more likely, except the meteor. As for the meteor, when Cattell speaks of its destroying the "human" species, his language betrays that even his loyalties are split. His program will not save the human species; it is designed to liquidate our species as soon as possible, perhaps long before a catastrophic meteor arrives.

No total refutation of Cattell is possible. Still, we have clarified what commitment to his one moral ideal entails: you really must believe that the human race has a duty to actively promote its own demise. Perhaps the science fiction scenario will come true: someday we may encounter a species who betters us in our own terms and who needs our living space. But there is nothing in "evolutionary ethics" that imposes an obligation to advance the equivalent of that day.

NIETZSCHE AND HIS SUPERMEN

I believe that what follows represents the substance of Nietzsche's moral and political ideals. His lack of precision allows interpreters like Kaufmann to find a more human face, but the dominant Nietzsche, taken at his word, is our very antithesis. This is fortunate. The ideal debate we should all carry on within ourselves must include a full range of antihumane opponents, and if we could find no real antithesis, one would have to be invented. Nietzsche's metaphysics and epistemology will be presented only insofar as he uses them to defend his ideals. This is sad because it cheats us of much of his brilliance: his critique of dualistic, idealistic, and materialistic metaphysics (giving up God to worship rocks); his analysis of Descartes's cogito, which anticipates Russell; his searching commentary on Kant's concept of the noumenal self. The omission of the doctrine of eternal recurrence is less sad. This was done because I have never found anyone who could make sense of it.

Nietzsche is the opponent who has given those of us with humane ideals our worst nightmares, not only because of the antihumane content of his ideals but also because he is so much more difficult to refute than those who base their elitism on race or class. To demonstrate his strengths and eventually his weaknesses, I will undertake four tasks: describe the foundation or core propositions of his ethics; show how these obviate arguments effective against our other opponents; summarize his thought more fully with emphasis on how his ideals are to be operationalized; show how we can use our agenda for moral debate against him.

Nietzsche's ethics rests on three propositions: only supermen merit moral concern; therefore, worrying about what people deserve applies only to supermen; therefore, supermen can treat herd men as means to their own ends, with the proviso that supermen should not do anything that would demean themselves in their own eyes. I believe that Nietzsche is correct in contending that before we apply moral categories we must make a prior assessment. We must decide for ourselves just what creatures are a form of life significant enough to merit moral concern. This can be shown by using a ladder of being running from insects, through higher animals, through ordinary human beings, through supermen, to Cattell's quantum-leap species of the future. The minority sect of Hindus called Jainists brush the path in front of them to avoid stepping on insects and wear masks to avoid breathing in microbes. Moving up the ladder, most animal rights advocates do not worry much about insects (they would spray mosquito larvae to prevent malaria), but they draw the line below the higher animals. Most humanists draw the line for possessing things like rights below the species *Homo sapiens*. Nietzsche chooses to draw the line for moral concern below supermen, according ordinary people only the derivative consideration (sadism is demeaning) humanists accord animals (Kaufmann, 1962, 24). In the absence of ethical objectivity, where anyone draws the line is a matter of personal commitment, and Nietzsche can argue that his delineation is no more or less arbitrary than our own. Cattell, of course, draws his line below a species so far beyond *Homo sapiens* that even the best of supermen cannot compete. A debate between Cattell and Nietzsche might be illuminating.

The fact that Nietzsche uses merit to delineate his circle of moral concern, a standard of merit only the great can meet, robs many arguments of their normal force. I have selected some arguments from the early works of Kai Nielsen (1957b, 1964, 1973). However, those familiar with the literature will know the heavy workload they bear in the defense of humane-egalitarian ideals.

First argument: human beings are moral agents in the sense that they choose good or evil; therefore, they deserve praise or blame and reward or punishment; therefore, they cannot be treated arbitrarily but fall under the protection of justice as fairness. And fairness dictates that people should not suffer for things that they cannot possibly do, for example, become creative geniuses. This is recognizable as a shortened version of Kant's argument for the third formulation of the categorical imperative: all human beings possess practical reason (reflective choice), which means we must presuppose their freedom, which means they fall under the categories of praise and blame, which means they should be rewarded only when praiseworthy and punished only when blameworthy. We have already anticipated Nietzsche's response: some may believe that ordinary people, who possess no more than the capacity to ponder choices, are important enough to count; however, he reserves his circle of moral concern for those who can meet a rather higher standard of human excellence than that. Sumner was caught in the net of justice as fairness because his preferred group consists of ordinary people who choose virtue over vice. Unless we have some case for our own delineation on the ladder of being, Nietzsche escapes. Fairness for ordinary people is simply not important. Moral concern is not a right but a "reward" for excellence.

Second argument: a criterion used to give certain people priority over others must be universalizable; like the classical racist, Nietzsche will have to choose between logical consistency and prices too heavy to pay. Let us apply this argument and see where it leads. Classical racists assert that whites are entitled to exploit blacks. When we asked racists whether they would deserve exploitation were their skins to turn black, they had to choose between two impossible alternatives: abandoning logic or saying that none of their personal traits counted against sheer blackness. But why were they caught in this dilemma? Because imagining a change in your skin color does not entail imagining any change whatsoever in your personal traits.

Certainly, we have a right to ask Nietzsche the same kind of questions. When he asserts that those who possess creative genius are entitled to use herd men as a means to their ends, we can ask him to imagine he was a herd man. Would he still say that supermen were entitled to use herd men as a means to their ends, even if this meant a total lack of concern for his own welfare or his own demise? But why should he hesitate? Unlike the racist, Nietzsche is being asked to imagine a revolution in his personal traits. He is being asked to imagine himself of perhaps below average intelligence rather than brilliant, enjoying ordinary work rather than the ecstasy of creation, with a pedestrian sense of humor rather than a keen wit. He is being asked to imagine his core personality so altered that he has changed into someone radically different from the sort of person he is; indeed, he has changed into the kind of person he loathes. He can reply simply that if he were a herd man he certainly should be exploited while reminding us that he is not really like that at all.

Third argument: the rule of universalizability in isolation has limits, but one is not really imagining oneself enduring the plight of another unless sympathy is brought into play. Surely, someone who feels sympathy for the plight of herd men would find it difficult to endure their suffering. In other words, if Nietzsche calmly asserts that people unlike himself should go under, we have a right to ask him to engage his emotions. We can ask him to vividly imagine the plight of his victims, empathize with them, identify with them on a one-to-one basis. If a superman made a real effort to feel what a herd man feels, were to experience personally the suffering of a herd man, would this not awaken sympathy and convince the superman that he should take into account what his victims want?

In response, I wish to distinguish between three things, namely, consequences, empathy, and sympathy. Nietzsche must face up to the full consequences of what his ideals entail when put into practice. If Nietzsche tried to minimize the sufferings of herd men, if he were to argue that ordinary people have dulled emotions, so that they feel things far less than the great, he would be vulnerable. However, let us assume that Nietzsche conceded that suffering is much the same for all people. There is no doubt that Nietzsche suffered personal tragedy and intense physical pain—we all do in the dentist's chair. If he experienced these things personally and believed ordinary people suffered much the same experiences, then he did have a real awareness of the pain his ideals might inflict on the masses. But why should this awareness shake his commitment to his ideals? Nietzsche never shied away from the fact that ordinary people do not want to suffer, it is just that, from his point of view, what ordinary people want or suffer does not count for much.

It may be said that this misses the point. Perhaps being aware of someone's suffering on this level is not enough, not enough to validate a claim of having attained empathy. And if Nietzsche attained true empathy with ordinary people, would that not necessarily awaken sympathy? The best way to test whether empathy and sympathy are necessarily conjoined is to imagine Nietzsche making empathetic demands on us. He might ask us whether we have ever fully identified with the sheer awfulness of ordinary people. Have we ever made an honest effort to access the minds of a family convulsed with mirth at a female impersonator or weeping sentimentally at endless re-runs of *This Is Your Life*; to merge with a mob mindlessly baying for blood at a Nuremberg rally; to duplicate the psyche of a bullying husband; to appreciate the idiot vanity of someone who offers the world no more than a pretty face and a cloying manner? He might assert that if we truly did all of this, we could not hold on to our egalitarian ideals, at least not while under the spell of these experiences, at least not if we repeated the experiment time after time. And he might conclude that if the tactic did not work, that merely showed we were incapable of true empathy.

If determining whether a series of empathetic experiments can weaken moral commitment is a legitimate test of commitment, we should not wait for Nietzsche. We should make such demands on ourselves and push them on others. If some of our humane comrades seem to falter in their commitment, we should urge them to immerse themselves in the awfulness of ordinary people, perhaps beginning with a close reading of the section on the common man in Wylie's *Generation of Vipers*. I doubt any of us would feel obliged to do this. Perhaps there is a core of validity here: if someone can only sustain a humane-egalitarian commitment by falsifying what people are like, turning workers into proletarian heroes or farmers into peasants sitting under an oak tree always deciding wisely, or believing that everybody is "essentially good at heart," then his or her commitment is built on sand. But if we have faced up to what people are like, warts and all, and still feel a lively sympathy, we need not undertake a concerted campaign to weaken our commitment by wallowing in human awfulness. Indeed, if some of our comrades approached us and said that under the spell of such experiences they doubted their ideals, we might say that this was a temptation to be resisted. We might say that this was no state of mind in which to make a binding decision, any more than one should decide on the existence of God when terrified of death. We might advise our comrades to calm down, reflect soberly, and see whether their commitment, despite what ordinary people can be like, was not still alive and meaningful.

If that is our view of empathy as a test of moral commitment, we can hardly object if Nietzsche adopts it. Imagine that Nietzsche, at our urging, did close the psychological distance between himself and a herd man suffused with suffering, not impossible because suffering probably serves as a psychic leveler, and experienced what? The self-sympathy of the herd man perhaps, because if Nietzsche had truly become that person, it would not be the distinctive Nietzsche experiencing anything. When he emerged from total empathy and recovered his own psyche, he might lose any feeling of sympathy at all. It is quite possible to attain real empathy with someone and then, when the spell is broken, be disgusted by the personality we entered into, as every actor who has played Uriah Heep will know. But let us assume that the resurrected Nietzsche did feel some lingering sympathy. I suspect he would react much as we would if empathy left us with a residual loss of sympathy for ordinary people. His psychological distance restored, he would soberly assess his feelings. He would find he still had a lively contempt for herd men, would be disgusted that for a moment he had felt sympathy for a creature so unworthy of sympathy, would deny that he was obliged to accept as final any decision he was tempted to make while captive of that emotion. He would contemplate anew the glory of the great, the awfulness of the masses, and assess with a cool head whether he really believed the sufferings of herd men should inhibit the goals of the great. Certainly, he would feel under no obligation to undertake a concerted campaign to weaken his commitment by constant or repeated identification with ordinary human suffering.

Those committed to humane ideals are obliged to try to convert others, particularly when reason fails, by inducing conversion experiences. But those with opposing ideals, so long as they have not hidden behind false assumptions about people or hidden from the human consequences of their ideals, have no obligation to cooperate. Sympathy for ordinary people is our best card, contempt for ordinary people is Nietzsche's best card: we are each obliged to play our own card by the ideals we hold, but neither of us is obligated to play both cards evenhandedly because neither of us holds both humane and Nietzschean ideals.

Having demonstrated why Nietzsche, above all, is a formidable opponent, it is time to let him develop the detail of his ethics. Toward the end of *Beyond Good and Evil*, Nietzsche tells us that a "distinguished soul" first clarifies for itself the question of rank. Who are its equals to whom it will accord respect and equal rights, and who are its natural inferiors who should sacrifice themselves to a being such as "we are"? It does not feel that the lot of the latter is hard or oppressive or arbitrary; it would say, "This is justice itself." Extending fairness to people in general is to treat them as the equals of their superiors, and this is unfair to supermen. The herd possesses a powerful herd need to obey. It was a sort of kindness when Napoleon stepped forward as absolute commander of the herd Europeans; indeed, he was the high point of the whole nineteenth century and created its most valuable men and moments.

Between unequals morality is no more than a kind of weapon. History shows the master moralities of rulers confident enough to despise the ruled and a slave morality espoused by the ruled or slaves or dependents of all kinds. It is the intrinsic right of masters to create values, and they create moralities of self-glorification. Although one may act toward lower beings as one sees fit, this does not mean sadism (Morgan, 1965, 371). The distinguished man may even aid the miserable, not out of compassion but out of a consciousness of riches to lavish. Slaves defend themselves against their superiors by identifying good with the slavish traits of ordinary people, compliance, patience, diligence, humility. Whenever slave morality predominates, there is a tendency to reconcile the meanings of the word "good" and the word "dumb" (Nietzsche, *Beyond Good and Evil*, secs. 199, 201, 226, 228, 260–261, & 265; *Genealogy of Morals*, I, sec. 13; *Thus Spoke Zarathustra*, II, On the Tarantulas; *Twilight of the Idols*, Skirmishes of an Untimely Man, sec. 48).

Christianity above all is a slave morality, one that attempts to give the best a guilty conscience. It holds up the ideal of a sublime abortion, a herd animal of good will, sickliness, and mediocrity (blessed are the meek). Christianity is a popularized Platonism that turns pure form and moral absolutes into all souls equal before God. God learned Greek to write the New Testament and learned it badly. Supermen must avoid self-deception, be too strong to be disarmed by guilt, and persist with their unique mission: they are the only ones who have the right to mold humanity for a higher purpose as artists use their materials. They must go beyond good and evil, beyond the herd animal morality of compassion and neighborly love that is conventional European morality to experiments with both "good" and "evil," embrace everything evil, frightful, tyrannical, brutal, and snakelike in man. A superman has no right to waste a superior, rare, and privileged nature out of concern for others. Even God could not become perfect if he were not permitted to sin (Nietzsche, *Beyond Good and Evil*, Preface, secs. 2, 23, 41, 44, 62, 65a, 121, 199, 219, & 221).

Nietzsche endorses caste societies, particularly those established by barbarian conquest, because a ruling caste knows that society exists only so that a select kind of creature can raise itself to a higher task. It also accepts the reduction of an enormous number of people to incomplete human beings, to slaves, to tools. The Germans must take the blame for inventing the printing press, thus the prevalence of newspaper reading, thus democratic "enlightenment." The result has been equality before the law, flattering the desires of herd animals, the socialist demand for social equality, the very rejection of the concepts "master" and "servant." Worst of all, compulsory education and universal literacy have corrupted not only writing but thinking, and this has reduced rare spirits to rabble (Kaufmann, 1954). The Brahmans of India knew how to educate the masses; they used religion as it should be used, to influence and control the ruled and sanctify their suffering. They even used religion to avoid the dirt of politicking by annexing to themselves the power to nominate kings. The problem for the future, the serious problem, is to breed a new caste to rule Europe. The Jews could have the ascendancy, literally the supremacy, because they are beyond doubt the strongest, toughest, and purest race in Europe. But they do not want it; all they want is assimilation. Perhaps we can interbreed Jews and the officers of the Prussian landed gentry, adding some intellectuality to a hereditary art of command (Nietzsche, *Beyond Good and Evil*, Preface, secs. 22, 61, 202, 251, & 257–258; *Thus Spoke Zarathustra*, I, On Reading and Writing; *Twilight of the Idols*, Skirmishes of an Untimely Man, sec. 40).

It is necessary to emphasize, for those who have heard garbled accounts of Nietzsche, that he would have despised the Nazis with their führer and anti-Semitism and vulgar German nationalism. Hitler would hardly qualify as a superman against a standard that goes beyond the military virtues to embrace the creative genius of Leonardo, and Goethe, and Beethoven. Nietzsche wants to banish the anti-Semitic crybabies, the Germans who are so weak that they fear the Jews as a stronger race. It is time to stop the literary obscenity of leading the Jews to the slaughter as scapegoats of every conceivable public and internal misfortune. The Germans should look at themselves with a clearer eye unclouded by patriotic drivel: they are a monstrous conglomeration of races perhaps not even predominantly Aryan. It is France that is the seat of the most intellectual and sophisticated culture of Europe (Nietzsche, *Beyond Good and Evil*, secs. 241, 244, 251, & 254; *Genealogy of Morals*, III, sec. 26; *Human, All-Too-Human*, sec. 475).

Nietzsche goes beyond delineation of his ideals to provide justifying arguments that function as substitutes for objectivity. Humane intellectuals exhibit a total dissonance between their metaphysics and their ethics. They would ridicule anyone who still believed in Plato's Forms or the Christian God, but they cling to a morality that makes sense only for believers. Love for mankind in general because everyone has a soul dear to God is a notion that makes some kind of sense, but love of mankind without this is simply stupidity and brutishness. Incredibly, humane intellectuals still suffer from "soul superstition." How could anyone love ordinary people without some concept that sanctifies them? Nietzsche is challenging us to review our commitments, look within ourselves and face what is really there, ask ourselves whether we would really be committed to egalitarian principles if our minds were not infected by a disreputable metaphysical residue. Utilitarianism, pasture-happiness for the herd, insipid and sentimental compassion, are these really what we admire most? The English do because they are not a philosophical race. After all, what are ordinary English people like? They are cattle taught to raise their voices in moral "mooing" by the Methodists and the Salvation Army, a penitential fit their highest level of achievement; just look at how even the most beautiful English woman walks.

Nietzsche feels that history is on his side. As more and more thinking people have the clarity and courage to face up to the moral implications of the demise of Platonic and Christian metaphysics, they will abandon an ethics that, its ontological foundations gone, rests on nothing except bad taste. Those with the right breeding will become "new philosophers" and hammer out a new conscience, a conscience that appreciates that a whole people is only nature's detour to six or seven great men (Nietzsche, *Beyond Good and Evil*, Preface, secs. 44, 60, 126, 186, 203, 213, 225, & 252).

The doctrine of the will to power also provides a justifying argument of sorts. Those committed to humane ideals call attention to the purity of their motives. They condemn those who exploit others, they praise themselves for helping those who need and deserve help. These pretensions of the humane cannot stand up to scrutiny. In fact, charitable people wish to own the needy: if thwarted, they will create a need for help, and if anyone else offers help, they become jealous. The charitable person, the possessive lover, a loving parent, a Catilina-type dictator, all merely want to control, all are motivated by the will to power. That is the cardinal drive of every organic being, and self-preservation is only one of its indirect and most frequent consequences. People differ primarily in terms of how many people they need to control and how completely. In real life, there are only strong or weak wills. In other words, how can exploitation be wrong if everybody exploits other people? And if we are all driven by the will to power, who would prefer a weak will to a strong will (Nietzsche, *Beyond Good and Evil*, secs. 13, 21, & 194)?

Before attempting to diagnose where Nietzsche is truly vulnerable, recall that he has taught us something: unless you can face without flinching every sad and silly manifestation of human behavior, your commitment to humane ideals is untested. However, George Orwell was not alone in passing that test. And whatever historical debt we may owe to the Greeks and to Christianity, plenty of us find our commitment to humane ideals enough without the prop of Plato's Forms or the notion of equality before God. The absence of ethical truth-tests affects all moral ideals and poses no special problems for humane ones. As to whether we are plants bound to wither when torn from our original metaphysical soil, the future will decide that. But I suspect that our roots go deep into human psychology, just as deep as those that feed the superman. In most societies, children internalize other-regarding oughts within the family, and some tend to generalize their moral concern outside that small circle, unless the struggle for existence is too intense, or unless social myths convince them that only a certain race, or class, or caste is fully human. The prevalence of humane ideals probably depends on things like mutual respect within families, reasonable access to a good life, and visible examples of blacks and poor people and untouchables with the kind of traits the myths tell us cannot be.

Nietzsche's argument, based on the theory of the will to power, is both weak and unnecessary. First, his theory is no better than any other theory of human motivation that reduces all human motives to one. There are many of these. Take, for example, the sophomoric thesis that all human actions, however other-regarding they may appear, are done because we "need" to do them and, therefore, that all human actions are selfish. What all such theories have in common is that they are all scientifically bankrupt. None of them generates a falsifiable prediction, that is, no conceivable human action is allowed to count against the theory (Warburton, 1992, 13–14). Second, even if Nietzsche's psychology had some scientific validity, committed people do not care whether or not all moral principles have a common origin; what they care about is how different they are in substance. Just as Nietzsche finds humane ideals insipid despite believing that they originate in the will to power, so we would find his ideals vicious even if someone could somehow trace all ideals back to a common source of compassion. Third, if all Nietzsche wants is a letter of intent that we will not question his motives, it is freely given. Within the context of their principles, all moralities produce people whose motives are pure. We choose to debate with our opponents not by casting aspersions on their integrity but rather by determining whose principles can pass certain tests of reason and evidence.

Turning to our agenda for moral debate, the universalizability item yields limited returns against Nietzsche, as we have seen. However, its use is legitimate, just so long as there is no attempt to bridge the psychological gulf that separates supermen and herd men. The best we can do is ask Nietzsche to imagine a Cattell-like world in which the kind of people he lists as protosupermen have become the norm; that is, the average person is a Leonardo or a Goethe. This is done not to suggest that such a world is probable. It is done to force Nietzsche to clarify his criterion for a superman, whether it is absolute or relative, whether Leonardo is a superman because of his quality or because of his percentile rank at the top of the human hierarchy. The Cattell-like world shows that either option would extract a price. If Nietzsche chooses absolute quality, then most people have become supermen, and there are few herd men for them to master or control. If he chooses rank, then the contemporary people he so admires have sunk into the herd and merit exploitation by the top few percentiles. Either Napoleon would have no herd army to command or would have to serve as a herd man in an army commanded by a super-Napoleon. However, I doubt these prices are so heavy as to demoralize Nietzsche. He would probably say that regard for excellence is at the very heart of his morality and that the superman of today would have to bow to the beyond-superman of a hypothetical tomorrow.

This brings us to the core of Nietzsche's ideals. No matter what criterion he uses to limit moral concern to supermen, no matter whether it incorporates absolute or relative merit, there is little point to the whole enterprise unless we can locate supermen in the real world or, alternatively, provide a plausible scenario for their emergence. Nietzsche recommends the caste societies that have been imposed by barbarian conquests. He says that these provide a vehicle by which rare creatures can rise to perform a higher task. However, the barbarian conquests he so admires did not really do anything to impose a genetic or cultural elite on a mass of herd men. Until about A.D. 1500, the date when Europeans achieved a technology potent enough to withstand nomadic cavalry, the horse was the greatest instrument of conquest in Eurasia. The only superiority required to be a barbarian conqueror was a homeland with abundant horses and pasture, agriculture not developed enough for large permanent settlements, and proximity to a civilization with advanced metallurgy.

It may appear that Nietzsche has handicapped his thesis by not endorsing more civilized conquerors, but the Romans showed no signs of genetic superiority to the Etruscans, Celts, or Greeks. The European conquest of the Americas was largely an accident of biogeography. The Europeans had dense populations, large centralized states with ocean-going ships, and iron tools. This advantage in population growth and technological development was enormously enhanced by the fact that Europe's indigenous animals, such as horses, oxen, mouflon sheep, pigs, and cows, and Europe's indigenous cereals, such as wheat, barley, oats, and rye, are relatively easy to domesticate. The indigenous animals of the Western Hemisphere, such as tapirs, bighorn sheep, peccaries, and bisons, and the indigenous plants, such as annual teosinte, maygrass, little barley, and wild millet, are very difficult to domesticate. The absence of pack animals and draft animals crippled transport and, therefore, trade, communications, and the beneficial flow of technology from one distant group to another (Diamond, 1991, chaps. 14 & 15; Sowell, 1998, chap. 5). I am not taking a dogmatic stance on the possibility of some genetic differences between conquering and conquered peoples, but whatever gap may have existed, it was light-years short of the gap posited between supermen and herd men.

Setting aside conquerors, whether barbarian or otherwise, Nietzsche's hopes for caste are based on illusion. Caste freezes in place an elite with no clear superiority; indeed, caste societies impede the evolution of a significant correlation between rank and merit more effectively than any other social experiment humanity has ever tried. Mascie-Taylor (1995) has said the last word about Sir Cyril Burt's sins in fabricating data, but this does not detract from the validity of Burt's pioneering social models. If one posits a moderate correlation between rank and merit, then a social mobility of 20 to 30 percent shifting class is needed in every generation, if even that moderate correlation is to be maintained (Burt, 1961). Burt's description of the historical prerequisites of a meritocracy has never been bettered: an elite established by force and blood relationship must give way to an aristocracy of property or wealth; ✓ finally, that must give way to an open society stratified by talent free to make its way (Burt, 1959). This is not to say that the correlation between merit and class has no upper limit (see chapter 8).

Caste must be abolished to achieve another of Nietzsche's objectives, that is, the maximization of great achievement. The best means to that goal is to tap the reservoir of talent existent throughout the whole of society. Only because Nietzsche's ban on education or literacy for the masses has been ignored do we have our own century's explosion of scientific and mathematical achievement. Look at the wonderful things dancing before our eyes, the prospect of a grand unified theory of all the forces of nature, the bold cosmological speculations about the origins of the universe, the solution of Faltings's theorem, the solution of Fermat's last theorem, the answer to Hilbert's question about Diophantine equations, the exciting and elegant progress on curves of genus 2 and above. The Brahmans of India were a dead hand on great achievement as much as any other caste. If education and literacy had been restricted to them, much of postindependence India's contribution to the arts, literature, film, science, and mathematics would never have occurred. As Nielsen (1985, 33) says, improving the lot of the masses revealed that they had always contained many creative people, unsung Miltons, undiscovered Goethes, quasi-Goethes, and mini-Goethes.

The real world confronts Nietzsche with a choice between two options: either caste without merit or merit with social mobility. And now our agenda ✓ can impose prices of crushing severity. The first option would mean jettisoning the ideal of excellence and tear the heart out of his value system. The second option retains that ideal but levies three demoralizing prices. First, an open society, one that forces all to compete with some semblance of equal opportunity, eliminates the social distance between the elite and the herd so dear to Nietzsche's heart. The select man will find that he, and particularly his children, can no longer simply issue commands, avoid the bad company of dwarfed beasts with pretensions to equal rights and demands, confine the ill-smelling task of studying the many to reading books (Nietzsche, *Beyond Good and Evil*, secs. 26, 203 & 257). Second, the prerogatives of supermen cannot be transplanted into a socially mobile society. Even bosses cannot use their secretaries as slaves or mere means to ends, much less a scientist a lab assistant, when the lab assistant might be a scientist tomorrow or when the scientist's son or daughter is likely to serve an apprenticeship as a lab assistant. Third, an open society cannot improve on a caste society in one important respect. It cannot provide a mechanism for conferring rule on supermen. Some individuals will scale the heights of achievement, but no one has ever found a way to give creative geniuses political or social control.

Even in his own day, Nietzsche could not specify any social group likely to become a superman ruling elite. His proposal to breed Jews with the Prussian military to seize control of a united Europe is surely tongue-in-cheek, a delicious slap at German pretensions and anti-Semitism. Military conquest promises nothing better for the future than it delivered in the past; witness Hitler and the imperial rule of Stalin.

Bertrand Russell (1946, 789) opines that Nietzsche had a romantic ideal, perhaps best represented by someone like Pope Julius II, fighting for Bologna one day and employing Michelangelo the next. If so, his ideal is truly consigned to the dustbin of history. No general today rides a horse around the field of battle and doubles as a munificent head of state. During Operation Desert Storm, Gen. Colin Powell never got closer to Iraq than Saudi Arabia, and his job as head of the chiefs of staff is rather like that of a top executive at General Motors. Gen. Norman Schwarzkoff, the commander in the field, played a role akin to someone running a complex computerized dating service operating under pressure. Total automation of reconnaissance and weaponry may soon mean that no "soldier," much less general, gets within five hundred miles of the enemy until the battle is over. General Powell knew he could not avoid the "dirt" of politics if he wanted to be president, and he found it not to his taste. As for a group like the Brahmans influencing popular culture behind the scenes, that role today is played by advertising executives, film producers, and pop stars. There is nothing in Nietzsche's writings to save him from the fate of Miniver Cheevy, child of scorn, who grew lean as he assailed the seasons. Someone who could not face loss of the "medieval grace" of iron clothing.

If Nietzsche can specify no actual or emerging elite that has been staffed by "a select kind of creature," what of the conscious creation of an ideal elite? This poses the problem of identification. It is hard to imagine any institutional method of stamping credentials, a sort of self-perpetuating fraternity plus sorority accepting or blackballing candidates, that could operate without self-destructive controversy. After all, the prerogatives of membership include control, enslavement, and sacrifice of those rejected. Nietzsche's own attempts at screening for creative genius do not inspire confidence. He does not provide a list of supermen (they belong to the future), but he does tell us whom he admires and rejects (Nietzsche, *Beyond Good and Evil*, secs. 199–200, 224, 245, 252–256, & 269). Those approved include some of the great names we would expect, although Alcibiades and Frederick the Great give pause. He likes Shakespeare despite the revolting vapors and closeness of the English rabble. Gogol is no better than Byron or Poe, a great stylist but child-brained. Rejected are Bacon, Hobbes, Locke, and Hume as unphilosophical, Mill, Darwin, and Spencer as mediocre intellects, Schumann because of petty taste. Bach, Newton, Leibniz, and Gauss go, as far as I can see, unmentioned. All of this suggests that no one can identify supermen except idiosyncratically.

Although Nietzsche has no plausible scenario for a public role for supermen, his ideals have implications for personal conduct or private ethics. Even here, the lack of an institutional method of identifying creative geniuses is significant because it leaves open only the alternative of personal or self-identification. This leaves every fool in Greenwich Village who paints him- or herself blue and rolls across a canvas free to claim the prerogatives of a superman. It conjures up the specter of these so-called artists murdering "ordinary" people in alleys to get money for paint and materials or even simply for inspiration. In other words, the only real-world consequence of putting Nietzsche's ethics into practice would probably be an increase in New York City's already robust random murder rate. What contribution this would make to great achievement is unclear. Self-identification would have a strong bias in favor of ersatz geniuses over genuine ones: the former are more numerous, they have worse judgment, and they are far more likely to want to claim the prerogatives of a superman. Russell (1946, 800) points out that Nietzsche turns his back on the psychology of actual living creative geniuses: "Love and knowledge and delight in beauty . . . are enough to fill the lives of the greatest men who have ever lived." Few among the great have ever believed that their creativity would be enhanced by embracing "everything evil, frightful, tyrannical, brutal, and snake-like in man." Setting aside Alcibiades and the generals, it is doubtful that anyone Nietzsche lists would have accepted the proffered role.

Those committed to humane ideals concede Nietzsche too much: they imagine a group of creative geniuses in power demanding the right to use everyone else and lament our lack of a refutation of that demand. In fact, Nietzsche had no concept that could perform the most fundamental task of justice: he had no ordering principle for human society that could operationalize his ideals. There is the analytic brilliance, the wonderful style, the challenge we must accept for our own peace of mind, namely, whether we have the courage to look humanity full in the face. Nietzsche will always haunt us as someone who loathed our ideals and to whom, in the absence of ethical objectivity, we can offer no reason to accept them. But as an opponent in moral debate, he lacks credibility. Neither Plato nor Thrasymachus would have taken him seriously.

WHAT THEY HAVE IN COMMON

Setting aside Cattell as an original, the thinkers criticized over the last two chapters use race, class, and admiration for greatness as foundations for antihumane ideals. They all prefer a fragment of humanity to the rest, and they all want a case for that group that goes beyond mere preference. Therefore, they all assert a perfect or near-perfect correlation between that group and merit and assign it a unique historical role. The favored group is either an actual group easily identified but whose merits have been exaggerated or an ideal group defined by merit but impossible to identify in practice. This gives antihumane ideologues something in common that gives us solace: a high vulnerability to critique in the light of reason and evidence. The fact we have been able to load them down with heavy prices is not accidental.

However, our agenda for moral debate is not a one-way street. The critics of humane ideals will use the very same items against us that we have used against our opponents. They will force us to ask ourselves whether or not we have a coherent concept of justice, and whether we can defend it against accusations of logical inconsistency, and what kind of society our ideals would produce, and whether we have averted our eyes from the consequences our ideals entail in practice. As usual, their case against us will have the underlying theme that we cannot face up to reality as revealed by social and biological and natural science. Moreover, they have in reserve a stunning criticism: that humane ideals are doing what our antihumane opponents have never been able to do; that our own ideals are creating, for the first time in human history, an elite both highly correlated with merit and identifiable. If they are right, humane ideals self-destruct in practice, which should be enough to demoralize almost everyone who looks within and finds a humane-egalitarian commitment.

8

Justice and Meritocracy

From a black perspective . . . the notion that a black [who passes for white] might reclaim his ethnic identity to take advantage of preferential admissions can only trigger an almost inexpressible sense of outrage.

J. C. Livingston, 1979

Turning an elephant loose in a crowd offers everyone, except the beast and his rider, equal opportunities of being trampled.

R. H. Tawney, 1931

A defense of humane-egalitarian ideals must answer critics, and that imposes a caveat. It would be quite wrong to imply that those critics necessarily have some kind of antihumane commitment. For example, Herrnstein and Murray (1994) clearly want to salvage humane ideals, it is just that they believe those ideals must be stripped of certain egalitarian excesses if they are to be viable in the real world. I believe that they are mistaken, that my own roughly Social Democratic ideals can survive our agenda and its items without radical surgery. As this implies, no version of humane ideals is likely to satisfy all who hold such, and, therefore, the best I can do is to present and defend my own.

To spell out any version of humane ideals fully would require something like a utopian novel about an ideal society. Since this book is about *method*, it will undertake the more modest task of illustrating how the method recommended functions in defending humane ideals. Since the method is open-ended, imposes the task of answering all objections, including future ones not yet put, the debate will reach no final and certain conclusion. I will defend one of my basic ideals, namely, a humane-egalitarian concept of social justice, in a particular context, namely, present-day America, against the most potent objections current. At the end of this chapter, and in subsequent chapters, I will make clear that a robust humane commitment endorses a number of basic ideals and that no one of them can really be defended in isolation from the others.

The humane-egalitarian ideal of social justice presented herein rests on sympathy for people in general, operationalized by leveling differences that are the effects of fortune. It includes affirmative action as a compensation for the luck of group membership, the welfare state as a compensation for the luck of genes, and redistribution of wealth as a compensation for the luck of personal circumstance. First, I will defend affirmative action for blacks living in contemporary America; then I will defend the ideal of equalizing environments, toward which the welfare state and redistribution of wealth are steps, against Herrnstein and Murray. These critics happen to be American, but the substance of their case, the meritocracy thesis, has been put forward by opponents of equality throughout the European world ever since the dawn of the industrial revolution.

BLACKS AS A DISADVANTAGED GROUP

Social science collects evidence on group differences. Sometimes it shows that putative differences between black and white Americans are illusions based on ignorance or bias. That can advantage blacks. Sometimes it shows that differences are real and must be accepted by all rational agents. As we shall see, if those agents are truly rational, they will then make certain choices to the disadvantage of blacks. Social science can do nothing about this except conceal the truth, and that it must not do. However, its practitioners must not close their eyes to the consequences of their science. They often say, "It makes no difference if we show that blacks on average are genetically inferior for intelligence, are less prudent and self-disciplined than whites, tend to be more criminal. Only a biased person will discriminate against people according to their group membership rather than judging them by their individual traits." I will show that this last assertion is false.

Social science also attempts to measure how much bias exists. Herrnstein and Murray (1994, 506) believe that while undeniably some bigotry still exists, the vast majority of Americans are fair-minded and free of racial prejudice. Rather than challenging that conclusion, I will treat it as a window of opportunity. If we can show that even in the absence of bias, individual blacks are gravely disadvantaged simply because of their group membership, that might be the strongest possible case for affirmative action. Therefore, the organizing concept of this analysis will not be racial bias but the cost of information.

Levin (1991) points out that race can be an information-bearing trait. He cites a variety of sources as showing that one black male in four is incarcerated at some time for the commission of a felony, while the rate for white males is only about 3 percent, and that a black male is ten times more likely than his white counterpart to be a criminal (Berger, 1987; Hindelang, 1978; Rushton, 1988; *U.S. News and World Report*, 1988; Wilson & Herrnstein, 1985). He endorses the practice of the New Jersey police of stopping young black males in expensive new cars for random drug searches. After all, police resources are stretched, and their efficiency in controlling the drug traffic is maximized by information that enhances the probability of finding illegal drugs. The dividends of targeting blacks extend to other areas of crime prevention. As police officer Mark Furhman of O. J. Simpson fame put it, if a black man is driving a Porsche and wearing a suit that costs less than $100, you stop him on the assumption that the car may be stolen. Anyone who listens to a police radio will discover that blacks who walk through a white neighborhood are labeled suspicious, while whites in a black neighborhood go without remark.

It is rational for police to use race as a low-cost information bearer to enhance their efficiency. Is it rational for blacks to resent this and take steps to make the information more expensive? A few examples may help. Irish Americans have a rate of alcoholism well above that of most ethnic groups. When resources are stretched, as always, and the highway patrol is conducting random checks for drunken drivers, they would do well to stop only Irish male drivers, particularly where Irish are heavily concentrated. The problem is that they cannot be identified by appearance, and stopping all drivers to verify whether or not they were Irish would be self-defeating. Irish could be forced, and everyone else forbidden, to drive green cars, but that law might be evaded. The rational solution would be shamrocks indelibly tattooed on the foreheads of all Irish males, perhaps luminescent at night. There would be a cost in this, but it could be shifted to the Irish themselves. Levin also notes that people associate insider trading with Jewish Americans. This association may not be based on evidence, and the resources of the Securities and Exchange Commission may not be stretched. But if those conditions hold, the utility of Stars of David becomes obvious.

Every black knows that Irish and Jewish Americans would raise the cost of collecting this sort of information to a prohibitive level by political action of the most impassioned sort. Their own efforts have had mainly a cosmetic effect: police omit race from the formula of criminal profiles but continue to use it in practice. Therefore, added to whatever humiliation blacks feel at random searches, there is a sense of overwhelming political impotence. Since blacks cannot use politics to raise the cost, it is rational to pursue other means both individually and collectively.

On the individual level, those stopped for random searches will tend toward noncooperation, verbal abuse, attempts at escape with attendant low-level violence. The police, being rational agents, are likely to anticipate this and resort to preventive measures, that is, they are more likely to handle and search black suspects roughly, even to perpetrate the occasional beating, hoping to intimidate and achieve control. The black community can collectively increase costs to the police by making it clear that if black suspects are abused, there is an ever-present chance of riot. You now have a significant level of random violence between police and black males, but there need be no animosity or real bias on either side. Black males may not dislike police simply because they are police nor police blacks simply because they are black. Both sides may recognize that the other's behavior is simply a rational response to objective group differences. David Stove (1995, 95) adds a point that takes us from theory back to reality, namely, that even rational behavior, just so long as it inflicts injury, can engender strong negative feelings between groups. It can indeed.

Police use race as an information bearer to justify giving blacks atypical attention. There is considerable debate about whether they use it as a rationale for atypical neglect. The incentives are complex. On the one hand, solving violent crimes in the black ghetto might require a disproportionate investment of time and energy and be given low priority. Livingston (1979, 44–45) reports a homicide detective who gave what he called a "niggericide," the killing of one ghetto black by another, a much lower priority than a normal homicide. The term is obnoxious, of course, and it is unlikely that it was used playfully. On the other hand, if promotion depends on a high rate of arrests and convictions, police would be motivated to pursue criminals in the ghetto with vigor. The National Black Police Association argues that blacks may suffer less from neglect than from too robust means of law enforcement. Since 1941, twenty-three black police, working undercover, have been shot by their white colleagues in New York City alone. Perhaps this is an unfortunate by-product of police profiles of blacks as criminals (Charles & Coleman, 1995).

Thomas Sowell shares little of the author's political program. However, he has done much to illuminate how the cost of information affects banks, landlords, employers, and retail outlets in their treatment of blacks. There are two relevant costs: the cost of classifying blacks as members of their group, which, thanks to their appearance, is nil; the cost of determining when a black is an exception to his or her group, which can be significant. For example, take a bank that has an excess of apparently sound white applicants for loans over the amount of funds it has to lend. The bank knows that blacks on average have less managerial experience, that their businesses tend to be undercapitalized, that their failure rate is higher, that their collateral is less salable; all in all, the bank knows that the risk of nonpayment is greater. It can conduct a thorough investigation of a particular black applicant to determine whether he or she is an exception to the group. But unless its competitors also do so, it has incurred an extra cost to its disadvantage. Therefore, the bank will tend to assess the black applicant as a member of his or her group and refuse the loan.

Landlords also use race as an information-bearing trait. They may prefer Asians, particularly females, because they afford a better chance of a tenant who is docile, will please neighbors thanks to sobriety and reticence, will be prompt and reliable in paying rent. They will not prefer young black males, who on average are more likely to be criminal, destructive, noisy, and insolvent. The cost of investigating every tenant as an individual is time-consuming, the cost of classifying blacks is negligible. It is easy to show that avoiding these costs is a rational factor not necessarily tied to racial bias. Sowell (1994, 111 & 114) cites the evidence of Light (1972) and Williams (1974) that successful black banks tend to invest outside the black community even more than white banks do. He cites Tucker (1990), who found that black landlords as well as white landlords prefer white tenants.

Clearly, the same factors extend to other areas. Retailers who provide goods and services in the ghetto bear higher costs, not only losses from theft and vandalism but from installing iron grates and hiring security guards. These higher costs are passed on to ghetto residents in the form of higher prices. The fact that employers use race as a cheap signal of an applicant's skills, motivation, and attitudes toward authority has been amply documented (Kirschenman & Neckerman, 1991; Kasinitz & Rosenberg, 1996; Kirschenman et al., 1996). They do not interpret a black skin as a signal of anything good. As Sowell (1994, 89) says, "It is bitter medicine to the fully qualified individual to be denied employment because of the racial, ethnic, or other group to which he belongs."

A phrase used above must not pass unnoticed: that the cost of classifying an individual as black is negligible. This puts blacks at a disadvantage compared to white ethnic groups because the cost of classifying the members of those groups can be expensive. When Mr. Bell comes to your door, it may be almost impossible to determine that his father is Mr. Bellini and that he has strong ties with suspect elements in the Italian community. This disadvantage is not trivial. Imagine an omnipresent mutation that left blacks exactly as they are except their appearances became a random sample of white America. Overnight the cost of classifying blacks as such, of identifying the people who had once been black, would be far too great for anyone to pay, whether police, bank manager, landlord, retailer, or employer. Disadvantage among no-longer blacks because of group membership would fade into the lesser disadvantages of class or neighborhood. Blackness really does make a difference.

The use of race as an information-bearing trait carries over to personal relationships. White parents concerned for their children's welfare will attempt to prevent them from marrying blacks. Since parents usually get to know their children's lovers without making a special effort, it might appear that the cost of judging potential partners as individuals, rather than as members of their group, is negligible. However, given the power of young love and the incomprehensible reluctance of young people to allow their parents to arrange marriages, the relevant information comes too late to be operationalized. Therefore, parents take preventive measures. First, they take steps to segregate their children from blacks of the opposite sex, particularly after puberty. Second, and far more important, white children are socialized with a taboo so powerful as to overcome sexual attraction and burgeoning affection. The effectiveness of these measures can be judged by the fact that only 6 percent of black men marry nonblacks and only 3 percent of black women. The latter is particularly significant, as we shall see, and contrasts with the rest of America's minorities: about 20 percent of Hispanic women and over 25 percent of Asian women marry out (Farley, 1995). The contrast is all the more striking given that many Hispanics and Asians are recent arrivals, while blacks are from families that have been in America for a rather long time. The paucity of black-white marriages in America cannot be assigned to lack of sexual attraction. The response of whites to black media stars, sports people, and prostitutes, and vice versa, provides evidence to the contrary.

The fact that black women do not have the option of marrying white men has devastating social consequences often not appreciated. Both black and white single mothers tend to be poor, and both are affected by a sexual revolution that makes men less likely to marry a pregnant partner. But black women are restricted to a pool of marriage partners much less likely to be in steady work. If you take the number of black men in steady work per 100 black women and deduct that from 100, you get a result that approximates the percentage of black single-mother homes. In the 1960s, when the number of males in steady work stood at 71 per 100 women, single-mother homes were about 25 percent. In 1990, when the number fell to 51 per 100, single-mother homes rose above 50 percent. These statistics, plus the poverty of black single mothers and the fact that they tend to have more children than other mothers, dictate that a high percentage of black children will be raised in poverty. Black women face a tragic choice: never have children at all, or have them with men too demoralized to be promising as permanent partners. No other group has been faced with that choice. At the turn of the century, when unemployment and alcoholism were prevalent among Irish-American men, Irish women simply married outside their ethnic group (Flynn, 1991, 130 & 135).

It may be suggested that the fact that black women have a mean IQ fifteen points below the white average accounts for any racial disparities. When you select out black women with an IQ of 100 so as to match the white average, the results look like this: 51 percent of black women unwed mothers, 10 percent white; 30 percent of black women with a history of being on welfare, 12 percent white; 14 percent of black women in poverty, 6 percent white (Jensen, 1998, 570, table 14.2). The reason the poverty percentage stands at "only" 14 percent is, of course, because we have selected out an elite well above black women in general in terms of family background and educational credentials.

BLACKS AND AFFIRMATIVE ACTION

My purpose has been to detail how much of the black experience in America is dictated purely by a rational response to objective group differences. Needless to say, three quarters of black males are never convicted of a felony, and most blacks are good workers, tenants, and neighbors. That is the whole point: they suffer because of bad luck in terms of group membership. A few white Americans will have such a strong sense of fair play that it will override self-interested decision making. Given what Adam is like and given what Eve is like, there will not be many. On the other hand, there may still be one or two racists left in American society, and, if so, racial prejudice will encumber blacks with additional negative experiences. However, the effects of racial bias are extraneous to the argument.

Blacks will suffer disadvantage until group differences alter. No one expects police to search white matrons in suburban neighborhoods for drugs as they do young black males. Remedial legislation to force banks, landlords, employers, and retailers to treat blacks as individuals or as typical consumers is clumsy and often counterproductive. Sowell (1994, 206–207) details how laws have been evaded when rational responses to group differences were at stake. The best historical example benefited blacks. Prior to the abolition of slavery, Southern cities passed law after law against teaching slaves to read or write, forbidding them access to pubs and prostitutes, forbidding paying them wages, all to no avail, because employers could hire skilled blacks more cheaply than they could their white counterparts. Legislation will never circumvent human ingenuity, abolish discretion, close off private networks, unless you recruit an army of secret police.

Since we cannot address adequately the specific evils blacks suffer, compensation must come in other areas. The public service is not subject to market pressures, and preferential entry into jobs can compensate for disadvantage in the private sector. Public housing can compensate for disadvantage in the private housing market. Efforts must be made to upgrade the ghetto, but for many the only solution is escape, and preferential access to education provides a means. The consequences of affirmative action programs must be carefully assessed because good intentions are not enough. They are meant, after all, to benefit blacks, not harm them. Blacks who have attended elite universities (and few would do so without affirmative action) have benefited both in terms of graduation rates and income (Kane, 1998). However, some were so unprepared that their courses became a bizarre non-learning experience (Sowell, 1972). It is no service to anyone to go to a university or have a job whose demands they cannot meet and to spend their time feeling humiliated and defeated.

A case for compensation must answer the question of how much. America already compensates blacks in a variety of ways. Perhaps compensation has already gone too far and should be diminished. The empirical task of assessing whether benefits conferred counterbalance disadvantages suffered because of group membership may be beyond the wisdom of a Solomon. Therefore, I will suggest a criterion for an easier task, namely, determining how many American whites *really believe* that compensation has gone too far. It consists of a question: How many whites would choose to become black, assuming continuity of those personal traits like intelligence and motivation most relevant to achievement? This is not like the questions Rawls (1972) poses, questions addressed to imaginary people ignorant of what they need to know to calculate their interests. It is addressed to contemporary white Americans: if they really believe blacks are advantaged beyond their competence in American society, then any rational white should find the black experience attractive. What is being chosen, of course, is a black life-history, to have had a black past, have a black present, and face a black future. It may be objected that a different socialization would have produced a different human being. Very well, we will guarantee not only continuity of personal traits but of core personality, so as to solve the problem of personal identity.

Ethnic identity or group pride can also act as a distracter. Many whites take considerable pride in being an Irish American or an Italian American. Many blacks know that it would be advantageous to be white but would not choose to join a group toward whom they have developed a certain degree of ambivalence. For whites with a significant degree of ethnic identity, the best way to honestly confront our question is this: assume you are being forced to give up your present ethnic identity; choose between being black and a white identity that awakens no special sense of belonging, perhaps being an Icelandic American.

Some of these complications can be avoided by reformulating the question: Were you and your partner to die soon after the birth of a child, would you prefer that child to be raised by black adoptive parents or white adoptive parents? (Assume the two couples were matched for personal traits and that the child would magically absorb the skin color of the parents, so as to eliminate any alienation arising out of different appearance.) Most people care as much for the welfare of their children as they do for themselves, and if few whites would choose the black option, there is a prima facie case that few of them believe that the black experience has become a privileged one.

The principle that blacks merit compensation because of bad luck in group membership may be accepted as a prima facie one, and yet objections may be posed as candidates to override it. A frequent objection is that blacks will sometimes be compensated at the expense of whites even more disadvantaged. That is true, and the ideal would be to collect information about individual differences that would allow us to isolate such cases and make exceptions. But if the price of this information is prohibitive, then we must choose between accepting affirmative action without it or abandoning affirmative action. The argument against abandoning affirmative action is clear: failure to compensate blacks because that would injure disadvantaged white individuals will leave an even greater number of black individuals injured without compensation. So is the price of the information prohibitive?

I believe it can be shown to be so by analyzing the case of veterans compensation (Ezorsky, 1991, 79 & 91). This program was by no means negligible. After World War II, America decided to compensate over ten million people who had served in the armed forces, a group that inclusive of their immediate families outnumbered blacks. Veterans received preferential entry into civil service jobs and targeted benefits, ranging from subsidized education and health care to pensions, special hospitals, and retirement homes. Veterans often benefited at the expense of nonveterans who were more disadvantaged. Ideally, there would exist some sort of ambulatory philosopher king, a source of walking wisdom, who would say, "This Boston Brahman had a cushy job in army supply, while this Polish American spent the war in Gary, Indiana, working in a dangerous steel mill." Therefore, no preference. That is not a realistic alternative. The only real-world alternative imaginable is a semijudicial inquiry with the brief of assessing the advantages and disadvantages of life histories. The cost of that sort of information about individual differences would include unacceptable invasions of privacy, enormous difficulties in securing testimony and assessing its reliability and relevance, huge expenditures in time and money.

Affirmative action, like veterans preference, the police, the banks, and the landlords, uses group membership as an information-bearing trait. Race tells us that some people on average have suffered much more because of their group membership than others. To burden affirmative action with collecting information about individual differences would sink it because the relevant information carries the highest cost imaginable. As we have seen, much lower costs would hamper crime prevention, disadvantage banks in favor of less scrupulous competitors, push landlords toward private networking rather than offering their premises to the public. American after American finds the cost of information about individual differences too high when disadvantaging blacks. To use such costs to forbid benefiting blacks makes an interesting exception to the rule. The real difference between veterans preference and affirmative action is that America really did want to confer a group benefit on veterans, and America is ambivalent about conferring a group benefit on blacks. This ambivalence is striking when we reflect on why blacks need compensation. The very essence of racial profiles is to confer a group benefit on whites while ignoring individual differences among blacks. They amount to nothing less than a systemic affirmative action program that gives whites special access to loans, housing, jobs, an advantageous marriage market, driving and walking the streets without harassment. Whites do not think of this as special access, of course, because it is only special compared to what blacks get.

When affirmative action for whites causes a problem, why is affirmative action for blacks objectionable as a remedy? The question that faces America is not whether it shall have affirmative action: it has had it for almost four centuries. Affirmative action for whites began the day the first black was brought to America as a slave and has persisted right up to the present. The only question is whether affirmative action for whites is to be balanced by a measure of affirmative action for blacks. It may be said that the case for veterans preference was based on the fact that they were better than others, suffered because they defended their country, while the case for affirmative action is based on the fact that blacks are worse than others. They suffer many of their ills because their group is the most criminal and dysfunctional. This reaction shows, more than anything else, how thoroughly judging people in terms of group membership permeates our thinking. In reply: individuals are not responsible for the behavior of their group; if innocent blacks suffer because of group profiles, no matter what the social reality behind those profiles, they deserve compensation.

Another objection pushed as a candidate to override the principle of compensating blacks is that benefits go disproportionately to the black middle class. Certainly, programs should be targeted to ensure that lower-class blacks benefit. Public housing is likely to attract a largely working-class clientele; special bonuses for teachers and administrators can be used to upgrade ghetto schools, clinics, and other amenities located in working-class areas; educational programs for basic job skills, budgeting, knowledge of welfare rights, and fertility control should be directed toward those areas. A good test of the sincerity of those who claim sympathy with lower-class blacks is whether they have no objection to preferential entry into the lower, as distinct from the upper, levels of the civil service. It is always hardest to benefit the most demoralized numbers of any group. It is not sensible to benefit no blacks at all because benefits cannot be class-neutral within the black community. Would it make sense to exclude middle-class blacks from benefits? Only if it could be done without excessive costs, which is highly unlikely, and only if it is contended that they have prospered to the point that they suffer no significant disadvantage because of their group membership. That contention suggests a variant of the original question we put to white Americans: How many whites who are clearly middle class would choose a black life history, assuming continuity of personal traits and core personality?

This last reminds us that our original question has gone unanswered. I prefer the adoption formulation of the question: How many whites would be indifferent as to whether their newborn child got white or black adoptive parents, assuming a match for traits and color? It would be difficult to conduct an honest opinion survey. But, as Plato in *The Republic* said of justice, has not the answer to this question been lying unnoticed at our feet all the time? I refer to the pathetically low rate of intermarriage between black and white Americans. White after white, despite powerful sexual attraction, has chosen not to make their children black because they know, they know very well, that to do so would be to give their children bad luck in terms of group membership. Anglo-Saxon Americans married the violent and drunken Irish, the hyperemotional and clannish Italians, the verminous and Pinochle-playing Poles. Did anyone marry blacks? They did not. And yet, during slavery, when they did not have to care about their children's prospects, white men fathered numerous black children.

I am not stating a general thesis, something like, whenever there is little intermarriage between white Americans and an ethnic group, whites must be skeptical about the life-prospects of the members of that group. Orthodox Jews and the Amish have built a fortress around themselves to preserve an atypical way of life. Obviously, their low rates of intermarriage do not signal whether they are regarded as disadvantaged or advantaged in terms of opportunity. Surely no one believes that such cases are relevant. Neither whites nor blacks have voluntarily turned their back on the mainstream of American society, and their failure to intermarry has its own peculiar significance. The intermarriage rate has risen over time (Staples, 1985, 1007–1008). It rose from almost nil to a few by 1980 to the levels quoted from the 1990 census. Census data for those twenty-five to thirty-four years give us a preview of the future. They put black men at 8 percent and black women at 4 percent. The same data put Hispanic women at 31 percent and Asian women at 45 percent (Farley, 1995). As the women of other groups rush toward total acceptance, black women remain a unique exception. Let us hope that someday their intermarriage rate will reach 30 percent, a figure that would indicate some white optimism about the prospects of black American children. For the present, when even middle-class blacks face this kind of rejection, the notion that whites believe blacks of any class are privileged is suspect. A society that acknowledges that the members of a group suffer much because of their group membership and yet gives high-minded reasons for refusing to compensate them as such forfeits a measure of respect.

This analysis does *not* assume that justice requires equal outcomes for black and white. It merely aims at a situation where whites believe there is an equal chance of equal outcomes, assuming traits relevant to competence are held constant. If such traits are unequally distributed between the races, outcomes will not be equal. It also makes no assumptions about the origin of group differences, about whether they are caused by genetic or environmental differences or a combination of the two. Perhaps the tenor of the analysis appears pessimistic. It recognizes that American whites often disadvantage blacks by choices motivated by self-interest, although some actors, such as the police, cannot be convicted of that. Pessimism should not be total. It is a happy paradox that people often ask government to coerce them into doing good. Many affluent people vote for progressive taxation who set aside little for private charity. People are even more ready to force other people to do good. Most of us will never lose a place at a university or a promotion or a job to a black. Willingness to sacrifice the interests of others for an ideal is not pretty, but it is politics and a kind of politics that does much good. Without the "little to lose" North coercing the "much to lose" South, blacks might have remained slaves for many decades.

EQUALITY AND MERITOCRACY

The humane-egalitarian ideal of social justice goes beyond compensation for the luck of group membership. It endorses the welfare state on the grounds that all people, unless they forfeit it by criminal or irresponsible behavior, should be able to live a decent life. They do not have to earn the right to do that by good luck in the genetic lottery; they do not have to have unusual talent or virtue. The humane-egalitarian ideal endorses the redistribution of wealth as a compensation for the luck of personal circumstance. There will be some people, of course, who earn high incomes despite below-average genetic endowment, despite humble birth, despite misfortune. But lucky genes and lucky circumstances are positively correlated with success, and redistribution of wealth helps rectify the balance sheet. Those of high income who are debited unfairly can afford it. The injury done them does not match the benefits conferred on the poor.

There is no sharp division of labor between the welfare state and redistribution of wealth. Using the former to ensure that all children benefit from a decent environment, irrespective of genetic inheritance, redistributes wealth to finance housing, schooling, nutrition, and health care for all. When progressive taxation, superannuation, and death duties are used to counterbalance the luck of personal circumstance, adults who benefit will count as one of their blessings an enhanced ability to benefit their children. Programmatically the two are functionally interrelated. Sometimes to make their two objectives clear they are equated with equalizing environments and abolishing privilege, and those labels are quite acceptable.

Humane-egalitarian ideals may include a coherent concept of justice, but can they accommodate what human genetics and social dynamics tell us about certain group differences? Herrnstein and Murray claim that they cannot and use the meritocracy thesis as the vehicle for their argument. I will rebut the meritocracy thesis and use that rebuttal to extract a bonus: a deeper insight into the dynamics of humane-egalitarian ideals. Herrnstein and Murray (1994, 105, 109, & 510) state the meritocracy thesis in four propositions: (1) if differences in mental abilities are inherited, and (2) if success requires those abilities, and (3) if earnings and prestige depend on success, (4) then social standing (which reflects earnings and prestige) will be based to some extent on inherited differences between people. They imagine a United States that has magically made good on "the contemporary ideal of equality." First, every child has equal environmental quality insofar as environment affects intelligence. Second, each person can go as far as talent and hard work can take him or her with neither social background, nor ethnicity, nor lack of money barring the way.

Herrnstein and Murray (1994, 91, 105–115, & 509–520) believe that America has realized the humane-egalitarian ideal in practice to a significant degree. The irony is that insofar as it is realized, America approaches a kind of caste society egalitarians would loathe. If environmental inequality is diminished, intelligence differences between individuals increasingly reflect genetic differences. If privilege is diminished, intelligence or IQ becomes an enhanced factor in social mobility, so that upper-class occupations become filled by the bright and lower-class occupations by the not bright. Genes for intelligence become more and more segregated by class. There is an elite class with good genes for IQ whose children tend to replicate their parents' high status because of luck in life's lottery, that is, because they inherit their parents' good genes. There is a large underclass with bad genes for IQ whose children suffer from cognitive disadvantage at birth and find it difficult to escape low status.

The meritocracy thesis strikes at the very heart of the humane-egalitarian ideal. That ideal is revealed to be counterproductive in practice. The abolition of inequality and privilege produces a class-equals-caste society with high status the inheritance of a few, dependency and low status the inheritance of many. How little this vision will appeal will vary from person to person, but it is safe to say that countless idealistic men and women did not lay down their lives for this.

Herrnstein and Murray select 1960 as the year by which America saw potent meritocratic mechanisms in place. This generates a prediction that can be tested against evidence. Recall what a trend toward meritocracy means. The more meritocracy, the more good genes for IQ go to high status occupa- ✓ tions, the more bad genes go to low status occupations. The genes are passed on from parent to child, so the more meritocracy, the more of an IQ gap between upper- and lower-class children. If Herrnstein and Murray are correct, the gap between upper- and lower-class children should show a visible jump when we compare representative samples of children tested recently with those tested in the premeritocratic era. The comparability of the most recent data rests on an assumption: that women show no less merit in attaining professional status than men. Social scientists who find life too dull or devoid of controversy are invited to step forward.

The best evidence comes from white American samples, and I (Flynn, in press) have analyzed these to show that they falsify the posited trend toward meritocracy. The correlation between child's IQ and parental occupational status has been surprisingly stable from 1948 to the present. The pattern is a mean IQ of 105 for upper-class children, 100 for middle-class children, 95 for lower-class children. The most parsimonious conclusion is this: nothing, nothing, absolutely nothing has happened.

However, the best that evidence can do is show that meritocratic trends do not exist at a particular time and place. This leaves the central contention of the meritocracy thesis untouched. That contention is that if the humane-egalitarian quest of abolishing inequality and privilege is successful, it will result in class stratification of genes for talent of which IQ is a marker. If such stratification has not occurred, the quest has simply been unsuccessful. Moreover, Herrnstein and Murray claim that a meritocratic future is inevitable. This means that the humane-egalitarian ideal has been given a reprieve both temporary and humiliating. It is a poor ideal that must pray for eternal failure in order to avoid unwelcome consequences. Therefore, we must go beyond evidence to analysis.

Meritocracy is psychologically incoherent: (1) the abolition of material-ist-elitist values is a prerequisite for the abolition of inequality and privilege; (2) the persistence of materialist-elitist values is a prerequisite for class stratification based on wealth and status; (3) therefore, a class-stratified meritocracy is impossible.

The major barrier to abolition of inequality and privilege is our obsession with money and status. Job creation, public health and education, and the welfare state have to be financed by progressive taxation, death duties, luxury taxes. Even limited objectives are costly, for example, giving America's depressed urban communities better housing, desirable not only for its own sake but also so that these communities can attract middle-class residents who bring with them their mores and job networks (Dickens, 1999). Which is to say that all of the steps needed to equalize environments involve massive transfers of wealth from some to others. They founder on the rocks of the love of money in one's own pocket, the lust for status superior to one's fellows, the desire to confer advantage for these things on one's family. The fact that universities now do a better job of matching credentials to academic performance does not abolish the enormous inequities of the larger society. Some parents are simply better placed to advantage their children. They provide educationally efficient homes that point children toward superior credentials (Flynn, 1991, 126–139), alter their children's appearance to make them more presentable, give them models of people in work, and pay off crippling debts. Best of all, their contacts and networks become their children's contacts and networks.

Even within the working class, youths can be divided into those who have functional and dysfunctional networks. Wial (1988) describes Boston youth fortunate enough to have fathers and uncles who tell them what skills they need (often learned informally on weekends), what behavior patterns are expected on the job, the importance of avoiding a criminal record, and information about job availability. The absolutely crucial role information plays is shown by the fact that recent studies suggest that about half of all jobs are found through connections (O'Regan, 1993, 329, table 1). Wial's young men viewed door knocking and answering newspaper ads as equally fruitless. They took it as axiomatic that decent jobs depend on two things only: connections and luck. Youths in families and neighborhoods without viable networks miss out on everything important, no good preparation, no good information, no interview with an employer arranged by a friend working for that employer (Dickens, 1999). Connections and luck are factors whose reach extends right to the top of the job hierarchy (Granovetter, 1974). In 1990 the National Center for Career Strategies stated that over 80 percent of executives find their jobs through networking and that about 86 percent of executive job openings do not appear in the classified advertisements (Ezorsky, 1991, 14–16).

An America in which everyone wants to win the glittering prizes of wealth and status will not pay onerous taxes (or show heroic virtue when tempted to seek special advantage) just so the competition can enjoy a level playing field. However, let us imagine that the value change needed to achieve equal opportunity has occurred: let us imagine what would happen were people to lose their obsession with money and status. The class hierarchy that ranks by income and an agreed pecking order of occupations would be diluted beyond recognition. People must *care* about that hierarchy for it to be socially significant or even for it to exist. Imagine a society in which the appreciation of beauty, the pursuit of truth, craft skills, being fit, companionship, personal traits like good humor and generosity, and so forth really counted for more than having above average income and possessions. Some people would be better than others at all of these things, but there would be at least a score of noncomparable hierarchies, and being better would not necessarily carry financial rewards. Even today there are executives who care less about promotion than running a good 10 k. The decline of elitist values, less joy in the sheer fact that you are better at something than others are, is also relevant. Superior performance would persist, but less status, less passion, less of a sense of being a better human being would attend superior performance.

In sum: either meritocracy posits a population who are materialist and elitist but who make financial sacrifices and sacrifice the prospects of their children just so others have a better chance to compete, or meritocracy posits today's class system as eternal, even though people have undergone a sea change that has eroded their love of money and status. The present class system cannot become just without a value shift, and a value shift would alter the present class system. Moral realists who believe the last sentence would be improved by calling that value shift a more accurate perception of moral facts are welcome to do so. After all, people have become less "morally depraved."

Meritocracy is also sociologically incoherent: (1) allocating rewards irrespective of merit is a prerequisite for meritocracy, otherwise environments cannot be equalized; (2) allocating rewards according to merit is a prerequisite for meritocracy, otherwise people cannot be stratified by wealth and status; (3) therefore, a class-stratified meritocracy is impossible.

This reveals an ambiguity at the heart of the meritocracy thesis, namely, failure to specify the quality of the equalized environments assumed. For most of us, giving everyone equal opportunity would mean everyone with access to quality health care and education; everyone reared in nondemoralized homes and communities, that is, by parents in decent housing and with decent jobs; everyone protected against handicaps like having to support an indigent parent or parents. If these things are enjoyed by 95 to 99 percent of the population, they can hardly be reserved to those of outstanding merit. Yet equalization of environments is to coexist with a large immiserated underclass, and that class must compete with an elite that has an environment so potent that they constitute a menace to democracy (Herrnstein & Murray, 1994, 509–526). The ideal that truly self-destructs in practice is the meritocratic ideal. Those who think it inevitable should give it a plausible social dynamic. They can begin by telling us how equality is to be achieved when a large underclass is already knocking at the door, or, conversely, how an underclass is to emerge if we keep topping up their environmental quality to maintain the level needed for equal opportunity. It is significant that Herrnstein and Murray imagine environments being equalized by magic. Magic's next task is to reconcile equality with a large underclass. Its final task should be to square the circle.

Our sociological analysis reinforces our psychological analysis. The higher we push the quality of environment all enjoy, the less attractive the prizes left for the winners. Many people of talent may want more than the not-unattractive norm, but how many will care about shaking the last dollar out of the money tree? Social scientists can go on publishing hierarchies that rank the whole population by occupational status, but these will fall short of ranking people by merit, much less genes for talent. An overenthusiastic sports master can force everyone to participate in the annual school run, but he or she cannot force them to train or try. The published results will not stratify people for genes for running ability. A decent life for all does not foster a Social Darwinist psychology or raise competition to fever pitch.

Now we have a better understanding of the dynamics of humane-egalitarian ideals. Rather than self-destructing in practice, they possess a self-correcting mechanism that avoids meritocratic excess. The truth is that we cannot push equality much beyond our ability to humanize. Every significant step toward equality must be accompanied by the evolution of values unfriendly to "success" as defined by the present class structure. Every significant step toward equality means a step toward a people less materialistic and elitist, more variegated in their interests and behavior, altogether more humane. Whatever dark spirits lurk in the depths of equality, meritocracy is not among them.

A final disclaimer: this analysis makes no prediction about how far we can go toward humanizing people away from materialistic and elitist values; it does not even say how far we should go. The caution does not come from recognizing that people disadvantage blacks because of rational self-interest. The fact that bankers, landlords, employers, and proprietors want to survive market competition is quite compatible with putting your woodworking hobby ahead of plotting to be president of General Motors. The caution comes from an inability to predict history. What the analysis does attempt is to describe the interaction between humane values and egalitarian ideals, to show that radical progress beyond the status quo for one assumes radical progress for the other. It attempts to show that when our critics write a scenario that assumes radical equality of opportunity conjoined with the present class system and its psychology, they simply are not thinking clearly.

CELEBRATING HUMANE IDEALS

The humane-egalitarian ideal of social justice has been defended. But justice is not the only great good, so a few words about whether that ideal requires unpleasant trade-offs with other basic ideals. Here I can only briefly indicate why I think such a thing unlikely.

Affirmative action, the welfare state, redistribution of wealth would impede the utilitarian goal of the greatest happiness if these programs wrecked the economy. If they avoid the existence of a large, unemployed, demoralized underclass, they should benefit the economy. The Organization for Economic Cooperation and Development (1999) lists the seven nations that have the highest per capita income; five of them have highly developed welfare states. Mobilizing support for compensating blacks would deter the pursuit of truth if research on the roles of genes and the environment were forbidden. That simply must not be allowed to happen. Sometimes an egalitarian society is said to be counterproductive to the creation of beauty. If so, as Huxley (1962) shows, the trade-off is limited and worth it. The proliferation of the lower classes is said to lower the perfection of the human species by threatening its genetic quality. The best way to prevent the lower classes from breeding is to give them a middle-class life-style. An egalitarian society is said to be a leveler that destroys human diversity. Few groups value the diversity poverty preserves. Any group that wishes can withdraw into its own subculture like the Hasidic Jews of Brooklyn or the Amish of Pennsylvania.

We close with a hymn to humane-egalitarian ideals. Those ideals possess not only goodness but beauty. They confront Fortuna with justice in all of her manifestations, and this confers a pleasing symmetry. They possess a great glory: a built-in self-correcting mechanism so that equality means people improved, not people degraded by some kind of social jackhammer that nails genes to class. The trinity will never be complete because we cannot claim ethical truth on their behalf. There is no such thing as ethical truth. However, those committed to humane-egalitarian ideals can make a truth-claim rare and precious: they can look reality and the truths of science full in the face and find nothing that makes them flinch.

9

Humanism and Postmodernism

The absence of a principle of justice, whether it occurs in a state or family or army or anything else, renders it incapable of common agreement . . . and sets it at variance with itself.

Plato, *Republic*, I, 351–352

Ex nihilo nihil fit.

Aquinas, *Summa Theologica*, I, Q.2.a.3

Humane-egalitarian ideals must accommodate everything known about the real world; and social, biological, and natural science expand knowledge at a fantastic rate. Therefore, many minds are needed to save humane ideals from obsolescence and vulnerability in moral debate. It is a pity that some who have a deep humane commitment walk away from their natural allies into a shadowland of unacknowledged ideals, principled resistance to the benefits of scientific knowledge, and arguments whose fallacies have been identified. I refer to those who classify themselves as postmodern or at least as influenced by postmodern thought.

Disliking the practice of criticizing unnamed thinkers whose views can be invented to suit the critique, I will analyze four thinkers of note who contributed to the April 1992 issue of *Political Theory Newsletter*. This was a special issue devoted to the "politics of difference." The four selected are Jane Haggis, Moira Gatens, Anna Yeatman, and Iris Marion Young. My analysis will argue three theses: that at least these postmodernists have in common a humane moral and political agenda, an agenda that should be made explicit;

that an empiricist like myself can share that agenda and should be exempt from the postmodern indictment of the Enlightenment; that ethical theory, the evolving traditional body of theory that both antedates and survives the Enlightenment, can clarify everybody's thinking. The aim of the critique is not negative but positive. Its ultimate objective is to encourage everyone who holds humane-egalitarian ideals to embrace logic and social science and become effective advocates on their behalf.

THE POSTMODERN AGENDA

These postmodern thinkers have formulated an agenda that has several dimensions. They want to engender a certain *ethical* sensitivity, a certain *historical* or sociological sophistication, and a certain *political* vision characterized by breadth and flexibility. They want all groups, but dominant groups in particular, to forgo the advantages of power in favor of concern for the welfare of other groups interfused with respect for group integrity. To illustrate this point, they often refer to Pakeha, the dominant European group of New Zealand, and Maori, the indigenous Polynesian minority, or to white Australians and Australian Aborigines. Other thinkers writing in a different locale would use other examples such as white and black Americans. Their real desire, of course, is to promote respect for group integrity universally. These thinkers also want everyone to recognize the complexity of group identity over time, see it as self-defining in relation to other groups, a shifting balance of similarities and differences always in flux. Finally, they want to help us break out of the straitjacket of the Lockean political vision, so as to imagine a series of political arrangements that give all groups parity, dignity, and some control over their own evolution.

The ethical dimension is omnipresent. Yeatman wants the powerful to cooperate in altering relationships of oppression, whether based on race, ethnicity, gender, disability, age, sexuality, or class. She wants good will between Maori and Pakeha with power and resources allocated so that both can maintain their own lingual and cultural sense of self. People who deliver services should value group differences, and the delivery should emphasize dialogue, expressed needs, negotiation, and flexibility. Young wants the relatively privileged to benefit the less privileged, recognize their claims to specific needs and compensatory benefits, and remedy group-based inequality. Maori and Pakeha should regard one another as *ethne* worthy of equal respect. Haggis notes that Young generalizes this last into a principle of equal respect for the "moral worth of all persons." Gatens wants an "ethics of difference" in which each group would accept responsibility for other groups whose ways of life intersect with its own. I will characterize these shared moral principles as a humane-egalitarian-tolerant ethic, with the last term carrying no hint of condescension but signaling a high moral value put on human diversity and group integrity (Yeatman, 1992, 6–9; Young, 1992, 12, 20, & 25; Haggis, 1992, 76; Gatens, 1992, 49).

The historical dimension is also omnipresent. Yeatman wants us to look history and "society" full in the face, that is, acknowledge group differences over time and the heterogeneity of social life. Rather than be like the Progressives, who saw the vibrant ethnic diversity of America as a problem to be solved by feeding everyone the dominant cultural diet, we should recognize that various groups value what makes them different, plus the fact that numerous individuals cannot be classified at all but have multiple, historically changing selves. Young warns groups against oversimplifying either their past or their present. She wants groups in conflict to see that their histories show positive interaction as well as antagonism, that they owe their very existence to defining their identity in relation to one another, that despite all their just grievances they are often inextricably interspersed and interdependent. She notes also that however groups define themselves there are always those who do not fit, if only because they are of mixed parentage. Gatens emphasizes how often history is written with nondominant racial and cultural groups, or women and the family, as passive objects, as if they had made no history and were merely swept along in its wake (Yeatman, 1992, 3, 5–6, & 9; Young, 1992, 15–16, 19, & 22; Gatens, 1992, 39–40).

The political dimension shows some variation, although this could be simply a matter that different contributors have developed different themes. Yeatman challenges the Lockean notion of citizenship. She believes it assumes that every individual must conform to society and the state and law in the same way or be excluded and that it promotes a bureaucratic centralized decision-making structure. Rather, we should conceive of civil society as a series of interconnected polities, some local, some regional, all acknowledging and affirming group differences. She wants a politics of voice and representation in which there is a continuing negotiation and renegotiation of settlements that various groups can accept if only provisionally. Young rejects both assimilation and separation in favor of a political vision in which different groups recognize that they participate in the same society and a single polity, but one with decision-making structures that foster discussion and acceptable outcomes. She applies this to Eastern Europe, where interdependence between even antagonistic groups is too great for separation to offer a real solution, and to Maori-Pakeha relations, where she rejects complete separation as a serious option. She favors biculturalism inclusive of Maori representation on decision-making bodies as a vehicle for debate, agreement, and disagreement. Gatens develops both themes, that is, rejects sameness as the price of social equality and assimilation as a strategy for suppressing differences. She urges us to remember that people are the result of long, different, and often brutal histories and to take seriously the varying practices and institutions of various groups (Yeatman, 1992, 1–3, 7, & 9; Young, 1992, 19–22 & 25; Gatens, 1992, 40, 43, 46, & 50).

This political vision, like every political vision, must confront the relationship between politics and ethics. As we have seen, Yeatman wants the powerful to abandon advantage seeking for cooperation, Young wants the powerful to recompense the less powerful, and Gatens reminds us that politics without ethics "too easily reduces to the question of who has the sword." It does indeed. This, it will be recalled, provides the great drama played out in Book I of *The Republic*. Thrasymachus dismisses talk about justice as academic because all actual human societies are ordered purely by the struggle for power. Plato shows him step by step that he is mistaken. Even a band of thieves that has declared war on everyone else must dilute its internal politics with ethics if it is to function.

All of which poses a question for these postmodern thinkers. They stress respect for diverse ethical systems, namely, the differing mores of different groups and different individuals who do not fit neatly into any group. However, are they really opposed to the universalization of *all* ethics, or do they not make an exception in the case of the humane-egalitarian-tolerant ethic they themselves hold? And if everyone is to accept that ethic, will not a lot of group differences have to be leveled? Some groups have mores that promote goodwill and cooperation, other groups do not. Benedict (1934, chap. 5) tells us that the Dobu of Melanesia put "a premium on ill-will and treachery and make of them the recognized virtues of their society." Haggis (1992, 75–76) makes the relevant point when she notes that Young's political vision

is based on universalizing an egalitarian morality and asks whether such a ✓
commonality can occur without denying difference.

I wish to drive the point home by distinguishing three kinds of universality: logical, epistemological, and practical. *Logical* universality is Hare's
rule of universalizability, which, stripped of its excesses, means that you
must be logically consistent when you make moral judgments. I will assume that postmodernists accept this rule. Recall that Young condemns
separatism in Eastern Europe. Presumably, if she wished to endorse the
creation of Pakistan as separate from India, she would feel the need to explain away the apparent contradiction. *Epistemological* universality is the
kind postmodernists reject, rightly in my opinion, because no one can make
a valid case for the objective status of the moral principles they hold. *Practical* universality is the goal of converting all humankind to one's moral principles. Thanks to their political agenda, postmodernists are committed to
the practical universality of their ethics as much as anyone else.

They might object that they are not committed to something quite as all-
embracing as described. If a group is powerless, like the Stone Age people
who live in the highlands of New Guinea, there is no harm in their having
an antihumane ethic. This is true but not very significant. The dominant
groups in industrialized nations have guns and missiles and oil and control
over the terms of trade, so surely we want all of them to be inhibited by a
humane-egalitarian-tolerant ethic. As for oppressed groups, part of the postmodernist agenda is to empower them, so if they have an exemption it is a
temporary one to be nullified as soon as possible. As Gatens (1992, 49) says,
no group can be exempt from accountability for their choices once they are
consequentially significant. This is already true for most oppressed groups:
Maori could choose to begin a campaign of random terror against Pakeha
tomorrow. And while humane values would not threaten their present-day
cultural integrity, this is because their traditional culture has already been
radically modified, beginning with the influence of Christian missionaries
in the nineteenth century.

HUMANE EMPIRICISTS AND THE SIX BALLS

Andrew Sharp (1992, 26, 30, & 37) points out that one need not walk the
path of the postmodernists to arrive at something close to their moral and
political agenda. As an Ulster Protestant (Orangeman) raised in New Zealand

and temperamentally marginalized by having a sense of humor, he early became aware and appreciative of group diversity. Irish Protestants, Irish Catholics, Jewish refugees, Maori on building sites, all appealed to him more than the dominant Anglo-Saxon type. Sharp is not unique. In America, Anglo-Saxon Protestants are a distinct minority, and American historians have created a whole literature that celebrates the heterogeneity of American society. They tell the story of its many ethnic groups without omitting the brutality, antagonisms, interdependence, and self-definition of groups in relation to one another, they sympathetically portray those who do not fit easily into any group, and they acknowledge that ethnic America made America what it is and made it something more than "white men" taming a "virgin continent."

None of these historians speaks the language of postmodernism. When they classify themselves at all it is as scientific historians; for example, Thomas Sowell says he uses the comparative method (he does so brilliantly) as the closest approach history can make to the controlled experiments of the exact sciences. Most of them are ethnic Americans who wrote out of a love for their own group, found that they could not write its history without writing that of other groups, found themselves empathizing with those groups, and then had the deeply moving realization, as Oscar Handlin puts it, that these people were American history. They began to cross-fertilize; for example, Nathan Glazer (a Jewish American) combined with Daniel Patrick Moynihan (an Irish American) to write the best analysis ever written of the ethnic politics of New York City. Mutual understanding emerged. It is not easy for some to understand how an Irishman's highest aspiration could be to be the best street fighter on the block. Moynihan paints a portrait of someone who may die poor but enjoys moments of glory unknown to a cost accountant. Sowell (a black American) has no difficulty understanding. The hill that separated the black and Irish neighborhoods in Harlem was called "San Juan Hill" because of the epic battles that raged on its slopes (Sowell, 1975, 115; Handlin, 1951, 3; Glazer & Moynihan, 1970).

Despite their similarities as ethnic historians, these scholars vary widely in terms of political vision. However, the ethnic groups themselves show a politics unfettered by the Lockean paradigm Yeatman rejects. They certainly developed a series of interconnected polities and a pattern of negotiated agreements minimally acceptable but always in flux. The city of Boston would have its Italian wards and its Irish wards, with reasonable treatment of the less numerous in each (so long as Italians did not have the temerity to want to become bishops), with ethnic businesses getting the paving contracts, with a kickback to the politicians, some of which was used to create an unofficial welfare state for desperate people neglected by the official state. They even transformed a political party, the Democratic Party, into an organizational polity within a geographic polity, one that supplemented a beneficially corrupted civil service as a major source of employment. New York's county committees grew to number 32,000 persons and had to hold their meetings in Madison Square Garden. They created a parallel school system outside the official system, whose priests, brothers, and nuns exhausted themselves in an unrelenting struggle to give their people the literacy and numeracy that would take them out of poverty toward the middle class (Glazer & Moynihan, 1970, lxxxiv & 223–231; Sowell, 1975, 75–79 & 183).

In other words, those who have been molded by ethnic history and ethnic politics have anticipated the historical and political dimensions of the postmodern agenda. As for the ethical dimension, that comes down to a matter of personal commitment. It is perfectly possible to confront the past and present of a heterogeneous society and have no higher principle than advantaging yourself or your group. Speaking for myself, I am happy to endorse the postmodern ethic of humane-egalitarian-tolerant moral principles as a foundation, but, as those words imply, an ethical system must then be constructed on that foundation. A fully articulated humane ethics is complex and consists of at least six great goods with multiple trade-offs between them. We are like jugglers who want to keep six balls in the air, sometimes one flying to the top, sometimes another, knowing that it is fatal to become preoccupied with one ball to the neglect of the others.

The six great humanist goods are at a minimum: the utilitarian ball or the greatest happiness principle; justice with more emphasis on desert than merit; the creation of beauty; the pursuit of truth; the perfection of the human species; a high regard for human diversity and the integrity of various groups. It is easy to demonstrate that there are trade-offs between these great goods, that the pursuit of one sometimes means some sacrifice of another. Had we the power to give Hitler bliss in 1945, say, a fantasy life in which he kept on killing Jews, I would have sacrificed some happiness for justice. In his utopian novel *Island*, Huxley (1971, 178) tells us that universal happiness is incompatible with tragic art but not with all art, which is fortunate, because if the latter were true we might demur. Even if it were proved that a happier humanity would all be of low intelligence, I would not wish to see the pursuit of truth come to a virtual halt and, that aside, would not welcome the degradation of the human species to a point at which no one aspired to more than watching *The Dating Game*. Finally, I would tolerate considerable internal misery within another society before I would interfere if interference meant shattering that society's cultural integrity.

Note how often I would trade off at the price of some sacrifice of the utilitarian ball. I would do so much less often at the expense of the tolerance ball. There is that shattering passage in Ruth Benedict when she talks to a chief of the Digger Indians, whose people have begun to prosper under Western ways. He is not worried about their physical survival or prosperity, but his heart is broken: "In the beginning God gave to every people a cup of clay and from this cup they drank their life . . . our cup is broken now, it has passed away" (Benedict, 1934, chap. 2). If alleviating mild privation among a people means the equivalent of exterminating them and replacing them with happy Europeans, the price is too great.

Nonetheless, the tolerance ball is not sacrosanct. If a people has the power to harm another, the utilitarian ball comes into play: the Masai evolved a warrior culture dependent on aggrandizing themselves at the expense of neighboring tribes, and that had to stop. There are also levels of intragroup misery, say, the more horrible forms of female circumcision, at which tolerance may have to give way. In other words, once postmodernists accept the fact that they want practical universality for their version of humane-egalitarian-tolerant ideals, they will have to face up to tradeoffs within its content. Some differences between peoples will have to be condemned.

The central critical point being made is this. Postmodern thinkers should be honest and confront the fact that they have self-imposed moral commitments just like the rest of us. They look within themselves and find certain moral ideals acceptable and other moral ideals loathsome. They cannot hide from this by some such device as recommending respect for all of the diverse moral principles that divide humanity. That merely leads to a truncated form of humanism almost totally dominated by the tolerance ball.

Certainly, they do not wish to share the fate of Kant, who always had to sacrifice all other humane goods to justice because it had been enshrined in the categorical imperative. They are in danger of making tolerance their categorical imperative. They will find and are finding the effects too suffocating (witness Haggis's query as to how much inequality can be tolerated). Their largely unacknowledged commitments to other great humane goods tend to surface, but precisely because they are unacknowledged, these goods remain shadowy and undeveloped. The trade-offs between other goods and tolerance are made, but made covertly and haphazardly rather than openly and systematically. The price of an implicit, rather than an explicit, commitment to full-fledged humanism is moral principles and moral judgments that may not even meet the test of logical consistency. And what is on the credit side of the ledger? Only the pretense that you have rejected the "monocultural" ethics of the Enlightenment.

POSTMODERNISM AND EMPIRICISM

My own approach to moral debate, whether humane ideals can accommodate everything that the social, biological, and natural sciences tell us, puts me squarely within the empiricist tradition stemming from the Enlightenment. I use the term "empiricist" not in its technical or narrow sense (for example, as excluding scientific realists) but in its broadest sense. Anyone qualifies who believes that observation plus deductive logic, sometimes elevated by fecund theory to the status of science, lends truth value to propositions about the physical universe and human behavior and, moreover, believes that no other method can do so. As we have seen, there appears to be no impediment to a humane empiricist endorsing, with the reservations of any independent thinker, the postmodern agenda.

This raises the question of whether empiricists should be exempted from the postmodern indictment of the Enlightenment. Frankly, I cannot discern whether these particular postmodern thinkers include empiricism among their targets. Therefore, I will note intellectual tendencies they do attack, use those to construct cases against empiricism critics might make, and attempt to answer those, drawing the conclusion that if they believe empiricism to be intrinsically flawed, they are mistaken.

Yeatman indicts a monocultural concept of reason, that is, the assumption that rational processes will lead to a rational consensus, as one that tends to identify women, children, and primitives as nonrational. She criticizes those who think in terms of natural essences and do not see that all states and all individuals are historical and contingent. Young indicts essentialism, a rational totalizing thought that posits real substances behind the apparent flux of experience, and a logic of identity, particularly the latter, as imposing good-bad dichotomies on categories defined as mutually exclusive (your ethnic group is superior, others are inferior; privileged groups are superior, dominated groups are inferior; societies are either civilized or primitive; men are rational, women are emotional). These good-bad dichotomies leave dominated groups with only three alternatives: assimilate and become good; separate and remain bad; or, if both are impossible, endure permanent inequality. Gatens criticizes the "master narratives" of the Enlightenment as inclusive of a commitment to the disembodied abstract subject that erases group and individual differences rather than engendering respect for such. Landes, another postmodern thinker, offers a variation on the theme of the sins of the Enlightenment. She indicts its "dialectic" as productive of the concept of an autonomous and rational subject (Yeatman, 1992, 5 & 9; Young, 1992, 13–18; Gatens, 1992, 40–41; Landes, 1992, 52).

Is there anything here that might be construed as a critique of empiricism? I will set aside two possibilities as nonstarters. First, Yeatman's indictment of the assumption that rational processes will lead to a rational consensus. If applied to morals, that assumption would constitute belief in ethical truth-tests or proofs, and, as Gatens points out, these have often been used to cast the mantle of objectivity over purely partisan moralities. Plato's World of Forms was used, at least to some degree, to rationalize the ascendancy of fourth-century Athenian aristocrats. I assume it will not be disputed that empiricism above all, with its emphasis on the scientific method as applicable to descriptive rather than prescriptive propositions, is unfriendly to ethical objectivity. Second, Yeatman and Young's criticism of Enlightenment thinkers for believing in natural essences and positing real substances behind the apparent flux of experience. Again, I assume as beyond dispute that beginning with Hobbes, empiricism led the charge against the doctrine of essences, and that ending with Berkeley, empiricism banished the notion of substances lurking behind the phenomenal world (Gatens, 1992, 44; Hobbes, *Leviathan*, part IV, chap. 46; Berkeley, *Principles of Human Knowledge*; Berkeley, *Three Dialogues*).

Any case against empiricism will have to be more subtle and, for the sake of clarity, should specify the putative connection between empiricism and invidious hierarchies or dichotomies. There are four possible connections. *Entailment:* the observational-deductive method assumes the possibility of ahistorical truths, or an ahistorical concept of reason, or an ahistorical rational subject. This in turn entails an ideal and a hierarchy based on how closely individuals or groups approach that ideal. For example, men, women, and children get ranked in a rationality hierarchy, with emotion downgraded; societies get ranked from civilized to primitive, with irrational beliefs downgraded. Moreover, the rationalist dichotomy of truth versus falsehood is re-inforced by deductive logic, which rests on the law of contradiction. This entails mutually exclusive and opposite categories, so if one group is good, other groups must be bad. *Cause-effect:* while empiricism may not logically entail a negative evaluation of persons or groups as nonrational, science can only be done in certain societies. Therefore, nonscientific societies will inevitably be condemned as causally counterproductive to the pursuit of truth. *Intrinsic habituation:* while empiricism may neither entail rationalist evaluations nor necessitate condemnation of nonscientific peoples, the dichotomy of "true or false" and the dichotomy of "this or that" have a subtle influence on thought and feeling. They tend to habituate empiricists toward invidious and mutually exclusive dichotomies. *Extrinsic habituation:* while none of the above is true, empiricism emerged during the Enlightenment. Therefore, like other schools of thought that emerged at that time, its advocates still show the influence of the moral and intellectual failings of the Enlightenment.

I will preface my reply to these possible indictments by conceding one point. The observational-deductive method of science does establish a kind of truth that the empiricist considers ahistorical. Those of us influenced by Lakatos would qualify this by saying that scientific theories are never proved true or false. However, those theories are preferred that generate fruitful hypotheses whose predictions are not falsified, as opposed to theories whose predictions are often falsified and therefore have to be patched up by sterile ad hoc hypotheses (Flynn, 1987d, 20). Further, below the level of theory, there are causal hypotheses and assertions that for all practical purposes are ahistorically true. William Graham Sumner's hypothesis, that most prostitutes in Boston were Anglicans because they were graduates of orphanages run by the Anglican Church, was infinitely closer to the truth than the clergy's hypothesis, that there was a latent corrupting content in their sermons. While the phenomenon being explained is time and place bound, the "fact" that Sumner was closer to the truth holds throughout all time. Dobu believe you cannot grow yams without magic (Benedict, 1934, chap. 5). They are simply mistaken, and the falsity of their assertions is timeless. In this sense, and only in this sense, does science allow reason and the rational subject who has mastered science to become ahistorical.

However, none of this logically entails making ahistorical truth or reason even one of your ideals, much less your sole ideal and what you use to rank people or societies. Ideals are values, and values are not entailed by any descriptive proposition, much less by an epistemology that sets out rules or a method for establishing the truth of descriptive propositions. You must commit yourself to the pursuit of truth as a moral principle; it does not logically impose itself on you. There are plenty of scientists who have never doubted that the observational-deductive method is the road to truth but whose behavior, sadly, shows they care little for the pursuit of truth. They are guilty of no logical mistake.

Still, I have acknowledged that humane ethics includes such a commitment, and it is certainly true that some people and some societies are causally more productive of truth than others, scientists more than artists, Swedish society more than Dobu society. If that were the sole ball in your ethical system, you would be forced to use it to rank people and groups. However, the antidote lies in the other balls. The creation of beauty elevates the artist to equality with the scientist and dignifies emotion in addition to reason. A high value on human diversity and cultural integrity allows us to appreciate the wonderful symmetry of Dobu society and the variegated passions of its people. Only a fanatic would want to Westernize it so as to produce an additional fifty child psychologists to swell the armies of science.

It may be said that all of this has to do with conscious ratiocination. Unconsciously, the truth versus falsehood and the A versus not-A dichotomies may be at work, habituating us to make invidious distinctions, entertain thought processes something like "men are A and like truth, so women as not-A must be like falsehood." This seems pretty feeble, but if such thought processes have been at work, now that we are aware of them that should be enough to build up our resistance. Moreover, if systematic observation, and appeals to truth, and logical consistency are unconsciously corrupting, postmodernists are at risk as much as empiricists because their own work is shot through with traces of such things. When Young addressed the sad history of group conflict in Eastern Europe, she consulted colleagues from that area to determine who did what to whom and when, rather than consulting polar Eskimos. Maori in New Zealand believe that the Treaty of Waitangi has not been honored, which is to say, they argue that the Crown did in fact make certain promises to Maori and that those promises have never in fact been fulfilled. Presumably postmodernists, as much as the rest of us, would be shaken if it emerged that the Treaty was not signed as alleged but was a forgery like the Protocols of the Elders of Zion. When Yeatman criticizes Locke's concept of citizenship, she cites the text of Locke to show that his concept differs from her own. She does not ignore the law of noncontradiction; that is, she would not feel comfortable saying, "My concept is identical with both Locke and not-Locke" (Young, 1992, 20–22; Yeatman, 1992, 2).

We are left only with the last of the imagined cases against empiricism, the weaker claim that empiricists were influenced by the racist, ethnocentric, and sexist biases prevalent in the Enlightenment. This is undoubtedly true, practically everybody was, and our best hope is that the present generation will be less susceptible than its predecessors. As empiricists they ought to be: they are in the best possible position to explode the unwarranted claims made to inflate the credentials of whites or Europeans or men vis-à-vis other groups.

Thus far, humane empiricism has been on the defensive, arguing that systematic use of science does not handicap it by imposing negative value judgments foreign to its ideals. To go on the offensive, what kind of price would postmodern thinkers pay if they were to reject science, particularly social science? For example, if Young wanted to make the best possible contribution to reconciling the warring factions in Bosnia, would she feel free to go beyond chatting with colleagues who happen to be from that area, would she feel free to explore fully, no doubt with a critical eye, the history, sociology, and psychology of the groups involved, consult a Thomas Sowell who had studied these groups rather than American groups?

Must the contribution of postmodernism be limited to one speech? A speech delivered to each and every group, endless repetition of phrases about the fragility and complexity of group identity and the fact that every group defines itself in relation to other groups? No doubt groups are in flux. But certainly, the interesting thing about ethnic groups is not that all of them are temporary and changing but rather the specifics of how they differ. The really interesting questions are questions like the following. Why has Italian-American identity been more persistent than Irish-American identity? In 1941, when America took sides with England against Germany and Italy, why did the responses of Irish and German and Italian Americans differ so much? Why did some condemn American entry into World War Two and suffer persecution as a result while others did not? Or, to focus on the present, why do Chinese Americans attain elite occupations disproportionately, why do they behave like a group with a mean IQ twenty points higher than they actually have (Flynn, 1991)?

Must postmodern thinkers remain mute about such questions? They might well answer in the negative, say something like, "Of course, we are not obscurantists, of course, we would make full use of social science, it is just that we wish to warn against its possible unconscious influence on our evaluations." Fair enough, the warning has been taken to heart. That done, can we conclude that your approach becomes identical with our own, that the distinctive contribution postmodernism has to offer has been exhausted, that we can leave it behind and stand together and use social science to defend humane-egalitarian-tolerant ideals against their opponents?

EX NIHILO NIHIL FIT

Whether or not postmodernists and empiricists find the same moral and political agenda equally attractive, they are united in their rejection of ethical objectivity. Therefore, both can profit from certain conclusions of the epistemology of ethics: that the rejection of ethical objectivity does not entail humane or egalitarian or tolerant values on the one hand or nihilism on the other.

The tolerance school argument surfaces whenever sociological relativism or epistemological relativism catches the imagination and seems to pose the threat of nihilism. In our century, the best example of someone who argued in favor of tolerance on the basis of sociological relativism was Ruth Benedict. Her greatest book, *Patterns of Culture*, closes with a rejection of "absolute definitions of morality" and "categorical imperatives" but holds out the hope of "rationally selected goals." She says that social relativity should not be construed as a doctrine of despair but carries with it its own values, namely, "tolerance for coexisting and equally valid patterns of life." The implicit connecting argument appears to be: all values are sociologically relative; therefore, we have no reason to favor one value over another; therefore, we have an obligation to be tolerant and treat all values as equally valid (Benedict, 1934, chap. 8).

The argument self-destructs as soon as it is realized that an obligation to be tolerant is itself a moral principle or value and not something else, say, a turnip. Therefore, it too is sociologically relative, and, according to the terms of the argument, we have no reason to favor it over intolerance. Some may think that while tolerance is not logically entailed by sociological relativism, it is an obviously appropriate psychological reaction. But actually, the reaction depends on the person: psychology sets no limits on itself. When it breaks free of logic, it can move anywhere from appreciation of diversity and tolerance to disgust for the "primitive" and a sense of arrogant self-approval.

William James (1897, 199–210) anticipated Benedict. However, he based the tolerance school argument on epistemological relativism rather than sociological relativism, which allows its flaw to be seen with even greater clarity. The argument: there is no defensible criterion of objectivity in ethics; therefore, we cannot label certain human demands or the demands of certain people as objective, thus putting them ahead of the demands of other people; therefore, we should treat all human demands as worthy of satisfaction without reference to what they are or whose they are. Once again, the argument self-destructs, this time when it is realized that treating the demands of people in general as worthy of satisfaction, even though I hold no moral principle to that effect, is to accept the objective status of those demands. Recall what objectivity in ethics is all about: an ideal or demand has objective status if all humanity ought to respect it whether they actually find it attractive or not. Therefore, James's conclusion amounts to asserting that literally all human demands have objective status. If we lack a criterion of objectivity in ethics, we can hardly go from saying that *certain* human demands cannot be labeled as objective to saying that *all* human demands have objective status (Flynn, 1973, 68–78).

Do postmodernist thinkers reflect echoes of the tolerance school argument? I am not sure. Yeatman (1992, 7) says that different social groups generate distinct perspectives on justice, there is a Maori view and a Pakeha view but no "God's-eye view," which means that "all then that is possible" is a mutual dialogue on "how they should decide and manage their life conditions." If the assertion about the relativity of justice is supposed to logically entail mutual respect and negotiating a mutually acceptable compromise, then this is the tolerance school error. If she is assuming that both parties share an unstated moral principle, "one should respect the integrity of other groups," then it is not. As we have seen, in the absence of such a principle, what is not only logically permissible but likely is that the stronger group will dictate terms.

Young believes that the fact that two groups define themselves, after mutual interaction, as both similar and dissimilar from one another is something from which "we can *derive* (emphasis mine) a social and political ideal of togetherness in difference," later defined as a "mutual recognition" of "group related rights." Actually, there is no bridge whatsoever linking the fact that Maori and Pakeha define themselves in terms of similarities and dissimilarities with the ideal of mutual regard for one another's rights. Or at least there is no bridge unless some middle term is inserted in the argument, namely, something that asserts group equality. This could be either the tolerance school argument (group differences themselves entail valuing groups equally) or a moral principle (when confronted with differences, we ought to extend mutual regard). Since Young provides no connecting link, we are left in doubt. It is interesting that Haggis interprets Young as rejecting a "universal moral point of view" and as positing the claim that "I want" can be translated into "I am entitled to." Such a claim is operationally identical with William James's conclusion that all human demands are worthy of satisfaction. The rejection of moral objectivity is identical with James's premise. However, since no connecting link is stated, we cannot say that the middle term would be the same as James's (Young, 1992, 16 & 20; Haggis, 1992, 75).

Gatens begins by endorsing the assertions of an aboriginal Australian who rejects universalizing ethics and wants recognition of the integrity of his own way of life. She says that an ethics of difference would acknowledge "a responsibility toward differently constituted 'others' whose 'ways of life' intersect . . . with our own." What is said to "entail" that responsibility is an awareness of how we became what we are; or, alternately, it is said we are accountable for the present in the sense that we are responsible for what we choose to actualize (Gatens, 1992, 40 & 48–49).

This argument, as I understand it, is not an example of the tolerance school argument. Rather, it moves from *causal* responsibility to *moral* responsibility: the fact that Pakeha and Maori have causally interacted to create the present, a situation in which their interests are inextricably linked and not fully compatible, means that both ought to work for solutions based on mutual regard. But like the tolerance school argument, the conclusion does not follow from the premise. The fact that I am causally responsible for certain consequences does not logically entail any particular evaluation of those consequences. For example, the fact that the Pakeha's coming to New Zealand has resulted in Maori being less well off than Pakeha does not entail that Pakeha ought to rectify the situation. That fact leaves you free to be a creature of self-interest, or condemn the Maori as an inferior race, or claim that the system rewards virtue and Maori are getting justice according to whether they are upper or lower class, or that benefiting Maori is no priority of Superman, or that affirmative action is indefensible once racial bias has disappeared. It is only if you supply the connecting link of a commitment to humane-egalitarian ideals that a humane response is dictated.

Humane empiricists might want to add a few qualifications to the notion that shared history creates moral responsibilities. For example, they might reject any implication that a Pakeha should feel guilt for anyone's behavior other than his or her own and might assert that we also have obligations toward distant groups, groups who have not intersected with us, such as Jews in Nazi Germany. But these are quibbles. It is perfectly sensible to acknowledge a special responsibility for those whom our actions directly affect, the lesson Dickens teaches so well in his caricature of Mrs. Jellyby, who shamefully neglected her own children because of her obsession with Africa. The main point is that causal interaction does not entail benevolent behavior without a principle, such as that "when I affect others I should ensure that the consequences are reasonably beneficial," a principle sadly lacking when Nazis intersected with Jews.

Gatens (1992, 49–50) is correct on one point of ethical theory. She argues that postmodernism in rejecting ethical truth-tests is not logically coerced into nihilism, defined as a "desert where it is no longer possible to . . . judge anything." We have already done enough to expose the nihilist fallacy for what it is. However, we now have a new insight into its logic: it is the mirror-image of James's version of the tolerance school error. James treated all human demands as if they had passed a nonexistent truth-test; the nihilist fallacy tells us that we must treat our most cherished ideals as if they had failed a nonexistent truth-test (Flynn, 1973, 20–22 & 76–77).

Critical analysis of arguments for the postmodern agenda reinforces critical analysis of the content of that agenda. Both evidence the same important truths. There is no substitute for moral principles because without them there can be no moral dimension to human life. For those who do not simply accept the mores of their group, they can only be got, without resort to self-deception, by looking within and finding a commitment. Empiricists and postmodernists are equally likely to find an appreciation of group differences, just so long as they have humane proclivities and have immersed themselves in the histories of various groups. Neither are going to get any moral principles from a moral vacuum, such as rejection of ethical objectivity, or from facts that in themselves are devoid of moral implications. The Angelic Doctor (St. Thomas) puts it without waste of words: ex nihilo nihil fit—from nothing nothing comes.

A RECRUITING PAMPHLET

I have no desire to put the tolerance school argument or an argument from causal to moral responsibility in the mouth of anyone who would reject them. Nonetheless, the arguments of Yeatman and Young and Gatens are either flawed or circular. They are either examples of arguments whose flaws have been identified by ethical theory or rest on a suppressed premise that endorses tolerance as a moral principle, which is to say that they assume what the argument is trying to prove.

The ambiguity of these arguments is not accidental. Principles not openly acknowledged cannot be openly argued for. At best, arguments are implied and therefore not refined by critical analysis, which maximizes the chance of error. At worst, you simply refuse to argue for your principles at all. These postmodernists may think better of the option of no argumentation than I do and may claim to have chosen it. They might say that the passages I have cited were not arguments for principles but rather affirmations of principle, that is, statements as to what their humane principles dictate concerning the negotiation of group differences. Granted that if no arguments have been offered, then accusations of circularity or any other defect of argument do not apply. However, the option of no argumentation is a very bad one. It leaves postmodernism in a posture of unilateral disarmament as far as moral debate is concerned, which could tip the balance toward those antihumane opponents who hold its moral and political agenda in contempt.

Humane empiricism affirms its ideals openly, argues for them unambiguously, and has no reluctance about making full use of logic and social science to defend them. Empiricism works in moral debate not because there is some kind of logical bridge from facts to values (there is none such) but because there are a thousand bridges from values to facts. This is clearly true of racists who value one race so much that they cannot help making spurious factual claims about the others. But it is also true of all political actors, including ourselves. Wishing everyone well, we spin factual hypotheses about what kind of society might reduce environmental inequality and privilege to a tolerable minimum. All of these bridging hypotheses, the hypotheses that link values with facts, can be tested against logic and science. That is where the real battle is joined: showing racists that they distort facts about the distribution of human traits; showing Sumner that his sociology and ethics conflict; showing Cattell the psychological tension between his desire to save the human species (from meteorites) and his desire to supplant it by an alien species; showing Nietzsche that caste and merit conflict; showing Americans that the case for affirmative action is not dependent on the existence of racial bias; showing Herrnstein and Murray that their scenario for meritocracy is psychologically and sociologically incoherent.

The defense of humane ideals needs every humane thinker down on the playing field, rather than half our comrades off in the hills, building bonfires to celebrate the demise of the Enlightenment and dancing by the light of the moon. This chapter has been a recruiting pamphlet directed at those whose depth of humane commitment is beyond doubt and who would make valuable allies. It can be reduced to a single sentence: throw the tolerance ball high, but do not neglect the other five; try on the powerful spectacles of ethical theory and social science before shutting your eyes against the clarifying vision they afford.

CONCLUSION

UNSOLVED PROBLEMS

10

The Personal and the Conventional

A word or two before we go concerning risks and unsolved problems. The risks of an empirical approach to defending humane-egalitarian ideals are obvious. What if the tide of evidence turns against us on some issue dear to our hearts, for example, the genetic equality of black and white? Myopia or nearsightedness is caused by a single gene that controls the shape of the eyeball. There is evidence that the gene responsible also has some positive influence on intelligence, and the frequency of myopia varies between racial groups. Jensen (1998, 149–150 & 487–489) hopes that the mapping of the human genome (genetic structure) will identify the genes that influence intelligence, that the gene frequencies between races can be determined, and that this will simply settle the debate about whether different races have differing potentials for intelligence.

Humane ideals have a capacity to face up to reality that most of our opponents lack. Even if blacks were proved inferior as a group, in the sense that only the upper 25 percent of blacks overlapped with the upper 50 percent of whites, the consequences would not be fatal. Humane ideals would survive because their champions could still ask, How can the handicaps of group membership be minimized? Affirmative action would still be on the agenda because so long as the merits of individuals are ignored because of their group membership, it is irrelevant why their group is devalued. It makes no difference whether the group's unfavorable social statistics are the result of environment only or of genes as well. Humanists could still ask, Whatever the make-up of a particular society, what will reduce inequality to more acceptable levels, and how can privilege be curtailed? Contrast this with the classical racist who must believe that every black is inferior to every white and whose whole world collapses under the weight of falsifying evidence.

Moral debate may give humane ideals an advantage, but this does not mean it can solve all important moral problems. Besting Nietzsche yields no tidy solution to just when abortion can be justified or what public policy about it should be. Two unsolved problems stand out because of the fundamental challenge they pose, not only for those who hold humane ideals but also for those who hold any moral principles whatsoever. One of these is familiar, the trade-offs that constitute the six-balls problem; the other is new, the problem of eroscentrism. The latter is best introduced through a discussion of its parent, the problem of egoism.

Egoism and eroscentrism differ in that egoism has no genuine moral dimension. All real-world people with pretensions to egoism would grant this; that is, they do not claim that their interests somehow deserve to come ahead of those of everyone else. Rather, they consider morality a sham some people are foolish enough to take seriously. If egoists were to state the primacy of their own interests as a moral principle, they would encounter difficulties. It is not that such a moral principle cannot be universalized in terms of bare logical consistency: an egoist would certainly praise anyone, not just him or herself, who accepted that his or her demands deserved to come ahead of those of all humankind. But the moral principle, "I deserve to come ahead of all humankind just because I am me," extracts the same price as pure color racism. The color racist, it will be recalled, ignores all the traits people actually use to assess one another (intelligence, humor, courage, honesty, and so forth) in favor of color alone, like the book reviewer who judges books purely on the color of the binding, never discussing character or plot. Moralistic egoism does the same: it tells all humanity that they should ignore the traits they normally use to assess people out of respect for the fact that I am me. Rather than pay such a price, better to give up moral claims entirely.

Claims that look like moralistic egoism are exceptions that prove the rule. Nero claimed that all his subjects should put his demands first, but not because his proper name was Nero, or because he had a unique physiognomy, or because he was born at a certain instant at a certain place, that is, not because of the trivia that singled him out as an individual. He said that Living Gods deserved to come ahead of mere mortals and claimed that he was the sole existent Living God, a claim that would have been rather easy to falsify once the criteria of divinity were spelled out. When believers in the invisible hand commend everyone acting on enlightened self-interest, they do not do so because that has moral dignity in itself. Rather, they argue that, thanks to the magic of the market, private selfishness is the best means toward an altruistic end, namely, the general prosperity and the general happiness. In sum, a moral dimension always involves either a claim to superiority that is in principle impersonal or a regard for the welfare of a group that transcends the individual.

The lack of a moral dimension engenders the standard refutations of egoism along the lines that the life-strategy of seeking self-interest will not really maximize self-interest. People who always put their own needs ahead of others cannot forge rewarding human relationships and, therefore, will live a socially isolated existence without friendship or loved ones. They can pretend a willingness to make sacrifices on behalf of others, but intimates will sense the falsity of the pretense. Moreover, sooner or later, a situation will occur in which self-interest and altruism conflict, and the egoists will be found wanting. It is here that the eroscentrist makes an appearance. He or she would seize on our indictment of egoism and turn it against us as follows: "You rightly emphasize that the circle of love makes life worthwhile, but does it make sense to put any moral obligations ahead of one's loved ones? I would sacrifice the lives of a million anonymous strangers to save one of my own children. I have no problem universalizing that assessment because I would expect anyone else to do the same. Indeed, there is something obscene about someone who honors obligations to humanity in general above the bonds of love. Love alone makes sense of morality. Anything else is a cold abstraction totally foreign to my nature."

It is important to understand eroscentrism. The eroscentrist is not saying that love tempts us to decide against larger obligations out of moral weakness but rather that it is morally right to do so, that the circle of love is the very foundation of morality. What obligations are recognized beyond that circle will vary, all the way from no obligations, to obligations always to be overridden when the well-being of loved ones is at stake, to obligations to be overridden except when the price in general suffering is huge, say, requires sacrificing ten million anonymous strangers to save one's own child. Two lines of criticism are possible, but neither carries much conviction.

First, we might try a variant on our argument against the egotist, namely, that the kind of person whose commitments are largely or wholly confined to a few misses out on a larger happiness enjoyed by those committed to humanity in general. This would be a sort of Aristotelian argument: a contention that eudaemonia attends an optimum road of human development inclusive of a larger generosity of spirit. This argument fails on one level because, even if true, it does not deny that eroscentrists can be happy, only that they fall short of realizing human nature's full potential for happiness. To people socialized within a tight circle, the notion that they should become virtuosos of happiness by denying their socialization would seem absurd. But on a more fundamental level, it totally misconstrues the nature of eroscentrism. Eroscentrists really do take morality seriously: they are not concerned with trying to maximize personal happiness; they really do believe that moral obligations lie primarily within the circle of love. Therefore, to tell them to compromise those obligations for the sake of an incremental gain in happiness is no more than an effort to tempt them away from the path of moral rectitude.

Second, we could argue that if everyone discriminated radically in favor of loved ones, the larger society that nourishes those loved ones would wither away. At a minimum, the eroscentrist can answer along the lines of Glaucon's use of the fable of the ring. Since no obligations beyond a circle of loved ones would mean a war of every small group against every other, you acknowledge some such, but only as a resented necessity having nothing to do with true morality. However, eroscentrism can go beyond such a grudging reply by drawing a distinction between self-sacrifice and the sacrifice of loved ones. Men and women can value their larger society and even act on a sense of obligation to risk their lives in a war for national survival. Eroscentrism does not forbid such behavior so long as the primacy of the circle of love is recognized. It would be wrong to leave one's children bereft of their parents. But regard for loved ones need not be carried to extremes, for example, young men or women eschewing self-sacrifice simply because their demise would cause sorrow for family and friends. Finally, eroscentrists can always count on the existence of noneroscentrists who reject their strictures on wider obligations. Unlike racism, or Social Darwinism, or Cattell's Beyondism, or humane-egalitarianism, eroscentrism has no proselytizing impetus. Its focus is not on converting all humanity to eroscentrism but on the needs of one's loved ones.

The reason that eroscentrism poses such a difficult problem is that it resonates in us all. It is not that we think it odd to extend moral obligations beyond the circle of love—every humane person does that. I never much liked the dour Bible-quoting Scandinavian Americans of rural Minnesota but thought they deserved something better than to be crucified when the tin mines gave out. Many Pakeha with little love for Maori culture hold moral principles that dictate state aid to help Maori preserve that culture. Kant feels we have moral obligations to all rational creatures, although he has trouble believing that people of good taste could love very many people, and, as he says, certainly sympathy with creatures like us is a sentiment we cannot presuppose in God (Kant, *Critique of Practical Reason*, AK. V, 35). However, even thoroughly humane people give some priority to love over wider obligations. None of us would sacrifice a million anonymous strangers for one loved one, but most of us would sacrifice ten or a hundred. Indeed, as Simon (1951, 41–42) has emphasized, human society would be an emotional desert if everyone became the kind of person who could easily will the death of a child because of principle. Therefore, every society develops conventions that sanction the primacy of personal ties to some degree. Middle-class parents are allowed to help their children with projects and homework, buy them books and electronic libraries, hire tutors for them, read over their M.A. theses and discuss the coherence of the argument. They are allowed to do a thousand things that help their children get the credentials needed to secure jobs and a good life, things that many working-class parents simply cannot do. The result is that, particularly in times of heavy unemployment, working-class children lose out and suffer from idleness and despair. Anyone with any imagination can think of other examples. To use humane-egalitarian morality to forbid these things would be to ignore Aristotle's dictum against moralities that require heroic virtue as the norm.

So humane morality has a place for eroscentrism. But what do we say when people carry it far beyond anything we can countenance? When the wife of a Ceausescu actively props up a regime that blights the lives of millions because of her fear, quite legitimate, that the conflagration of bringing it down would threaten her children's liberty and survival. When an advertising executive, too old to secure another well-paid post, promotes smoking in order to earn the money to send her daughter to Harvard. Certainly, everyone with a humane commitment wants to win an ideal debate with those who carry eroscentrism to these extremes. Yet our agenda for moral debate is helpless: their position is logically coherent; I can see no bridge between their values and social reality that science can falsify. It looks as if the line drawn between eroscentrism and wider obligations must be purely personal. Each of us can only look within and say, "No, that is too much, even for the sake of those I love more than anything else in the world." The disappointment is not that we must look within (we must do that for all of our ideals), the disappointment is that we have no evidential case against those who look within and find something we loathe.

The problem of the six balls is easily solved if you elevate one ball to act as a criterion to prioritize the other five. The temptation to do this is strong, as evidenced by the fact that both humane and antihumane thinkers have taken that option. Utilitarians choose the greatest happiness ball, even though they must then twist and turn to explain why one innocent person should not suffer much to afford a slight rise in the happiness of many. Kant chose the justice ball and rejected the slightest mitigation of punishment even if such would reform the criminal and afford wider benevolent consequences. Nietzsche may have flirted with choosing beauty (note that his list of proto-supermen is dominated by artists and omits the great names of science and mathematics). Milgram exalted the pursuit of truth to the point of degrading his subjects: he tested hypotheses about respect for authority by using authority figures to get subjects to give what they thought might be fatal electric shocks. Cattell chose the perfection of human nature, with the consequence that he endorsed suffering and injustice for humanity in general, just so long as this would speed evolution into a higher species. Some postmodern thinkers elevate tolerance to the point that they are helpless to condemn a society that practices female circumcision (Kant, *Metaphysics of Morals*, AK. VI, 331; Nietzsche, *Beyond Good and Evil*, secs. 199–200, 224, 245, 252–256, & 269; Patten, 1977).

The description of the consequences of the above choices, plus the analysis of previous chapters, should discourage humane thinkers from elevating one ball. Even when done by the utilitarians, or Kant, or humane postmodernists, this robs humane ideals of their rich diversity. The only way to preserve a full-bodied humanism is to retain the freedom to make trade-offs between great goods when they conflict. Thus far, the examples given of trade-offs have been mainly intersocietal: the example of the Allied occupation of postwar Germany, where a balance had to be struck between bringing every last person guilty of complicity with the Nazis to justice and benevolent goals like feeding the hungry and reconstructing a social order, or the example of eliminating female circumcision in a preindustrial society, despite the inevitable cultural trauma that attends altering a central social practice.

However, there are plenty of less dramatic cases on the local or professional levels, for example, whether to allocate a lot of money to relocate the municipal art gallery (the beauty ball) even though there never seems to be enough money for public housing (the utilitarian ball). Or take an academic department that controls a fund that has been accumulating capital. One professor proposes a scholarship for a former student, highly intelligent, who has a unique opportunity to pursue postgraduate study only if financial support is available immediately. Another is outraged that there is no time to publicize the award so that all former students can apply. How do we balance the fact that publicity is unlikely to elicit a more worthy case, and that a chance to do the most good will be missed, against the unfairness of a covert award?

Unless such trade-offs are to be made on a personal basis, an overriding criterion is needed to say when benevolence should give way to justice, or tolerance to benevolence, and so forth. What would something have to look like in order to play that role? First, it would have to have a certain breadth. It would have to be a criterion of value broad enough to cover all the diverse kinds of good represented by the six balls, that is, benevolence, justice, the integrity of truth, the majesty of beauty, the ideal of making people less imperfect, the wonderful diversity of which human nature is capable. The breadth needed gives it a striking resemblance to Plato's concept of the Chief Good, which had to be broad enough to cover all the diverse goods in the World of Forms. The fact that the concept of the Chief Good proved bankrupt (chapter 2) is discouraging. Second, it would have to have a peculiar content. On the one hand, its content would have to be nonpartisan vis-à-vis the six balls, that is, not dominated by either benevolence or justice or truth or beauty. On the other hand, its content would have to be "partisan enough" to discriminate in favor of one ball over another when handing down decisions. The resemblance to the contradiction that bedevils ethical truth-tests is obvious. And even if it could be found, would its content not duplicate the darker side of truth-tests? If, like them, it must provide overriding reasons for calling acts good, once again we would find ourselves unable to say something was good simply because it was benevolent, or just, or productive of truth, or productive of beauty.

Aristotle's solution to the problem of the conflict of great goods was pragmatic. Be happy if you live in a humane society whose conventions govern the trade-offs and if most of you find those conventions personally acceptable. The Aristotelian solution works best in a time of stability rather than in a time of flux. The conventions of modern technological society alter at too fast a pace, leaving us with many conscious trade-offs, all being fought out in the political arena. The only pragmatic solution for a time of flux is to write utopian literature. In his utopian novel *Island*, Aldous Huxley (1962) attempts to maximize the correlation of benevolence with justice, with the pursuit of truth, with human diversity, with the perfection of human nature, culminating in everyone having the introverted mystical experience. He grants that the creation of beauty might suffer. Perhaps someone happy and perfect could not write Beethoven's music or Shakespeare's plays because these may require a tortured psyche. But he sees no reason why the more tranquil forms of great art should not survive and argues that since the package so fully realizes humane ideals, some sacrifice of the beauty ball is acceptable. If he is correct, if we can imagine an ideal society whose conventions create a way of life acceptable to the judge that resides within each humane person, then utopian literature can provide a substitute for Aristotle. We can use our ideal society as a pattern laid up in heaven, as something whose conventions anticipate the trade-offs we encounter in our actual society, as something that can impose order on change and guide us to minimally acceptable solutions.

However, conventions that seek the endorsement of humane people on a person-to-person basis can never satisfy a philosopher. No philosopher will ever feel that convention can compare with a principle that can be stated, clarified, and assessed, ideally in the light of impersonal reason. If anyone can shatter my pessimistic analysis of the possibility of an overriding criterion that can balance the six balls, his or her contribution will be more than welcome.

Is there any palliative that can mitigate our sense of failure? There is this: our inability to solve the problems of eroscentrism and the six balls confers no advantage over ourselves on our ideological opponents because they will be equally disturbed and impotent. Trade-offs between the six balls will surface within a community no matter how it is delineated, that is, they will surface within the white race, or the middle classes, or supermen. Unless antihumane ideologues take one ball, as Cattell did with human perfection and as Nietzsche tended to do with beauty, and elevate it into the arbiter of all the rest, they will have no solution to offer. And even if they do that, they gain no real advantage because, as we have seen, they thereby exchange a rich diversity of ideals for a suffocating uniformity. That is a price to which they are welcome. In addition, they have no unique flexibility: any humane ideologue who thinks the exchange worthwhile can elevate one ball, just as easily as the antihumane. Anyone tempted to do so, however, should recall what happened to Kant's ethics when he elevated the justice ball.

As for eroscentrists, who limit their moral obligations to the circle of loved ones or put all other ideals below those obligations, they are as impervious to antihumane ideals as they are to humane ones. They will put their loved ones not only ahead of concern about humankind in general but also ahead of the historic mission of the German people, or rewarding the virtues of the middle classes, or a meritocracy of supermen, or sacrificing our species to produce a higher one. All of these ideals will seem bloodless to eroscentrists because none make a claim on their affections comparable to their loves, and all deny center stage to the emotion they consider the only relevant foundation for ethics. Such people will sacrifice the lives of thousands of their fellow Germans for the sake of one of their own children, refuse to label their child unfit because of lack of thrift, see Napoleon die rather than their partner, use a World Research Center veto to prevent a failed group from being phased out if that group includes one of their own.

Another palliative: if the only solution to the six-balls problem would have to be something akin to an ethical truth-test, and if the only solution to eroscentrism would have to be literally an ethical truth-test, then we have learned something about the darker side of that. Self-imposed duties, rather than duties imposed by an alien criterion of moral rectitude, are at least our very own. And would we really be happy if the great problems of ethics were all solved and our generation had nothing to do but work out the applications? What drama can match a voyage of discovery that reveals whether or not the ideals we find within can survive honest confrontation with the truths of logic and social science? Every one of us can say along with Stephen Dedalus, "I go to encounter for the millionth time the reality of experience and to forge in the smithy of my soul the uncreated conscience of my race."

A summary to make an end. The central themes of this book can be stated in ten sentences. From time immemorial, concealed behind the search for ethical objectivity or some kind of moral reality, there has existed an agenda that structures moral and political debate. No committed person of any persuasion has ever refused to argue over its items because doing so forfeits prices too great to bear; arguing over it brings into play another set of prices that can be devastating. All of us, whether postmodern or empiricist, should conduct an ideal debate that uses that agenda to test ideals, whether humane or antihumane. Our opponents suffer from a disadvantage: either they take some existing race or class or other group and inflate its virtues, or they posit an ideal elite whose members they cannot identify. Therefore, we can use logic and social science against them. However, no matter what points we score, we can never tell them that they ought to accept humane ideals. The only hope of converting them is by inculcating a commitment to humane ideals, and the only hope of doing that is by praxis or following the example set by Martin Luther King Jr. Although we have escaped the darker side of ethical truth-tests and preserved our ideals as a source of reasons for the moral rectitude of acts, we must give up the universalist language ethics has hitherto employed. At present, neither we nor our opponents can solve some serious problems, problems like eroscentrism and the six-balls problem. Humane utopian literature can do something to make the task of juggling the six balls more bearable.

Before saying good-bye forever to ethical truths, honesty and civility dictate acknowledging the thinkers who struggled so hard to create them for us. The passion that drove them is not foreign to ourselves. When racism and sexism and cruelty and false pretensions to superiority, all so prevalent, choke us with moral indignation, anything less than the categorical ought seems absurd: that all-embracing rational ought that activates a moral ought that "commands" everyone to make the world a little bit better. And yet we cannot suppress the knowledge that ethical truth involves a deception that diminishes the intellect and a logic that diminishes our ideals. Torn between our hearts and our heads, ethics will always be a kind of tragedy. The millennia cannot weaken the tie that binds us to Plato if only because, right at the beginning, his genius tried to write a happier ending. So we go on boats against the current, beating back ceaselessly into the past.

References

A NOTE ON CITATIONS OF PLATO, KANT, NIETZSCHE, AND OTHER GREATS

The citations of these thinkers allow the reader to use any available current edition or translation. All citations of Plato (*The Republic, Phaedrus, Timaeus, Meno, Phaedo, Parmenides, Sophist,* and *Statesman*) refer to the relevant dialogue and the pages of the standard medieval edition, whose page numbers are duplicated in every respectable current edition. They are always put in the margins of the text rather than at the top or bottom.

The Akademie edition is the standard edition of Kant's works. Almost all of my citations (*Critique of Practical Reason, The Groundwork of the Metaphysics of Morals, The Metaphysics of Morals*) refer to its volumes and pages. These too are duplicated in every respectable current edition. Those who lack German, as I do, will easily find English translations of all of Kant's works except *The Metaphysics of Morals*. It is divided into prefatory material (preface to Part I, introduction), Part I on justice, and Part II on virtue. For the prefatory material and Part I, see John Ladd (Trans.), (1965), *The metaphysical elements of justice*, New York: Liberal Arts Press; for Part II, see James Ellington (Trans.) and Warner Wick (Ed.), (1964), *The metaphysical principles of virtue*, New York: Liberal Arts Press. The only exceptions to citing the Akademie edition are the essay on benevolent lying, for which the reference is to Abbott, the only English translation, and the *Lectures on Ethics*, for which the reference is to Infield for the same reason.

When citing Nietzsche (*Beyond Good and Evil, The Genealogy of Morals, Thus Spoke Zarathustra, Twilight of the Idols,* and *Human, All-Too-Human*), I utilize his division of his books into sections. The sections range from a few lines to a few paragraphs, and they are either titled or numbered. Sometimes the number sequence runs throughout the work. Sometimes it terminates and begins again as you go from one larger unit to another, for example, from the preface of *The Genealogy of Morals* to the First Essay, to the Second Essay, to the Third Essay. I use Nietzsche's units of internal organization rather than citing pages because the latter would be peculiar to a particular edition. I follow the same procedure in chapter 9 when citing St. Thomas Aquinas, *Summa Theologica*; Thomas Hobbes, *Leviathan*; and Bishop George Berkeley, *Principles of Human Knowledge* and *Three Dialogues Between Hylus and Philonous*.

WORKS CITED

Abbott, K. (1927). On a supposed right to lie from benevolent motives. In *Kant's theory of ethics* (6th ed., pp. 361–365). London: Longmans. (Original work published 1909)

Benedict, R. (1934). *Patterns of culture*. Boston: Houghton-Mifflin.

Berger, J. (1987, June 19). *New York Times News Service*.

Brink, D. O. (1989). *Moral realism and the foundations of ethics*. Cambridge: Cambridge University Press.

Broadie, A., & Pybus, E. M. (1974). Kant's treatment of animals. *Philosophy, 49*, 375–383.

Burt, C. (1959). Class differences in general intelligence: III. *British Journal of Statistical Psychology, 12*, 15–33.

Burt, C. (1961). Intelligence and social mobility. *British Journal of Statistical Psychology, 14*, 3–24.

Cattell, R. B. (1938). *Psychology and the religious quest*. London: Thomas Nelson.

Cattell, R. B. (1972). *A new morality from science: Beyondism*. Elmsford NY: Pergamon.

Cattell, R. B. (1987). *Beyondism: Religion from science*. New York: Praeger.

Charles, N., & Coleman, C. (1995, September). Crime suspect. *Emerge*, 24–30.

Davie, M. R. (Ed.). (1940). *Sumner today: Selected essays of William GrahamSumner, with comments by American leaders*. New Haven: Yale University Press. All citations of Davie refer to Sumner's own words, not to commentaries on Sumner.

Dawidowicz, L. S. (1976). *The war against the Jews, 1933–1945*. New York: Bantam Books.

Diamond, J. (1991). *The rise and fall of the third chimpanzee*. London: Radius.

Dickens, W. T. (1999). Rebuilding urban labor markets: What community development can accomplish. In R. F. Ferguson & W. T. Dickens (Eds.), *Urban problems and community development* (pp. 381–485). Washington DC: Brookings Institution Press.

Dougherty, S. J. (1983). *William Graham Sumner and Social Darwinism*. Dunedin, New Zealand: B.A. honors thesis, Department of Political Studies, University of Otago.

Dykstra, V. H. (1955). The place of reason in ethics. *Review of Metaphysics, 8,* 458–467.

Ezorsky, G. (1991). *Racism and justice: The case for affirmative action*. Ithaca NY: Cornell University Press.

Farley, R. (1995). *State of the union: America in the 1990s*. New York: Russell Sage Foundation.

Flynn, J. R. (1973). *Humanism and ideology: An Aristotelian view*. London: Routledge.

Flynn, J. R. (1976). The realm of the moral. *American Philosophical Quarterly, 24,* 273–286.

Flynn, J. R. (1979). Kant and the price of a justification. *Kant-Studien, 70,* 279–311.

Flynn, J. R. (1980). *Race, IQ, and Jensen*. London: Routledge.

Flynn, J. R. (1984). The mean IQ of Americans: Massive gains 1932 to 1978. *Psychological Bulletin, 95,* 29–51.

Flynn, J. R. (1986). The logic of Kant's derivation of freedom from reason: An alternative reading to Paton. *Kant-Studien, 77,* 441–446.

Flynn, J. R. (1987a). Flynn replies to Nichols. In S. Modgil & C. Modgil (Eds.), *Arthur Jensen: Consensus and controversy* (pp. 234–235). Lewes, Sussex: Falmer Press.

Flynn, J. R. (1987b). Massive IQ gains in 14 nations: What IQ tests really measure. *Psychological Bulletin, 101,* 171–191.

Flynn, J. R. (1987c). Race and IQ: Jensen's case refuted. In S. Modgil & C. Modgil (Eds.), *Arthur Jensen: Consensus and controversy* (pp. 221–232). Lewes, Sussex: Falmer Press.

Flynn, J. R. (1987d). The ontology of intelligence. In J. Forge (Ed.), *Measurement, realism, and objectivity* (pp. 1–40). Dordrecht, Netherlands: Reidel.

Flynn, J. R. (1989). Rushton, evolution, and race: An essay on intelligence and virtue. *Psychologist, 2,* 363–366.

Flynn, J. R. (1990). Explanation, evaluation, and a rejoinder to Rushton. *Psychologist, 3,* 199–200.

Flynn, J. R. (1991). *Asian Americans: Achievement beyond IQ.* Hillsdale NJ: Erlbaum.

Flynn, J. R. (1992a). Cultural distance and the limitations of IQ. In J. Lynch, C. Modgil, & S. Modgil (Eds.), *Education for cultural diversity: Convergence and divergence* (pp. 343–360). London: Falmer Press.

Flynn, J. R. (1992b). Flynn replies to Lynn. In J. Lynch, C. Modgil, & S. Modgil (Eds.), *Education for cultural diversity: Convergence and divergence* (pp. 378–382). London: Falmer Press.

Flynn, J. R. (1994). IQ gains over time. In R. J. Sternberg (Ed.), *The encyclopedia of human intelligence* (pp. 617–623). New York: Macmillan.

Flynn, J. R. (1998). IQ gains over time: Toward finding the causes. In U. Neisser (Ed.), *The rising curve: Long term gains in IQ and related measures* (pp. 25–66). Washington DC: American Psychologoical Association.

Flynn, J. R. (1999). Searching for justice: The discovery of IQ gains over time. *American Psychologist, 54,* 5–20.

Flynn, J. R. (in press). IQ gains over time: Intelligence, race, and meritocracy. In S. Durlauf, K. Arrow, & S. Bowles (Eds.), *Meritocracy and equality.* Princeton NJ: Princeton University Press.

Fromm, E. (1941). *Escape from freedom.* New York: Holt, Rinehart & Winston.

Fromm, E. (1955). *The sane society.* New York: Rinehart.

Gatens, M. (1992). Embodiment, ethics, and difference. *Political Theory Newsletter, 4,* 39–50.

Gauthier, D. (1986). *Morals by agreement.* Oxford: Clarendon Press.

Gewirth, A. (1978). *Reason and morality.* Chicago: University of Chicago Press.

Gewirth, A. (1984). Replies to my critics. In E. Regis (Ed.), *Gewirth's ethical rationalism: Critical essays with a reply by Alan Gewirth* (pp. 192–255). Chicago: University of Chicago Press.

Glazer, N., & Moynihan, D. P. (1970). *Beyond the melting pot* (2nd ed.). Cambridge: MIT Press.

Granovetter, E. M. (1974). *Getting a job: A study of contacts and careers.* Cambridge: Harvard University Press.

Haggis, J. (1992). The politics of difference. *Political Theory Newsletter, 4,* 70–78.

Handlin, O. (1951). *The uprooted.* New York: Grosset & Dunlap.

Hare, R. M. (1963). *Freedom and reason.* London: Oxford University Press.

Hare, R. M. (1973). Rawl's theory of justice. *Philosophical Quarterly, 23,* 241–252.

Harman, G. (1977). *The nature of morality: An introduction to ethics.* New York: Oxford University Press.

Herrnstein, R. J., & Murray, C. (1994). *The bell curve: Intelligence and class structure in American life.* New York: Free Press.

Hindelang, M. J. (1978). Race and involvement in common law personal crimes. *American Sociological Review, 43,* 93–109.

Hitler, A. (1943). *Mein Kampf,* R. Manheim (Trans.). Boston: Houghton-Mifflin.

Hofstadter, R. (1959). *Social Darwinism in American thought* (rev. ed.). New York: Braziller.

Huxley, A. (1962). *Island.* London: Chatto & Windus.

Infield, L. (Trans). (1930). *Lectures on ethics* (Kant's "unpublished" lectures). London: Methuen.

James, W. (1897). The moral philosopher and the moral life. In *The will to believe and other essays in popular philosophy* (pp. 184–215). New York: Longmans. (Original work published in *International Journal of Ethics* [1891, April])

Jensen, A. R. (1998). *The g factor.* Westport CT: Praeger.

Jonsen, A. R., & Toulmin, S. E. (1988). *The abuse of casuistry: A history of moral reasoning.* Berkeley: University of California Press.

Kane, T. J. (1998). Racial and ethnic preferences in college admissions. In C. Jencks & M. Phillips (Eds.), *The black-white test score gap* (pp. 431–456). Washington DC: Brookings Institution Press.

Kasinitz, P., & Rosenberg, J. (1996). Missing the connection: Social isolation and employment on the Brooklyn waterfront. *Social Problems, 3,* 180–196.

Kaufmann, W. (1954). Thus Spoke Zarathustra, First Part, Editor's Note No. 7, On

Reading and Writing. In W. Kaufmann (Ed.), *The portable Nietzsche*. New York: Viking Press.

Kaufmann, W. (1962). *Nietzsche: Philosopher, psychologist, antichrist* (7th ed.). New York: World Publishing Company.

Kavka, G. (1986). *Hobbesian moral and political theory*. Princeton NJ: Princeton University Press.

Keller, A. G., & Davie, M. R. (Eds.). (1969). *Essays of William Graham Sumner* (Vols. I & II). Hamden CT: Anchor Books. All citations of Keller & Davie refer to Sumner's own words, not to editorial comment.

Kirschenman, J., & Neckerman, K. M. (1991). "We'd love to hire them, but . . . ": The meaning of race for employers. In C. Jencks & P. E. Peterson (Eds.), *The urban underclass* (pp. 203–232). Washington DC: Brookings Institution Press.

Kirschenman, J., et al. (1996). *Space as a signal, space as a barrier: How employers map and use space in four metropolitan labor markets*. Unpublished paper prepared for the Social Science History Association Meetings, October 1996.

Landes, J. B. (1992). Rethinking Habermas's public sphere. *Political Theory Newsletter*, 4, 51–69.

Levin, M. (circa 1991). *Responses to race differences in crime*. Unpublished manuscript.

Light, I. H. (1972). *Ethnic enterprise in America: Business and welfare among Chinese, Japanese, and black*. Berkeley: University of California Press.

Livingston, J. C. (1979). *Fair game? Inequality and affirmative action*. San Francisco: Freeman.

Mackie, J. (1951). The place of reason in ethics. *Australasian Journal of Philosophy*, 29, 114–124.

Mackie, J. (1977). *Ethics: Inventing right and wrong*. New York: Penguin.

Mascie-Taylor, C. G. N. (1995). Intelligence and social mobility. In N. J. Mackintosh (Ed.), *Cyril Burt: Fraud or framed?* (pp. 70–94). London: Oxford University Press.

Moore, G. E. (1903). *Principia ethica*. London: Cambridge University Press.

Morgan, G. A. (1965). *What Nietzsche means*. New York: Harper & Row. (Original work published 1941)

Mounce, H. O. (1970). *Moral practices*. London: Routledge.

Nakhnikian, G. (1959). An explanation of Toulmin's analytical ethics. *Philosophical Quarterly*, 9, 59–79.

Nielsen, K. (1957a). Justification and moral reasoning. *Methodos*, 9, 77–109.

Nielsen, K. (1957b). The functions of moral discourse. *Philosophical Quarterly*, 7, 236–248.

Nielsen, K. (1958). Good reasons in ethics. *Theoria*, 24, 9–28.

Nielsen, K. (1964). The good reasons approach revisited. *Archiv für Rechts und Sozialphilosophie*, 50, 455–484.

Nielsen, K. (1973). *Ethics without God*. London: Pemberton.

Nielsen, K. (1984). Against ethical rationalism. In E. Regis (Ed.), *Gewirth's ethical rationalism: Critical essays with a reply by Alan Gewirth* (pp. 59–83). Chicago: University of Chicago Press.

Nielsen, K. (1985). *Equality and liberty: A defense of radical egalitarianism*. Totawa NJ: Rowman & Allanheld.

Nielsen, K. (1989). *Marxism and the moral point of view*. Boulder CO: Westview Press.

Nielsen, K. (1994). How to proceed in social philosophy: Contextual justice and wide reflective equilibrium. *Queen's Law Journal*, 70, 89–137.

Oakeshott, M. (1962). *Rationalism in politics and other essays*. London: Methuen.

Olmsted, F. L. (1969). *The cotton kingdom*. New York: Modern Library.

O'Regan, K. M. (1993). The effect of social networks and concentrated poverty on black and Hispanic youth unemployment. *Annals of Regional Science*, 27, 327–342.

Organization for Economic Cooperation and Development (1999). OECD *surveys 1998–99: New Zealand. Appendix: Basic statistics, international comparisons, gross domestic product per capita*. Paris: OECD.

Paton, H. J. (1954). An alleged right to lie: A problem in Kantian ethics. *Kant-Studien*, 45, 190–203.

Paton, H. J. (1967). *The categorical imperative* (6th ed.). London: Hutchinson.

Patten, S. C. (1977). Milgram's shocking experiments. *Philosophy, 52*, 425–440.

Persons, S. (Ed.). (1963). *Social Darwinism: Selected essays of William Graham Sumner*. Englewood Cliffs NJ: Prentice-Hall. All citations of Persons refer to Sumner's own words, not to editorial comment.

Popper, K. (1945). *The open society and its enemies*. London: Routledge.

Prange, G. W. (Ed.). (1944). *Hitler's words*. Washington DC: American Council on Public Affairs.

Rawls, J. (1972). *A theory of justice*. London: Oxford University Press.

Rawls, J. (1985). Justice as fairness: Political not metaphysical. *Philosophy and Public Affairs, 14*, 223–251.

Regis, E. (Ed.). (1984). *Gewirth's ethical rationalism: Critical essays with a reply by Alan Gewirth*. Chicago: University of Chicago Press.

Rhees, R. (1965). Some developments in Wittgenstein's view of ethics. *Philosophical Review, 74*, 17–26.

Rushton, J. P. (1988). Race differences in behaviour: A review and evolutionary analysis. *Personality and Individual Differences, 9*, 1009–1024.

Russell, B. (1912). *The problems of philosophy*. Home University Library. The most accessible edition is London: Oxford University Press, 1967.

Russell, B. (1946). *History of Western philosophy*. London: Allen & Unwin.

Sacksteader, W. (1951–1952) [Review of the book *An examination of the place of reason in ethics*]. *Ethics, 62*, 217–219.

Shannon, D. A. (1960). *The great depression*. Englewood Cliffs NJ: Prentice-Hall.

Sharp, A. (1992). Representing *Justice and the Maori*: On why it ought not to be construed as a postmodern text. *Political Theory Newsletter, 4*, 27–38.

Simon, Y. R. (1951). *Philosophy of democratic government*. Chicago: University of Chicago Press.

Sowell, T. (1972). *Black education: Myths and tragedies*. New York: David McKay.

Sowell, T. (1975). *Race and economics*. New York: Longman.

Sowell, T. (1994). *Race and culture*. New York: Basic Books.

Sowell, T. (1998). *Conquest and cultures*. New York: Basic Books.

Stapledon, O. (1968). *Last and first men*. New York: Dover. (Original work published 1931)

Staples, R. (1985). Changes in black family structure: The conflict between family ideology and structural conditions. *Journal of Marriage and the Family*, 47, 1005–1013.

Stove, D. (1995). *Cricket versus republicanism and other essays*. Sydney: Quakers Hill Press.

Sturgeon, N. L. (1988). Moral explanations. In G. Sayre-McCord (Ed.), *Essays on moral realism* (pp. 229–255). Ithaca NY: Cornell University Press.

Sumner, W. G. (1883). *What social classes owe to each other*. New York: Harper.

Sumner, W. G. (1940). *Folkways: A study of the sociological importance of usages, manners, customs, mores, and morals* (rev. ed.). Boston: Ginn.

Tawney, R. H. (1920). *The acquisitive society*. New York: Harcourt, Brace & Howe.

Tawney, R. H. (1931). *Equality*. London: Allen & Unwin.

Toulmin, S. E. (1950). *The place of reason in ethics*. London: Cambridge University Press.

Tucker, W. (1990). *The excluded Americans: Homelessness and housing policies*. Washington DC: Regnery Gateway.

U.S. News and World Report (1988, August 22). The black-on-black crime plague.

Veblen, T. (1899). *The theory of the leisure class*. New York: Macmillan.

Wadia, P. S. (1965). Professor Toulmin and "the function" of ethics. *Philosophical Studies*, 14, 88–93.

Waismann, F. (1965). Notes on talks with Wittgenstein. *Philosophical Review*, 74, 12–16.

Warburton, A. (1992). *Beyond Kaufmann: Walter Kaufmann and Nietzsche's ethical theory*. Dunedin, New Zealand: B.A. honors thesis, Department of Political Studies, University of Otago.

Wial, H. (1988). *The transition from secondary to primary employment: Jobs and workers in ethnic neighborhood labor markets*. Ph.D. dissertation, Department of Economics, MIT, Cambridge MA.

Williams, W. E. (1974). Some hard questions on minority businesses. *Negro Educational Review, 25*, 123–142.

Wilson, J. Q., & Herrnstein, R. J. (1985). *Crime and human nature*. New York: Basic Books.

Wittgenstein, L. (1965). A lecture on ethics. *Philosophical Review, 74*, 3–12.

Yeatman, A. (1992). Minorities and the politics of difference. *Political Theory Newsletter, 4*, 1–10.

Young, I. M. (1992). Together in difference: Transforming the logic of group political conflict. *Political Theory Newsletter, 4*, 11–26.

Subject Index

Author Index

SOCIAL SCIENCE + LOGIC 99

98

126 NIETZCHE
130
* 143   /
155   /
164
166
169 *

176 - 177

187

193
194 *

Printed in the United States
114413LV00004B/136/P

9 780803 217959